SCM STUDYGUIDE TO EARLY CHRISTIAN DOCTRINE AND THE CREEDS

SCM STUDYGUIDE TO EARLY CHRISTIAN DOCTRINE AND THE CREEDS

Piotr Ashwin-Siejkowski

scm press

British Library Cataloguing in Publication data

A catalogue record for this book is available
from the British Library

978–0–334–04200-6

First published in 2010 by SCM Press
13–17 Long Lane,
London EC1A 9PN

www.scm-canterburypress.co.uk

SCM Press is an imprint of
Hymns Ancient and Modern Ltd

Typeset by Regent Typesetting, London
Printed and bound in Great Britain by
CPI Antony Rowe, Chippenham SN14 6LH

Contents

Illustrations

Acknowledgements

This book is an outcome of my teaching and learning from outstanding scholars and publications, which I have been privileged to encounter in recent years. Hopefully, this *Studyguide* will inspire my readers in their study of the history of the early Church and Patristic theology.

I would like to thank to Dr Natalie Watson, the Senior Commissioning Editor of SCM Press, for her interest in this project, then for her continuous encouragement and practical comments on the first draft of the book. I wish to express my gratitude to two anonymous reviewers whose comments helped me to prepare the general outline of the book. As in the case of my previous publications, I must pay tribute to the big-hearted staff from the Library of University of Chichester; thanks to them I was able to collect all necessary academic resources which I used in my research. Among many very generous people who helped me with the manuscript, I am indebted to Shirley Walls, Mary Comerford, Pam Miles, Professor Richard Rondel and Elizabeth Foster. Their kindness inspired my effort: thank you.

With gratitude to the students of Patristic Theology
at the University of Chichester 2001–2009

Abbreviations: Important ancient Authors and Documents Quoted in the Book

Acts of the Christian Martyrs

MartPol.	Martyrdom of Polycarp
MartPerp.	Martyrdom of Perpetua and Felicitas

Ancient Christian Sermons

1 Clement	The Letter of Romans to the Corinthians known as First Clement
2 Clement	An ancient Christian sermon known as Second Clement

Ambrose of Milan

ExLk	Exposition of the Gospel of Luke
ExPs.	Exposition of the Psalms
Ep.	Letters
Virgins	On Virgins

Athanasius of Alexandria

AHeathen	Against the Heathen
Dec.	On the Decrees of the Synod of Nicaea
EpBEL	Epistle to the Bishops of Egypt and Libya

EpSerapion	Epistles to Serapion
IncarnationL.	On the Incarnation of the Logos
OrAA	Orations Against the Arians
OV	On Virginity

Athenagoras of Athens

| Res. | On the Resurrection of the Dead |
| Supplication | Supplication for the Christians |

Augustine of Hippo

AJ	Against Julian
BCD	Brief on the Conference with the Donatists
CG	City of God
Conf.	Confessions
Enchir.	Enchiridion
For.	On Forgiveness of Sins and on the merits of Infant Baptism
GraceCh.	On the Grace of Christ and Original Sin
IS	On the Immortality of the Soul
OFC	On Faith and the Creed
Serm.	Sermons
Soliloquies	Soliloquies
Trin.	On the Trinity
TR	On True Religion

Basil of Caesarea

AEun.	Against Eunomius
Ep.	Letters
Hex.	Hexaemeron
HomPs.	Homilies on Psalms
Moralia	The Moralia
OHS	On the Holy Spirit

Clement of Alexandria

Exhortation	Exhortation to the Greeks
ExTh.	Excerpts from Theodotus
Strom.	Stromateis
Tutor	Tutor

Cyprian of Carthage

Ep.	Letters
EpTh.	Letter to the People of Thibar
OM	On Modesty
OUCh.	On the Unity of the Church

Cyril of Alexandria

DialTrin.	Dialogues on the Trinity
2 EpN	Second Letter to Nestorius
3 EpN	Third Letter to Nestorius
Ep.	Letters
ExpGJ	Exposition of the Gospel of John
ExpGLk	Exposition of the Gospel of Luke
ExpIsa.	Exposition of Isaiah
IncarnationOB	On the Incarnation of the only-begotten
OTF	On the True Faith
PH	Paschal Homilies
Worship	Worship of God in Spirit and Truth

Cyril of Jerusalem

CL	Catechetical Lectures

Epiphanius of Salamis

Chest	Medicine Chest

Ephrem the Syrian

HP	Homilies on Paradise
SF	Sermons on Faith

The Epistle of Barnabas

EpB.	

Eusebius of Caesarea

EH	Ecclesiastical History
LC	Life of Constantine
OEC	Oration in Praise of the Emperor Constantine

Gregory of Nazianzus

Ep.	Letters
Or.	Orations
Poems	Poems

Gregory of Nyssa

AApp.	Against Appollinaris
AE	Against Eunomius
AMac.	Against the Macedonians
CO	Catechetical Orations
ComSS	Commentary on the Song of Songs
LM	Life of Moses
OLP	On the Lord's Prayer
OMM	On the Making of Man
OSR	On the Soul and the Resurrection

Gregory Palamas

Ep.	Letter

Gregory the Great

MDJ	Moral Discourses on Job

Hermas, The Shepherd

Man.	Mandates
Par.	Parables
Vis.	Visions

Hippolytus of Rome

AN	Against Noetus
Heresies	On Heresies

Ignatius of Antioch

Eph.	Letter to the Ephesians
Mag.	Letter to the Magnesians
Phil.	Letter to the Philadelphians
Pol.	Letter to Polycarp

| Smyr. | Letter to the Smyrnaeans |
| Tral. | Letter to the Trallians |

Irenaeus of Lyons

AH	Against Heresies
Fr.	Fragments
Proof	Proof of the Apostolic Preaching

Jerome

AJ	Against Jovinian
Ep.	Letters
Lives	Lives of Illustrious Men

Jewish and Christian Apocrypha and Pseudepigrapha

AI	Ascension of Isaiah
ApJ	Apocryphon of John
1 Enoch	First Book of Enoch
2 Enoch	Second Book of Enoch
EpAp.	Epistle of the Apostles
SO	Sybilline Oracles
TTP	Testament of the Twelve Patriarchs

John Chrysostom

BI	Baptismal Instructions
Hom1Cor.	Homilies on the First Letter of Paul to Corinthians
HomL	Homilies on Lazarus

John of Damascus

| Orth. | On the Orthodox Faith |

Josephus

| JA | Jewish Antiquities |
| JW | Jewish War |

Justin Martyr

| 1 Apol. | First Apology |

2 Apol.	Second Apology
Dial.	Dialogue with Trypho

Lactantius

DP	On the Death of the Persecutors

The Macarian Tradition

Hom.	Homilies

Marcus Victorinus

AA	Against Arius

Melito of Sardis

HP	Homily on the Passion

Methodius of Olympus

Symp.	Symposium

Minucius Felix

Oc.	Octavius

The Nag Hammadi Library

AcJ	Acts of John
ApJames	The Apocryphon of James
2 ApJames	The Second Apocalypse of James
ApPeter	The Apocalypse of Peter
BThC	The Book of Thomas the Contender
CGP	The Concept of our Great Power
EPP	The Epistle of Peter to Philip
EthB	Eugnostos the Blessed
GE	The Gospel of the Egyptians
GPh.	The Gospel of Philip
GTh.	The Gospel of Thomas
GTruth	The Gospel of Truth
STGS	The Second Treatise of the Great Seth
TS	The Teaching of Silvanus

TTruth	The Testimony of Truth
TP	Trimorphic Protennoia
TRes.	The Treatise on the Resurrection
TT	The Tripartite Tractate

Origen

AC	Against Celsus
ComEph.	Commentary on the Letter to Ephesians
ComGJ	Commentary on the Gospel of John
ComGLk	Commentary on the Gospel of Luke
ComGMat.	Commentary on the Gospel of Matthew
ComSS	Commentary on the Song of Songs
CommSPsalms	Commentary on selected Psalms
HomJer.	Homilies on Jeremiah
HomLev.	Homilies on Leviticus
HomNum.	Homilies on Numbers
OP	On Prayer
Princ.	On the Principles

Papias

| Fr. | Fragments |

Pelagius

| ExRom. | Exposition of the Letter to Romans |

Philo of Alexandria

Abraham	On Abraham
Confusion	On the Confusion of Tongues
Dreams	On Dreams
Embassy	On the Embassy to Gaius
Heir	Who is the Heir of the Divine Things?

Pseudo-Justin

| OR | On the Resurrection |

Rufinus of Aquilea

| ChH | Church History |

Shenoute

IAA	I Am Amazed

Syriac Literature

BookCT	Book of the Cave of Treasures
BS	Book of Steps
Dem.	Demonstrations of Aphrahat's the Persian Sage
HaH	Hymns against Heresies
HN	Homilies on Nativity
HV	Hymns on Virginity
Hymn	Hymn on the Church in Qennešrin
Tr.	Treatises

Tatian

Orat.	Oration to the Greeks

Tertullian

AJ	Against the Jews
AM	Against Marcion
AP	Against Praxeas
Apology	Apology
Bap.	On Baptism
Crown	On the Crown
Flesh	On the Flesh of Christ
Idol.	On Idolatry
Mod.	On Modesty
Mon.	On Monogamy
OR	On the Resurrection
OS	On the Soul
OVV	On the Veiling of Virgins
Pen.	On Penitence
Prayer	On Prayer
PH	Prescriptions of Heretics
Scapula	To Scapula
Scorpiace	Scorpiace

Theodore of Mopsuestia

CH	Catechetical Homilies
ExEph.	Exposition of the Letter to the Ephesians
Fr.	Fragments

Theodoret of Cyrrhus

ComPs.	Commentary on the Psalms
ExRom.	Exposition of the Letter to the Romans

Other

HRT	*Harvard Theological Review*
JTS	*Journal of Theological Studies*

Starred terms and names in the text are covered in more detail in the Glossary (some, relating to Ecumenical Councils, are alternatively covered in that section at the back of the book). Underlined terms are discussed in nearby boxes in the text.

Chronology of Ancient Theologians and Documents

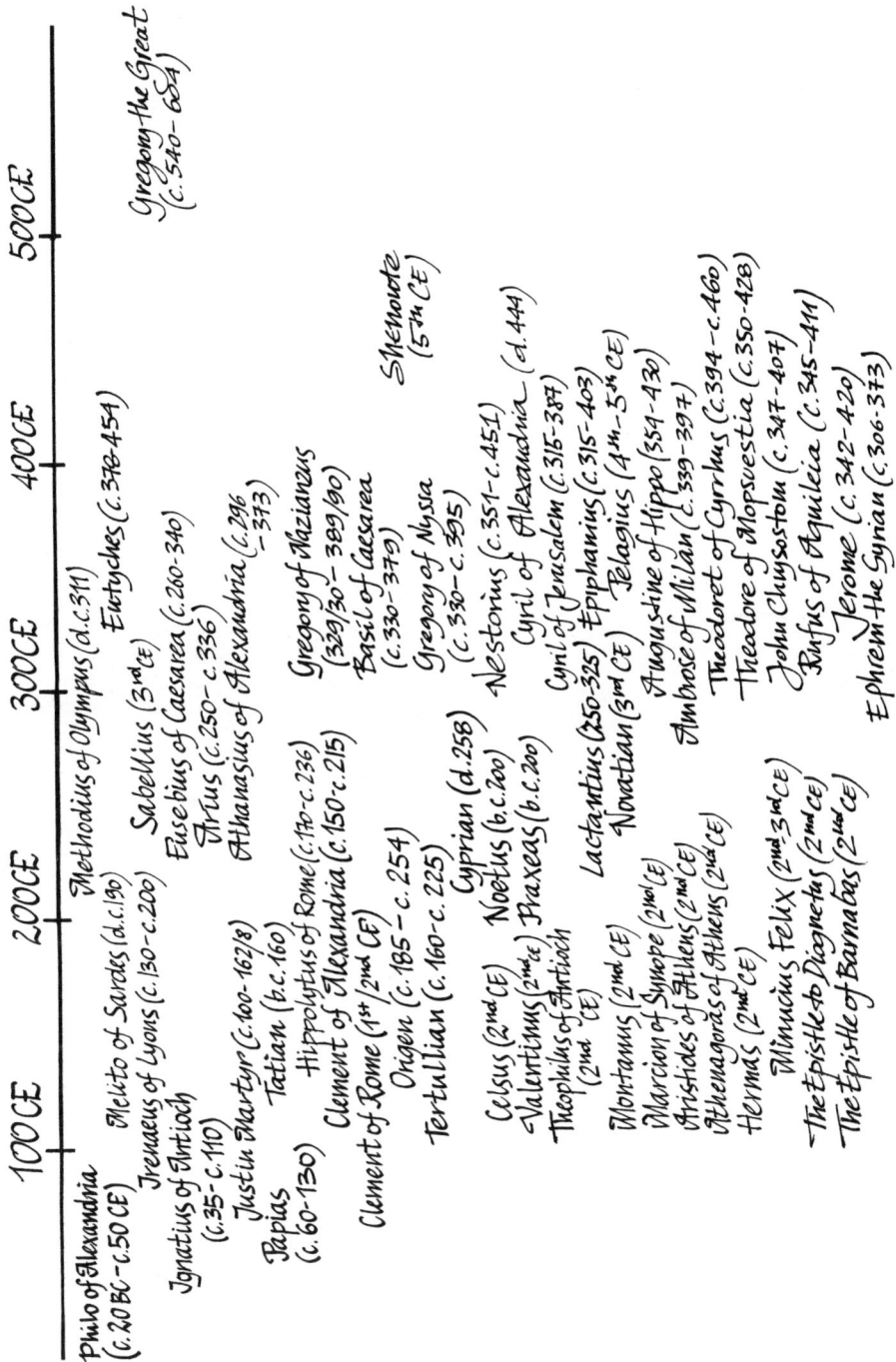

Philo of Alexandria (c.20BC–c.50 CE)

Melito of Sardes (d.c.190)

Irenaeus of Lyons (c.130–c.200)

Ignatius of Antioch (c.35–c.110)

Justin Martyr (c.100–162/8)

Papias (b.c.160)

Tatian (b.c.160)

(c.60–130)

Hippolytus of Rome (c.170–c.236)

Clement of Alexandria (c.150–c.215)

Clement of Rome (1st/2nd CE)

Origen (c.185–c.254)

Tertullian (c.160–c.225)

Celsus (2nd CE)

Valentinians (2nd CE)

Noetus (b.c.200)

Praxeas (b.c.200)

Theophilus of Antioch (2nd CE)

Lactantius (250–325)

Novatian (3rd CE)

Montanus (2nd CE)

Marcion of Sinope (2nd CE)

Aristides of Athens (2nd CE)

Athenagoras of Athens (2nd CE)

Hermas (2nd CE)

Minucius Felix (2nd/3rd CE)

The Epistle to Diognetus (2nd CE)

The Epistle of Barnabas (2nd CE)

Methodius of Olympus (d.c.311)

Eutyches (c.378–454)

Sabellius (3rd CE)

Eusebius of Caesarea (c.260–340)

Arius (c.250–c.336)

Athanasius of Alexandria (c.296–373)

Gregory of Nazianzus (329/30–389/90)

Basil of Caesarea (c.330–379)

Gregory of Nyssa (c.330–c.395)

Nestorius (c.351–c.451)

Cyril of Alexandria (d.444)

Cyril of Jerusalem (c.315–387)

Epiphanius (c.315–403)

Pelagius (4th–5th CE)

Augustine of Hippo (354–430)

Ambrose of Milan (c.339–397)

Theodoret of Cyrrhus (c.394–c.460)

Theodore of Mopsvestia (c.350–428)

John Chrysostom (c.347–407)

Rufus of Aquileia (c.345–411)

Jerome (c.342–420)

Ephrem the Syrian (c.306–373)

Shenoute (5th CE)

Gregory the Great (c.540–604)

100 CE

200 CE

300 CE

400 CE

500 CE

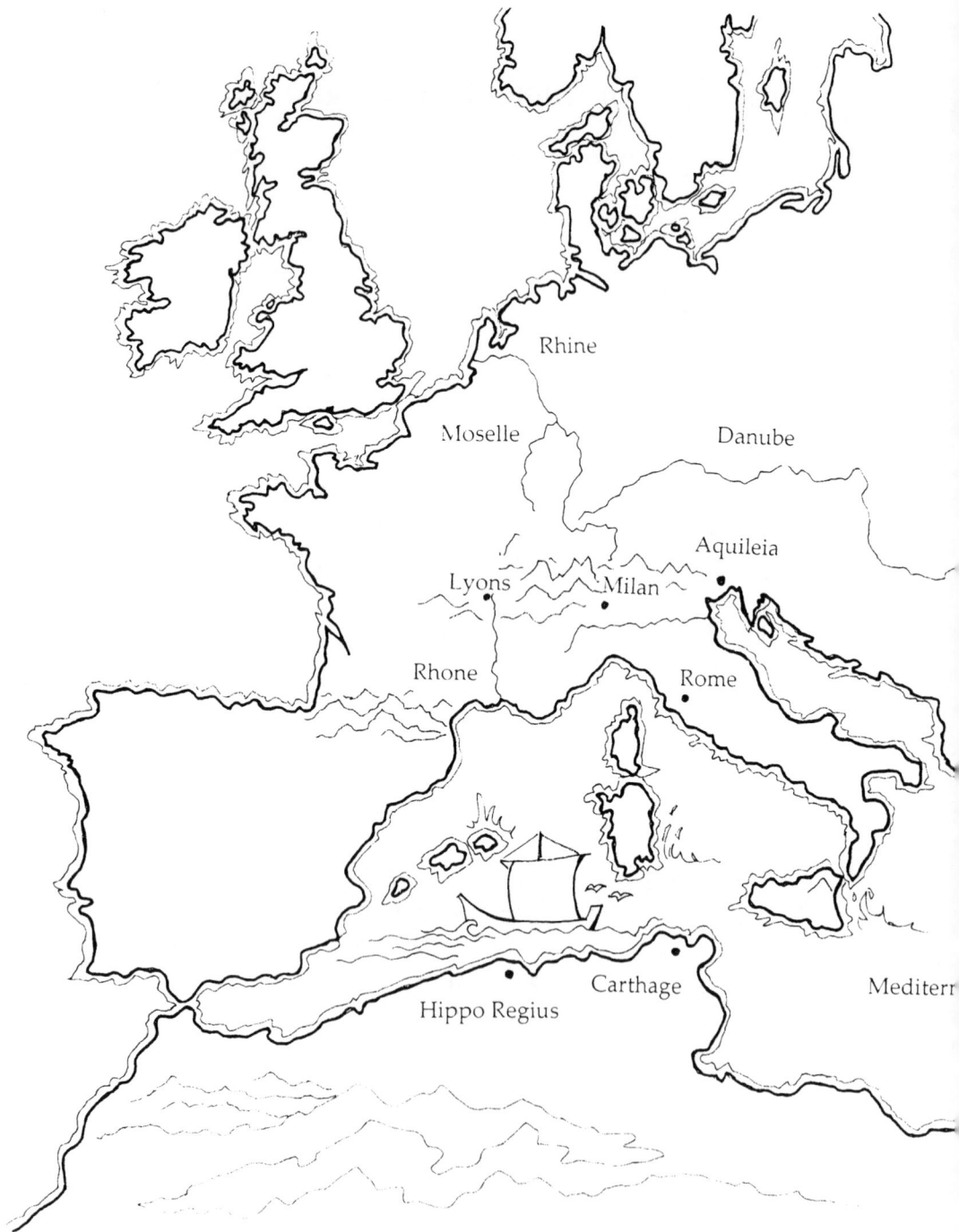

Rhine

Moselle

Danube

Lyons

Milan

Aquileia

Rhone

Rome

Carthage

Mediterr

Hippo Regius

Geographical Locations Cited in the Book

Black Sea

Sinope

Tigris

Constantinople

Nazianzus

Chalcedon Nyssa Caesarea

Nicaea Cyrrhus

Smyrna Sardes Mopsuestia

Athens Ephesus Antioch

Damascus Euphrates

Salamis

Caesarea Jerusalem

...anean Sea

Alexandria

Nag-Hammadi

Nile Red Sea

Introduction

The purpose of this book is to introduce the readers to a number of the important statements from the ancient Creeds, or 'rules of faith', and their original and complex context. Early Christianity presents a fascinating mosaic of various doctrines and a polyphony, sometimes cacophony, of theological voices. Within this plurality of views, gradually the mainstream theological position emerged, which soon acquired the very significant and powerful label of 'orthodoxy'. This title became a synonym of the Universal/Catholic Church. By way of introduction, I wish to make three important points.

From Oral Tradition to Formalized Creeds

The Patristic era, which in this Studyguide encompasses the first five centuries of the Common Era, was one of the most fruitful, creative and important phases of Christian history. But those ancient theologians, orthodox and heretic alike, understood their role first and foremost as commentators on the Scriptures. None of them invented 'Christianity'; all of them claimed to understand God's plan of salvation revealed in Jesus of Nazareth as identified by them with God's Saviour. Thus, our search for the origin of Christian doctrine should begin with Jesus, the rabbi. But immediately we face the first and most difficult problem: Jesus' teaching was preserved among his disciples and then in the first generation of Christians as so-called 'oral tradition'. These earliest Christians tried to memorize and pass on the individual sayings of their Lord, such as 'blessed are those who have not seen and yet have come to believe' (John 20.29), or 'it is more blessed to give than to receive' (Acts 20.35). In the light of such elementary pieces of evidence we know that Jesus did not create any dogma, including an intellectually advanced deliberation on his own identity. Nor did he comment on the nature of God, the special role of his mother, the value of grace or even his view on the afterlife. Jesus' parables contained rather an educational value and were not a coherent theological doctrine. However, in the second half of the first century and continuing into the second century these sayings were collected by diverse groups of Christians who used them to compose a particular story about Jesus, known to us as the 'Good News' or Gospels. In the fourth century, the Church affirmed the authority of only four Gospels as divinely inspired sources of revelation, but this selection reminds us of the much greater number of Gospel narratives which did not find their place in the canon of the New Testament. Still, among these earliest sayings recorded and collected into a particular Gospel there are the seeds of future dogmas; the first and most important example is Peter's famous proclamation which names Jesus of Nazareth, the man standing in front of him, as the Son of God and the Saviour (Matt. 16.16). Still surprising to many readers, the Gospels were not the first Christian testimonies about Jesus. Paul's correspondence is chronologically earlier than any Gospel. Paul, a Jewish convert and theologian, reflected on many occasions about the significance of Jesus' appearance as the Saviour. It is in Paul's theological elaboration that Jesus becomes the Saviour of all humankind, not only the Saviour of the Jews, but of all, including Greeks (in other words pagans) and even the departed. It is also clear from Paul's correspondence with various Christian communities that those earliest Christians already had various questions arising from the ethical implications of being followers of the Lord. It is thus with Paul's commentaries and proclamations that some clearer views on Jesus emerged and became the framework of the emergent doctrine of the Church. Very soon the liturgical practice of baptism, which was an act of being introduced to new Christian life, needed clarification as to its significance, and the earliest proclamation of God as 'the Father, the Son and the Holy Spirit' became ascribed to this Christian ritual. At this stage Jesus' testimony about 'his Father' and the forthcoming 'Spirit – the Comforter' recorded in many of the original sayings was enough to introduce a new and significant terminology and at the same time to produce a summary of faith in the Father, the Son and the Holy Spirit. Soon this summary became the basis for Creeds, which developed further detail.

The next important stage in the development of Christian identity came when the missionaries of the new religion encountered both their closest Jewish opponents, as well as pagan neighbours. Declaration of faith in the crucified-but-alive Lord called for more than just the emotional proclamation: 'Jesus is the Lord. Amen.' Among the new converts to this Jesus movement were intellectuals with a philosophical education who tried to explain the core of the Christian faith in terms of their cultural background. During the second century we may observe a number of further doctrinal clarifications, which either protected 'authentic' Christian faith from errors or proclaimed that faith in a language which assimilated terminology not found in the Scriptures, but was helpful and known to people of this time. For instance, in this period Jesus of Nazareth already proclaimed as 'the Son of God' and 'the Saviour of humanity' also becomes known as 'the Word of God', a person different from 'the Father' and not a synonym of 'the Holy Spirit'. In a natural way, each new generation of Christians brought into their experience of faith new theological concerns. In the fourth century one of these concerns was a simple question: is 'the Word of God' begotten or created? Again, after a passionate debate especially among Christians representing the Eastern, Greek-speaking world, one opinion prevailed and then was declared by the Creeds as the measure of Christian correctness and identity. As before, new terminology was introduced to support and explain the new theological formula. In this way the nature or natures of Jesus of Nazareth and their relationship become even more elaborated. The Council of Nicaea (325 CE) defined the relationship between Jesus, the Son of God, and his divine Father. However, the new theological formula expressed by the Creed that took its name from this Council left room for further questioning explored by the theologians of the next century.

With the growing alliance between the Christian faith and particularly the Platonic philosophical tradition, even more advanced notions became part of the Creeds. They provided more information about the nature of the Saviour, while at the same time elaborating with more detail on the Holy Spirit, the Church, divine grace, human freedom, original sin and, ultimately, everlasting life. In the middle of the fifth century, with the Council of Chalcedon (451 CE), the Church formalized the original theological intuition into a compound, formal and systematic collection of statements which now shaped the theological sensitivity of Christians. Jesus Christ was now proclaimed as one person with two co-existing natures: human and divine.

The early Christian Creeds came into being as a response to questions asked during the first five centuries. Their statements were the official responses of the

Catholic Church to alternative theologies understood to be erroneous. Without basic knowledge of their background and the crises which produced each statement, these ancient Creeds remain silent, incomprehensible relics of the past, still used in the liturgy of all Christian denominations, but rarely commented on or discussed. This Studyguide aims to allow these ancient credal statements to speak out in their original, historical and fascinating context.

Attitude of a Critical Reader/Student

Christian doctrine has evolved through ardent debate between what have later been labelled as 'orthodox' and 'heretical' views. However, readers should beware: although the picture is intricate, our access to the original documents is rather limited and biased. Often, the theologians representing the Great, later known as Catholic, Church were not concerned about the objectivity of their account of the theological arguments of their Christian adversaries. The writings and testimonies of those labelled as 'heretics' were destroyed. The persecuted opponents, among them many nameless martyrs, were denied the right to leave their legacy. Finally, the voices of Christian women are hardly heard in this dominantly male choir of Church authorities. Therefore, we have to read the Church fathers with a careful, critical and contextual eye, without assuming that only their views contain the 'whole truth and nothing but the truth'. In brief, we need to be aware that this fascinating picture known as 'Patristic theology' is only a part of the richness of early Christian life and experience of God. I would therefore like to encourage my readers to approach the subject with an attitude which is critical, contextual and creative. This is necessary to assess the natural historical limitations, but it also helps to select the aspects of the belief which are still relevant to the modern reader.

The critical approach enables us to reassess the values of the credal declarations and accommodate them into a new context. Creeds are only signposts towards the divine, not divine themselves.

The contextual approach suggests an effort to know more about the culture, philosophy, mentality, rhetorical purpose and competitive context which created these expressions of Christian faith. Without that necessary knowledge the Creeds are alienated from their natural milieu: they are soundless, colourless and bland.

The creative approach suggests a possible inspiration found 'among' and 'in' these ancient assertions to question our understanding of the divine and Christian revelation. All three approaches may offer a new fresh way of studying theology.

Aim of this Studyguide

The history of the early Church may look like an overwhelming panorama full of details, difficult names and events in distant places. It may present itself as the labyrinthine architecture of an ancient building, with too many levels, rooms and corridors.

One of the Greek myths presents a romantic story of Ariadne's love for Theseus. According to this ancient legend, Daedalus built a labyrinth for the King of Crete. The labyrinth's construction contained a system of corridors and rooms from which no one could escape, and it also concealed the Minotaur, a beast which fed on lost visitors. Eventually, the Minotaur was killed by the brave Theseus. In order to help him find his way out of the labyrinth, his lover Ariadne gave him a thread of wool. I hope that readers attracted to the history of early Christian theology by its significance, mystery and beauty will find that this Studyguide provides them with a 'thread of wool', which will allow them to explore some aspects of the complexity of Patristic thought. I hope also that this introduction will protect them from the unpleasant experience of being lost in a multitude of details. The structure of the book, clear content of each chapter, helpful questions, selection of relevant original documents in translation, the explanations of vocabulary within each chapter and, finally, the Glossary, all these, and many more resources, should assist the reader throughout the whole of the journey inside the ancient palace.

Having said that, I take full responsibility for the selection of themes, authors and documents discussed in this book, while, obviously, I had to leave out many other significant resources. But this book is only an introduction which I hope will encourage readers to pursue further academic research in Patristic theology.

We all have to face our personal Minotaur, even if, at the end of the day, the monster reflects only our fear and ignorance. Studying, learning and sharing our academic passions with others is the greatest reward of conquering the Minotaur.

Piotr Ashwin-Siejkowski
1 July 2009

1

Belief in God the Father Almighty

See also chapters 2, 3, 7, 10, 11.

Consider this Task

Write a short summary of your interpretation of the term 'god'. Which philosophical or religious tradition(s) do you find most helpful in your understanding of 'god'?

Introduction

This first credal statement introduces one of the main theological axioms of the early Church: the Christian understanding of the divine. Early Christian proclamation, although it originated in the Hebrew Scriptures and theology, also reinterpreted the Christian legacy in the light of the new revealer: Jesus of Nazareth and his teaching about God. This central message soon encountered a non-Jewish audience, Graeco-Roman culture and the philosophical, inquisitive mentality that went with it. From that cultural encounter Christian faith in God was transformed into a new systematic theology. It gradually assimilated some of the philosophical, <u>Middle Platonic</u> concepts of the divine (such as 'transcendence') and absorbed linguistic notions (for example, 'a divine person', see chapter 2) which were not known in the original Hebrew context.

> **Middle Platonism**: school of philosophy (first century BCE – second century CE) which highlighted the transcendence of God.

In relation to the credal statements, the first pronouncement came into being as a response to a variety of philosophical and theological debates during the first five centuries. Some of the most difficult challenges came not from the Jewish theologians and <u>pagan</u> philosophers, but from fellow Christians who questioned the original message and put forward alternative interpretations.

> **Pagan**: term denoting the traditional religions and myths of the Graeco-Roman world and people who respect them.[1]

Those attempts were later labelled as 'heresies' by the Church.

Heresy (Gr. *hairesis* – 'choice', 'a thing chosen'): an erroneous teaching or the formal denial of a defined doctrine of the Church. As the emerging Catholic Church claimed teaching authority, it used this term to denote disagreement with some alternative views and doctrines.

Nevertheless, those ancient quarrels had significant consequences with regard to the orthodox view of God promoted by mainstream Christianity in teaching, preaching and liturgy, and later in iconography.

Orthodoxy (Gr. *orthos* – 'straight', Gr. *doxa* 'opinion'): therefore straight/correct thinking and teaching. In the Patristic period, orthodoxy was understood as the correct teaching of the Church, contrasted with the heresies of various schools of thought.

To a modern, critical reader two characteristics of the divine person as 'Father', 'the Almighty' sound rather disconcerting as synonyms of a 'male', 'autocratic', 'powerful' ruler. This critique is understandable, but we have to take into account the rhetorical function of the male God-language in its original context. This chapter addresses the vital phases of the emergence of the Patristic understanding of the fatherhood of the first person of the Trinity. In its initial stage the first credal statement summarized the decisive continuation of the Christian faith within Jewish monotheism (the One God), while it also hinted at discontinuity within that tradition by reference to Jesus' teaching about his 'Father' (for instance Mark 14.36). In the later Patristic theology, the same title received further clarification in relation to a more elaborate understanding of two other divine persons: the Son and the Holy Spirit. Throughout that period the emphasis on the fatherhood of God played an important role in Patristic teaching and liturgy as a part of a concerted effort to advocate and promote divinity as 'the greatest perfection' and unquestionably sovereign over all creation. As a result that rhetoric overemphasized masculine traits and gender of the divine.

Opening Question

What are the main limitations of thinking about God in exclusively male terms?

Development of the Argument

The concept that the Ultimate Source of reality might be called by the highly androcentric title 'the Father of all' had a long pre-Christian history in Greek philosophy[2] and among some Jewish authors such as *Philo of Alexandria.[3] The earliest Christian theology tried to assimilate some of their most valuable elements and apply them in a new religious and pedagogical framework. Along-side this earliest effort appeared a significant alternative presented by Gnostic theologies. The <u>Gnostic</u> narratives produced a number of eclectic theologies of God, where Jewish and Greek notions amalgamated into complex myths.

Gnostic/Gnosticism: term describing a great range of beliefs and theologies which in its Christian form flourished in the second century CE. Often these beliefs showed a tendency towards dualism with radical distinction between the good spiritual and evil material elements: the invisible, good world and the visible universe; the soul/spirit and matter/body.

The rest of the chapter traces some of the most important stages of that process of assimilation and verification, which characterized the theologians of the Church.

The Holy One

The Christian intuition also reaffirmed the earlier Hebrew theological axiom that the divine Creator revealed himself as the 'living God' (e.g. Deut. 5.26; Ps. 84.2; Isa. 37.4; Hos. 2.25; Matt. 16.16; 26.63; Acts 14.15; 2 Cor. 3.3; 6.16; 1 Tim. 3.15; 4.10; Heb. 3.13; 9.14; 10.31; 12.22; Rev. 7.2). As a direct consequence of the priority given to the self-revelation of that God, biblical knowledge about

God was not the outcome of theoretical speculation. It was rather a result of a very personal, intimate experience of the divine, parental care, which revealed God as 'a person' rather than as an awesome, abstract power. For Jews and then later for Christians, God the Almighty was holy (Hebr. *kaddosh*) rather than an abstract awesome cosmic power.

> As the Scripture says: 'ten thousand times ten thousand stood around him and thousands of thousands served him, while crying out Holy, holy, holy is the Lord of Hosts, all creation is full of his glory [Isa.6.3].' Let's then gather together like them in unity of voices and attention of hearts, let's cry out to him sincerely with one mouth so we may share his great and wonderful promises.
>
> 1 *Clement* 34.6–7, trans. P. A.-S.

God was the intelligent and good Creator, absolutely holy, but in direct, compassionate and parental relationship with his creatures (e.g. Gen. 9.9–17; Isa. 49.14–15; Luke 15.8–10). The encounter with the Holy One was an overwhelming mystery, which brought to light his affectionate love and protection, then called for respect, trust and faithfulness. Although Jews and Christians shared this attitude towards the divine Creator, as common religious ground it was limited since only Christians accepted Jesus of Nazareth's role as the true Revealer of his divine Father.[4] From now on, the emerging theology of the Church explored and then pronounced the particular nature of God as 'the Father' of Jesus and 'the Father' of all who recognized in Jesus the 'Anointed' (Gr. *Christos*), that is the promised Saviour.

The Absolute

Among the earliest Christian authors and their documents, the emphasis on Christian monotheism appeared closely linked with God's title as the 'Father Almighty', and together with other characteristics played an essential role in constructing the intellectual comprehension of the Absolute. This new theology faced many critics and philosophical problems. Unlike some common beliefs such as pantheism (Gr. *pan* – 'all', 'everything', *theos* – 'god') and astrological determinism personified in a female deity, Christian theology emphasized the fatherhood of God. Against pantheism, the early *apologists claimed that matter was not co-eternal with God or even that it was his 'body' and 'garment'. Equally strong opposition was expressed against determinism.[5] God's oneness meant that he was not only chronologically, but also ontologically prior to creation; that is, God's nature cannot be compared with the nature of the universe as the latter is totally dependent on the former. Prior to any other element of reality, his unlimited might had called everything into existence. Contrary to popular polytheism, which included a number of female deities, the Christian claim emphasized the uniqueness of 'God Father Almighty' as he surpassed other 'gods', 'goddesses' and evil beings interfering in human affairs. Finally, against idolatry, the Christian apologists highlighted God's spiritual nature, invisibility and transcendence.

> I have given sufficient proof that we are not atheists, but hold God to be one, unbegotten, eternal, invisible, suffering nothing, comprehended by none, circumscribed by none, apprehended by mind and reasoning alone, girt about with light and beauty and spirit and power indescribable, creator of all things by His Word, their embellisher and master.
>
> Athenagoras of Athens, *Supplication* 10, trans. J. H. Crehan

The Supreme God and Gnostic Polyphony

So far pagans and Jews represented the only opposition to the emerging Christian faith. However, there were also those within Christian communities who subscribed to a rather different understanding of God. Among those Christians who later became labelled by their opponents as 'Gnostics' there was a pluralism of views on the nature of God. Still, this pluralism of theologies can be summarized by a common belief that God is the totally transcendent Supreme Being. The best name to denote the divine existence of 'the unknown God' was 'Father and Mother'.

> This is the first Thought, his image [Gr. *ikon*]; she became the womb of everything, for it is she who is prior to them all, the Mother-Father [Gr. *metropator*), the First Man, the holy Spirit, the thrice-male, the thrice powerful, the thrice-named androgynous one, and the eternal aeon among the invisible ones, and the first to come forth.
>
> The Nag Hammadi Library, *ApJ* 5.5, trans. F. Wisse

As the Supreme God is other-worldly, the Gnostic narrative introduced further divine figures and mediators between the lower and higher level of beings. Among them the central place was given to a creator of the visible reality, who received the Platonic characteristics of craftsman (Gr. *demiurgos*) and was seen as an evil god of this material, visible world. The Supreme God was beyond any form of 'revelation' or even the Other; he/she did not try to communicate with human beings. It was only through the mission of the Redeemer (see chapter 2) that knowledge (Gr. *gnosis*) about the origin and structure of reality as well as about the way of escaping from the current condition was passed on to certain elect Christians. The Supreme, Unknown God remained unknowable by any human notion or comprehension.

> He Who is ineffable. No principle knew him, no authority, no subjection, nor any creature from the foundation of the world excerpt he alone.
>
> *EthB* 71.15, trans. D. M. Parrott

It must be noted that some Gnostics were influenced by dualism and, as in the case of *Marcion, claimed the existence of the evil God, the Creator of the universe and the good, loving God revealed by Jesus Christ. Against those 'internal' enemies the credal title 'God – the Father – Almighty' highlighted that God is the ultimate Administrator and Ruler of the visible and invisible worlds and his governance fulfils the plan of salvation (see chapter 3). This plan included all beings, visible and invisible, material and spiritual. It also called them to the ecclesiastical authority established, as some theologians argued, by the will of the divine Father. To illustrate this important internal Christian struggle we turn to one of the most significant theologians of the second century.

Irenaeus of Lyons: God the Good Creator

In *Irenaeus' theology the title 'good Creator' received special attention and played an important role as a rhetorical weapon against his opponents. Irenaeus' treatise *Against Heresies* expressed a very personal and pastoral concern about the correctness of the beliefs in his local flock. The author quotes the views of his adversaries representing various Gnostic schools, and then tries to respond to their misinterpretation of what for him seems to be the 'apostolic' teaching and the genuine faith. From this work we may see that during Irenaeus' episcopacy at Lyons, there must have been a great deal of competition between various Christian factions. However, our views on this conflict are partial and dependent on the record of only one group, namely that which expressed Irenaeus' stance. Still, some of Irenaeus' observations find backing in Coptic documents from the *Nag Hammadi Library. In this highly polemical context, Irenaeus asserts the understanding of God as the Father Almighty, as he wishes to highlight that this very God is the only and good Creator of the material and spiritual universe, whom Christians call 'Father'.

> It appears to be One God the Father, not made, invisible, Creator of all things; above whom there is no other God, and after whom there is no other God. And, as God is a rational being, therefore by the Word [Gr. *logos*] he created all that is made. God is Spirit, and by the Spirit he adorned all things, as the prophet says: 'By the word of the Lord were the heavens established, and by his spirit all their power.' [Ps 33.6] [. . .] His apostle Paul rightly says: 'One God, the Father, who is over all and through all and in us all.' [Eph. 4.6] For 'over all' is the Father; and 'through all' is the Son, for 'through him' all things were made by the Father; and 'in us all' dwells the Spirit, who cries 'Abba Father' [Gal. 4.6], and fashions man into the likeness of God.
>
> Irenaeus of Lyons, *Proof* 5, trans. P. A.-S.

This good God is a caring parent of all. In the same breath, Irenaeus adds that the good God and only God has called into being all reality 'out of nothing' (Lat. *ex nihilo*). Only he, the Father Almighty is able to do what otherwise is impossible according to the classical axiom 'nothing comes from nothing'

(Lat. *ex nihili nihil fit*).[6] The Father's might is able to create worlds in a way that is unique and inaccessible to any other being, according to his free will, his reason/mind and his plan of salvation (see chapter 3). The fatherhood of God is elevated by Irenaeus as the principle of the inner life of what, or rather who, will be named 'the Trinity'. But the Bishop of Lyons also sees God as the male Architect of reality.

It has to be said that Irenaeus' theology responded to many alternative Christian views. These views represented a form of radical dualism separating the spiritual sphere from the material world. Consequently, Gnostic dualism completely detached the invisible, perfect realm ('light') from the visible, material world ('darkness'). While the higher and spiritual realm was a sphere of goodness and beauty, the visible world was the work of an evil creator. According to this dualistic view, the creation of the visible world took place as the result of a malicious act. The Gnostic view of God emphasized that the Absolute remains beyond any comprehension, as all human notions come from contact with visible, material reality. Therefore the divine Being, true God, is beyond any name given to him or her by theology. Totally transcendent and alien to this world, nevertheless, the divine Father–Mother was the true Parent of the Gnostic. Some Gnostics claimed that the divine Parent was androgynous, and that view was seen as scandalous by Christian apologists such as Irenaeus. The emphasis on the male characteristics of God the Father presented by those theologians aimed to save the legacy of the original 'apostolic' faith as understood by them, while 'feminization' of the divine being was stamped with the mark of 'heresy'.[7]

The Puzzle of Concepts: Patripassianism, Modalism and Monarchianism

The second important debate in the early Church dealt with yet another deadly threat. At this point, an introduction to some new terms and schools of thought is called for. During the second century of the Common Era, the fledgling Christian communities flourished around a specific scriptural narrative or a charismatic leader who claimed to present a genuine teaching of the Saviour and his apostles. One of the new challenges came with the appearance of a certain theologian *Noetus, a native of Smyrna (Asia/Turkey). As in many similar cases, we do not have his writings, but we depend on his opponents for a summary of his teaching, in this case on *Hippolytus of Rome. According to Hippolytus' charge, Noetus introduced himself as 'the new Moses'[8] and claimed that Jesus of Nazareth was himself 'the divine Father', and that it was 'the Father' who was born, then suffered and died.[9] This extraordinary opinion ascribed to Noetus seemed to defend God's oneness (monotheism) against possible accusations that Christians acknowledged the existence of 'two gods' within the divinity: the Father and the Son. Soon, Noetus' theory received the label of *'Patripassianism' (Lat. *pater* – 'father', *passio* – 'suffering') and was rejected by the Church. In a parallel way to Noetus, another theologian of the same period, Praxeas, known this time from Tertullian, held similar views. Both radical theories entered the vocabulary of heresies under the name of *Modalism (Gr. *modus* – 'mode') as they amalgamated divine persons into one Absolute, and by this they undermined the real differences between the Father, the Son and the Holy Spirit. To Noetus and Praxeas, the scriptural names 'the Father' and 'the Son' show only two different modes of being of the One God. To the theologians, such as Hippolytus and Tertullian, this kind of theory contradicted the core of Christian revelation about the nature of the Trinity.

> Yet, the shoot is not shut off from the root nor the river from the spring nor the beam from the sun, any more than the Word is shut off from God. Therefore according to the precedent of these examples I profess that I say that God and his Word, the Father and His Son are two: for the root and the tree are two things [Lat. *res*] but joined, and the spring and the river are two manifestations, but undivided; and the sun and its beam are two aspects but they cohere. Everything that processed from something must of necessity be another besides that from which it proceeds, but it is not for that reason separated [from it . . .] In this way the Trinity, proceeding by intermingled and connected degrees from the Father, in no respect challenges the monarchy, while it conserves the state of the economy [on economy, see chapter 3].
>
> Tertullian, *AP* 8, trans. E. Evans

Yet another theory, which appeared during the second century, has to be mentioned. The more sophisticated version of the previous view is known as *Monarchianism (Gr. *monos* – 'alone', *archo* – 'rule', 'govern') thanks to another theologian, *Sabellius. According to the account presented by his adversary Tertullian, Sabellius taught that the divine being is one <u>substance</u>, but with three operations comprehended by human beings as the three names.

> **Substance** (Gr. *ousia*): the term had many meanings in its original philosophical context. It was even confused with *hypostasis*. Later, post-Nicene theology emphasized its meaning as 'substance'. See the term *homoousios* in chapter 2.

If we can say anything about God, or Godhead, the correct statement would describe his nature as the One God appearing in this visible world and performing the acts of salvation as the Father who created the world, as the Son who redeemed it, and then in the last phase, as the Holy Spirit who sanctified what had been redeemed. These three actions point to their three sources, which are not separate ontological beings (persons), but rather three expressions of the same single reality.[10] This radical theory or Christian version of monotheism addressed not only the theology of the Church about the co-existence of three divine persons, but also attacked any dualism within divinity. The ultimate emphasis was laid on God's unity, to which any plurality is only external and related to our human perception of God's plan of salvation in history.

If some radical theologians, such as Marcion, suggested the co-existence of two principles of visible and invisible reality, to many theologians neither Modalism nor Modalistic Monarchianism was an option. A 'third way' seems to underlie the writings of such theologians as Tertullian (representing Latin Christianity) and *Origen (representing the Greek-speaking theologians). Tertullian, a highly skilful orator, attacked Modalism in his treatise *Against Praxeas*. At first, Tertullian reaffirmed the value of 'monarchy' within God, with the central position of the Father. But at the same time he goes further than Irenaeus in highlighting the usefulness of the term 'plan of salvation' in description of the three divine persons. To Tertullian, the opening idiom of 'monarchy' denotes the inner unity of empire and its concentration on a single individual that is the monarch. But like earthly rulers, the monarch may share his power with his son or any other agent of his choice.[11] In God's case, the Father Almighty shared his might with his divine Son and the Holy Spirit. It should be noticed that, for Tertullian, it was in no way inappropriate to present God as the Father/Monarch while his Son and the Holy Spirit, although they are of the same divine substance of the Father, fulfil the role of his generals. Tertullian accepted that God the Father is then greater than the Son, not in the sense of perfection, chronology or ontological significance, but rather as the ultimate source of all being and the author of the plan of salvation. Tertullian highlighted in his theology the harmony between divine monarchy (i.e. unity in God) and economy (i.e. functions of all three persons in salvation), while emphasizing the reality of each person against his adversaries. The fatherhood of God was to Tertullian the source of all, first and foremost of his Son, an exceptional title applicable to only one person of the Holy Trinity. Tertullian was the first theologian to write in Latin, and he coined a number of important theological terms still in use in the Christian West. The whole process of salvation has been expressed as 'the mystery of economy'. It was based on the fundamental unity of God's *substantia* (constitutive material of thing)[12] and the real difference between the three *personae*, which from now on begins to denote a distinct individual existence of each divine person among Latin authors.

Origen: God the Father and his Existence

Another vital input to the understanding of God's fatherhood in the pre-Nicene period came from the genius of Origen. He was the most remarkable theologian in third-century Christianity, and some aspects of his highly elaborated theo-logy, such as pre-existence of souls and hope of universal salvation, gave rise to many controversies in the forthcoming centuries. In the current context, Origen's attack on Modalism emphasized that the Father, the Son and the Holy Spirit have their own individual being or 'real existence'.

Real existence (Gr. *hypostasis*): (1) 'primordial essence', (2) the principle of individualization, (3) a subject.

Early Christian theologians struggled with the ambiguity of the term as meaning (1) appeared in the theology of Monarchianism. On the other hand, overemphasis on meanings (2) and (3) led to belief in two or three gods, i.e. tritheism. In relation to the distinction between the Father and the Son, this term denotes 'a person'. See the term *prosopon* in chapter 2.

Origen tried to hold together two crucial elements of his theory: real existence of each divine person and their eternal, mutual communion. In this view, God is a community of the three divine beings and each one is unique; but this does not mean that Christians worship three 'gods'. As Origen explains in his treatise *On Prayer*, Christian worship should address 'the God, the Father of all'.[13] It shows rather that those three divine individuals belong to one and the same species and they are not 'parts of the divine' or alien to each other. Each divine being is or rather has his own character, while at the same time, they share, like a family, the same divine status. Within this 'family' there is, in Origen's view, a clear structure and function, where the Son in his existence was dependent on his Father.[14] Unlike Tertullian, Origen was very careful to avoid the use of the term 'shared nature' or '<u>consubstantial</u>' (Gr. *homoousios*).

Consubstantiality: in the material world, for instance, a wooden spoon and a wooden table are 'consubstantial' as both items are made of the same, not similar, material substance, namely wood. Similarly, all men and women share the same nature as human beings ('human race'). In the spiritual realm, not limited by time or space, beings such as angels share the same nature. Finally, in relation to the Trinity, the Patristic notion of 'consubstantial' suggests that all three persons share the same divinity, which is their nature.

This idiom had a material connotation and therefore was not applicable at all to God, at least in Origen's view. As an erudite critic of Gnostic theology, Origen was also aware that 'shared nature' or 'to share the same being' suggested some form of 'multiplication' close to the Gnostic concept of generation of the divine aeons through the act or process of begetting. Consequently the crucial distinction between the divine Father and the divine Son is real not just conceptual;[15] they are two 'things' (Gr. *pragmata*) but at the same time one in harmony of minds and wills.[16] The notion of God's fatherhood plays the crucial role of distinction between the existence of the Father and the Son. This term and name expresses the 'exceptional way' of existence of the second divine being. Again, it is rather clear, as in the case of Tertullian, that Origen believed in the subordination of the Son to his Father, but it does not mean that the Son was 'less' divine than his Father. All this theological, philosophical and rhetorical effort pictured God as a hierarchy of beings, where the central and first place belonged to the Father.

> But whereas the offspring of men or of the other animals whom we see around us, correspond to the seed of those by whom they were begotten, or of the mothers in whose womb they are formed and nourished, drawing from these parents whatever it is that they take and bring into the light of day when they are born, it is impious and shocking to regard God the Father in the begetting of his only-begotten Son, and in the Son's substance as being similar to any human being or other animal in the act of begetting; but there must needs be some exceptional process, worthy of God to which we can find no comparison whatever, not merely in things, but even in thought and imagination, such that by its aid human thought could apprehend how the unbegotten God becomes Father of the only-begotten Son. It is an eternal and everlasting begetting, as brightness is begotten from light. For he does not become Son in an exceptional way through the adoption of the Spirit, but is Son by nature.
>
> Origen, *Princ.* 1.2.4, trans. G. W. Butterworth

Athanasius and the Arian Controversy

The image of God reinforced by these important elaborations showed God as a powerful, male Principle of the universe, while the emerging notion of the Trinity presented God as a hierarchy of three beings. At its apex was the Father, then the Son contemplating his Father and finally the Spirit who continues the mission of the Son, now in the Universal Church. But with the Arian controversy, and especially Athanasius' response, yet another aspect of God's fatherhood established its position in Catholic theology in the centuries to come. Tertullian's and Origen's theories of the relationship between God the Father and the Son emphasized the subordination of the latter to the former. Equally, Origen's ambiguity on the origin of the second person, the Logos' generation or creation,[17] as well as his strong accent on the Son's individuality, left the Alexandrian milieu with a specific legacy. This legacy included yet another aspect of approaching Godhead in a particular, apophatic way, which emphasized the limitation of all human characterizations of God.

Apophatic (Gr. *apophasis* – 'negation', 'denial'): a synonym for 'negative theology', which characterized the way of approaching God by critical rejection of the claim that human concepts may comprehend the essence of God. *Apophatic* theology argues about the inadequacy of human notions which are unable to denote the divine; therefore it concludes with God's ineffability.

In addition, exegesis of the Scriptures focused on Christ,[18] and the Alexandrian liturgy established the central position of the Son as the only Mediator surrounded by the archangels and angels and other good spirits. This image showing a divine hierarchy may suggest that the divine Father remains a distant Absolute beyond comprehension, while the Logos holds the second place as his most perfect reflection/creation, then on the third level we may see a place for various degrees of pure angels.[19] Origen, however, was not the direct source of what became known as Arian theology.

Arius was a presbyter and theologian of Alexandria who radicalized answers to certain questions which had previously been left open. In his view, the fatherhood of God is only a metaphorical title, as Godhead can neither share his nature with any other 'divine being', nor beget in an anthropomorphic way any offspring. Arius' radical, but coherent, exegesis of the Scriptures and this theological construct, as far as we can assess it on the basis of some excerpts from his opponents, shook the foundations of Christian belief. The most acute defence of the fatherhood of God came from Athanasius of Alexandria,[20] who was for many years almost the sole adversary of Arius and his supporters. The notion of 'the Father' was amplified by the pro-Nicene theology as it served a specific theological purpose. For Athanasius, the essence of his opponents' heresy was their denial of the eternal fatherhood of God, which he pointed out while recording a number of Arian declarations of faith in the Creeds.[21] Athanasius used the concept of God's eternal fatherhood as the key theological notion to prove the Son's eternal generation and participation in the same divine nature. In his *Orationsagainst the Arians* his argument runs that his adversaries the Arians, like the contemporary pagan philosophers, are unaware of the true nature of God, because like them, they are too stubborn to recognize the specific nature of the Son.[22] Both groups of intellectuals, in Athanasius' criticism, were so obsessed with logical investigation into the natural world that they did not take into account the divine revelation given by the Son. To Athanasius, the title 'Father' thus becomes a synonym for the essence of Godhead and the most appropriate name revealed by his Son to Christians.

> If God is simple as he really is, so consequently while calling him Father, we are not saying something about God, but naming his very essence.
>
> Athanasius of Alexandria, *Dec.* 18.28–30, trans. P. A.-S.

Still, Athanasius as a highly intelligent theologian and ecclesiastical admin-istrator wished to attain much more. As noted by one modern commentator: 'at stake was nothing less than the standards by which a father's potency, a son's legitimacy, and a leader's fitness would be judged'.[23] Athanasius' point of view prevailed and, with it, the status of his theological and political championship became the example of orthodoxy in the forthcoming centuries.

Seeing God the Father More Clearly: the Cappadocians

The last important phase of Patristic theology, which sealed the significance of the title, gained an important contribution from the *Cappadocians. While the development of the doctrine of the Trinity reached its climax in Latin Patristic theology with one of the greatest works in the history of the Church, Augustine's *On the Trinity*,[24] the Eastern branch of Christianity was privileged to have the works of three outstanding theologians commonly known as 'the Cappadocians'. They were: *Basil of Caesarea, his brother *Gregory of Nyssa and their close friend *Gregory of Nazianzus. The substantial contribution of the theologies of Augustine and the Cappadocians to the doctrine of the Trin-ity will be discussed in chapter 6 of this book; here I simply wish to sketch out a very important thought on the fatherhood of God presented by the Greek theologians. One of the most characteristic features of their theology of God was the accent on God's ineffability. The 'negative theology', which we have already encountered with Origen, highlighted that the human mind with its intellectual skills cannot reach or penetrate the essence of God. Consequently all human concepts of God must be carefully examined and verified, leaving theologians with certain knowledge about 'who God is not', rather than with an ultimate knowledge of God's nature. The human mind is inadequate in the light of God's light or rather darkness, while his essence remains unknowable. Therefore using, for instance, a particular male title in relation to God was inappropriate and biased, but equally imagining that God could be female, or neuter led to the same mistake of applying anthropomorphic images to the divine being, who must be beyond any concepts.[25] It was simply an error, at least according to Gregory of Nyssa, to apply any particular gender to God.[26] The scriptural title which denotes God as 'the Father' is a metaphor which defines God's nature as an archetype of parenthood to all creation, not an indication that Godhead has male gender. For the Cappadocians as defenders of pro-Nicene doctrine, the nature of God as the One who gave life to his son by eternal generation out of his own nature contains fatherhood and motherhood equally.[27] It is remarkable that with the highly sensitive, inspiring and mature theology of the Cappadocians the nature of God unveils itself as free from gender, therefore free from the 'patriarchal' model which dominated the vast majority of Patristic literature which was deeply rooted in the imagination of the majority of theologians of this period.

Conclusion

For many reasons the Patristic narrative about God used images and language which highlighted specific characteristics of the nature of God, such as 'fatherhood' and 'might'. But this theological and philosophical construction has to be assessed in the direct context of its historical origin, various challenges and their rhetorical as well as pedagogical functions. Although from our modern perspective and experience of the divine, this special theological construct of God as the Father Almighty seems to be rather narrow and exclusive, it points to the ancient Christian intuition that the only possible way of distinguishing between the divine persons is on the basis of their relationships, particularly between the first and the second persons of the Trinity. In addition to the scriptural revelation of this divine and unique relationship between Jesus of Nazareth and his Father, an ongoing history of salvation provided Patristic theologians with some insights into the individualities of all three divine persons. Yet the distinctive nature of the Holy Spirit did not appear in the context of the fatherhood of God, but had to wait for a later theological questioning. The Patristic understanding of God gradually developed into the more advanced concept of God as Trinity while unveiling more details about the specific status of each person.

Questions for Discussion

- Which are, in your view, the most important aspects of the Patristic notion of God?
- What in your view are the most challenging aspects of the Patristic theory of God?
- Can 'the apophatic theology' be helpful in constructing a positive, coherent and convincing narrative about God?
- Who among the ancient theologians discussed above is closest to your own views on God?
- 'If God is male, the male is God' (Mary Daly) – do you agree?

Further Readings

For beginners

E. Fergusson, 2003, *Background of Early Christianity*, 3rd edition, Grand Rapids, MI: Eerdmans.

J. Behr, 2001, *The Way to Nicaea: The Formation of Christian Theology*, Crestwood, NY: St Vladimir's Seminary Press.

For more advanced students

W. A. Dembski, W. J. Downs and J. B. A. Frederick (eds), 2008, *The Patristic Understanding of Creation: An Anthology of Writings from the Church Fathers on Creation and Design*, Riesel, TX: Erasmus Press.

J. M. Soskice, 1992, 'Can a Feminist Call God "Father"?', in Alvin K. Kimel Jnr (ed.), *Speaking the Christian God: The Holy Trinity and the Challenge of Feminism*, Grand Rapids, MI: Eerdmans, pp. 81–94.

P. Widdicombe, 1994, *The Fatherhood of God from Origen to Athanasius*, Oxford: Oxford Clarendon Press.

On Athanasius and the Arian Crisis

L. Ayres, 2006, *Nicaea and its Legacy: An Approach to Fourth-Century Trinitarian Theology*, Oxford: Oxford University Press, pp. 140–4.

V. Burrus, 2000, 'Fathering the Word: Athanasius of Alexandria', in Burrus, *'Begotten Not Made': Conceiving Manhood in Late Antiquity*, Stratford: Stratford University Press, pp. 36–79.

R. Williams, 2004, 'Athanasius and the Arian Crisis', in G. R. Evans (ed.), *The First Christian Theologians*, Oxford: Blackwell, pp. 157–67.

On the Cappadocians

B. Daley, 2000, *Gregory of Nazianzus*, London and New York: Routledge.

A. Meredith, 1999, *Gregory of Nyssa*, London and New York: Routledge.

P. Rousseau, 1998, *Basil of Caesarea*, Berkeley and Los Angeles: University of California Press.

F. M. Young, 1983, *From Nicaea to Chalcedon: A Guide to the Literature and its Background*, London: SCM Press, pp. 92–122.

On Gnosticism

C. Markschies, 2003, *Gnosis: An Introduction*, 2003, trans. J. Bowden, London and New York: T&T Clark, pp. 1–27.

On Irenaeus of Lyons

E. Osborn, 2005, *Irenaeus of Lyons*, Cambridge: Cambridge University Press.

On Origen

L. Ayres, 2006, *Nicaea and its Legacy: An Approach to Fourth-Century Trinitarian Theology*, Oxford: Oxford University Press, pp. 20–30.

R. Williams, 2004, 'Origen', in *The First Christian Theologians*, ed. G. R. Evans, pp. 137–9.

Internet Resources

The nature and attributes of God (Catholic Encyclopaedia):
http://www.newadvent.org/cathen/06612a.htm

Notes

1 As noted by Gillian Clark, this term is rather problematic as it reflects Christian disparagement of non-Christians, yet it is hard to find an alternative. In this study the term 'pagan' denotes the representative of Graeco-Roman culture and religions. For further details, see G. Clark, 2004, *Christianity and Roman Society*, Cambridge: Cambridge University Press, p. 35.

2 For example Plato, *Timaeus* 28 C.

3 For example *Dreams* I, 141.

4 More in: J. Barr, 1988, 'Abba Isn't "Daddy"', *JTS*, NS, 39, pp. 28–47. As noted by Francis Martin, the word 'Father' is applied 22 times in the Old Testament, but 170 times in the Gospels; see his 'The use of *Father* in the Second Temple Period', in F. Martin, 1994, *The Feminist Question: Feminist Theology in the Light of Christian Tradition*, Edinburgh: T&T Clark, p. 275 and K. E. Børresen, 1983, 'God's Image, Man's Image? Female Metaphors Describing God in the Christian Tradition', *Temenos* 19, pp. 17–32.

5 For example, Justin, *1 Apol.* 43–4.

6 *AH* 2.10.4.

7 For more information, see R. Williams, 2001, 'Defining Heresy', in A. Kreider (ed.), *The Origin of Christendom in the West*, Edinburgh: T&T Clark, pp. 313–35.

8 *AN* 1

9 *AN* 1.

10 Epiphanius, *Chest* 62.1.1—8.5.

11 *AP* 3.

12 Tertullian was rather materialistic in his ontology. The notion of 'substance' even applicable to God, meant for him 'body', as without body an object or an individual would be an abstract.

13 *OP* 15.1. This treatise discusses in many places various aspects of the Fatherhood of God.

14 Origen, *Princ.* 1.2.9.

15 *ComGJ* 10.37.212.

16 *AC* 1.23.

17 *Princ.* 4.4.1. On this point, see R. Williams, 2001, *Arius*, London: SCM Press, p. 141.

18 For instance, the divine Wisdom/Logos as 'the first Creation', cf. Wisd. 7.25–6.

19 Origen's later theology seems to bring the Father and the Son closer together, while the position of the Holy Spirit in this relation remains much less specified, apart from the fact that the Holy Spirit was a distinct person (Gr. *hypostasis*).

20 More on Athanasius, in K. Anatolios, 2004, *Athanasius of Alexandria*, London and New York: Routledge.

21 Cf. *Dec.* 6; *OrAA* 1.5–6, 1.9.29; *EpBEL* 12.

22 *OrAA* 1.33.81.

23 Burrus, *Begotten not Made*, p. 78.

24 For an example of Augustine's assimilation of the title 'Father' (Lat. *pater*) in relation to God, see, for example, *Soliloquies* 1.2, where the Bishop of Hippo addressed God with a number of characteristics which exemplify the divine fatherhood.

25 Gregory of Nazianzus, *Or* 31.7.

26 Gregory of Nyssa, *AE* 2.419 and *ComSS* 7. For more, see V. Burrus, 2000, 'Son's Legacy: Gregory of Nyssa', in *Begotten Not Made*, pp. 80–133.

27 For more information, see J. Pelikan, 1993, *Christianity and Classical Culture: The Metamorphosis of Natural Theology in the Christian Encounter with Hellenism*, New Haven, CT: Yale University Press, pp. 87–8.

2

Jesus Christ – Son of God – Our Lord

See also chapters 1, 3, 4, 5, 6, 7, 8, 9, 10, 11.

Consider this Task

Remind yourself of the meaning of 'the Messiah/Saviour' and 'salvation' in the Bible. Find out more about the biblical concept of 'the Messiah/Saviour' and about God's Word (Gr. *logos*) in the Prologue to John's Gospel.

Introduction

The second statement shared by the ancient Creeds naturally has its origin in the belief about the fatherhood of God as it highlights the central role of God's Son: Jesus of Nazareth. Like the first declaration of the Creeds, the second article was also the subject of many heated debates and controversies during the first five centuries. However, even more than the previous credal declaration, the present statement absorbed many rather complicated philosophical notions, which soon became established terminology in mainstream Christianity. This credal article expresses not only an emotional attachment to Jesus of Nazareth (e.g. Rev. 22.20), but it also hints at a great number of exegetical, theological and even philosophical assumptions, which supported the claim that Jesus of Nazareth was the divine Word (Gr. *logos*) and the <u>Saviour</u>.

> **Saviour**: a person whose life, teaching and deeds offered liberation and rescue from sin and its consequences, such as condemnation and death. The origin of the Saviour was not necessarily divine or heavenly.

Consequently, these assumptions have to be noted in order to assess the complexity of the credal statement. This chapter is a reminder of the most important phases of the development of <u>Christology</u>, which began with Jewish-Christian theology and reached its climax with the definition of the *Council of Chalcedon (451).

> **Christology** is often used to describe the theology of the person of Jesus of Nazareth as the divine and human in his two natures. In the present study, I shall use this term also as a description of some controversial, alternative models of presenting Jesus.

Opening Question

In the light of the four Gospels, do you think that Jesus thought of himself as divine? What evidence from Scripture supports your position?

Development of the Argument

The scriptural references to Jesus of Nazareth, both those later qualified as 'canonical' and the Christian apocrypha (see chapter 3), provide strong evidence which identifies Jesus of Nazareth with the Messiah/Christ.

> **Canon** (Gr. *kanon*, – 'reed', or 'measuring rod'): the official list of the 27 books of the New Testament as 'inspired by God' was affirmed and promoted by *Athanasius of Alexandria in his *Festival Letter* (367), which gives the earliest reference to the present NT canon.

The majority of these ancient documents expressed an emotional attachment to Jesus rather than a refined theological and philosophical theory of his being. The earliest post-apostolic literature reflected the loud acclamation that 'Jesus is the Lord' and did not contain any speculation about the nature of the Saviour. Soon a more extended explanation of this acclamation was called for under growing pressure from some alternative Christian views on the Saviour as well as in the light of Jewish and pagan critique of this belief. Later Patristic doctrine of Jesus Christ assimilated further very sophisticated philosophical notions of those elements which constituted 'human' and 'divine' beings, which were ultimately included in the dogmatic statements of the Ecumenical Councils on the person of the Saviour.

Jesus: Angel/Messenger

One of the main concerns of early pre-Nicene Christians was to clarify the mission and distinctiveness of their Lord. Accepting that Jesus' life, death and resurrection fulfilled the prophecies of the Hebrew Bible, this affirmation called for a specific interpretation of the Scriptural prophecies. The urgent task was to highlight God's act of salvation accomplished through Jesus of Nazareth. To Christian *apologists, Jesus became the universal 'channel' of salvation, the ultimate 'revealer' of God and the unique Messenger of God's will. This last notion appeared in a different context in the earliest Christian documents. For some among the Jewish Christians the crucial imagery of Jesus Christ was connected with the function of an angel of God (Hebr. *mal'ak Yahweh*), which exceeded in might and authority all other angels of God. This early Christian tradition emphasized two important functions of Christ-Angel/Messenger, while suggesting the third crucial point. First, he was the ultimate manifestation of God, the ultimate Messenger of the greatest authority. The most venerable Angel brought to humanity a new illumination, and this motif, although with different semantics, was common ground among various Christian traditions.[1] Second, the same symbolism helped to affirm Jewish monotheism, while assimilating a new Christian emphasis on the central role of the Son. Third, this notion suggested the pre-existence of the Glorious Angel-Christ before he became Jesus of Nazareth, although at this stage of the development of the doctrine the origin of the Messenger remained an open question.

Jesus: God's Word

One of the most significant understandings of Jesus of Nazareth among second-century theologians was expressed by the title 'God's Word' (Gr. *logos*). This title appears in, for instance, the Prologue of John's Gospel (1.1, 14), but it hints at a larger, Greek and philosophical view of the role and nature of the mediator between a transcendent God and humanity/creation. In this philosophical tradition, which was assimilated into Hebrew theology by *Philo of Alexandria, the Logos was God's Mind, the principal Servant and the Instrument of the creation of the world, and then he was the main governor over the created universe. One of the most important witnesses of the application of this title and its content to a Christian theology of Jesus was *Justin Martyr. In his defence of Christianity as true and most noble religion, Justin argued on many occasions that Jesus of Nazareth is God's ultimate 'message', 'word' and 'revealer' of the Absolute.

> God's Son, who is rightly called 'Son', the Word, who was with God and was begotten before the creation, when at the beginning God created and ordered all things through him, is called 'Christ'.
>
> *2 Apology* 6, trans. P. A.–S.

Justin's philosophically inclined intellectual pagan audience would have found in his apologetic treatise a number of arguments which aimed to convince them that the Absolute revealed himself in the fullest way through Jesus of Nazareth, who was more than just a sage. Jesus, God's Word, was at the centre of the history of salvation, while his life and teaching presented the fullness of God's communication with all humanity.

Divine or Human? A Way Out of the Christological Dilemma

The earliest theological reflection on the nature of Christ developed along at least three competing paths and produced three Christological models. This should not be understood to suggest that those early interpretations established their 'profile' as 'a theological school'. Rather, the pluralism of theological views is evidence of the mosaic of theologies which flourished in various geographical places and intellectual milieux. One tendency affirmed the Saviour's pure divinity unmixed with humanity, and this view became known as 'docetic' Christology.

> Docetism/docetic (Gr. *dokein* – 'seem to be' or 'to appear'): the proponents of this view believed that the divine Saviour only 'appeared' in human flesh, but was not really incarnate.

In consequence, docetic Christians claimed that Jesus' suffering and death was apparent, not real. The Saviour could not suffer in human body because the material element, including flesh, is evil. Consequently, the divine Redeemer did not have a physical body or mix with the evil element of matter. The radical dualism which underpinned the separation of 'light' and 'darkness', 'good' and 'evil', 'spiritual' and 'material' or 'earthly' was the basis for docetic Christology.

Another early Christian opinion rejected any 'divine' element in Jesus of Nazareth and focused on Jesus' nature as human but equipped with supernatural charisma. Jesus was 'a mere man' living according to the Jewish law.[2] This view was called *'Ebionitism' (Hebr. *ebyon* – 'poor men'). It characterized some Jewish-Christian groups and later become known in another version as 'Adoptionism'.

> **Adoptionism**: the early Christology which proclaimed that Jesus of Nazareth was a mere human being 'adopted' by God as his messenger and who consequently acquired divine powers.

The Ebionite Christians saw Jesus as a mere human being, yet another prophet who spoke for God but was not divine.

The third option, which tried to steer between the extremes of these two views, can be found among some of the *Apostolic Fathers. Their interpretation of the Scriptures emphasized the greatest paradox of Christian faith in Jesus: he was at the same time human (mortal, limited in knowledge) and divine (immortal, omniscient), born in time (has his beginning, finite) but pre-existed the creation of the world (he does not have a beginning, infinite). In brief, Jesus' status and nature do not have any analogy in the visible and invisible worlds, as he is unique.

This synopsis shows that among these three tendencies two overemphasized either the divine or the human element (or nature) in Jesus Christ, while the third tried to establish some balance between the two radical opinions and interpret the Scriptures in a way which bound together divinity and humanity in Jesus Christ. The third way, which became the view of the Church, assumed as its axiom the greatest paradox of Christian faith: that in Jesus two natures are united in one person.

Irenaeus of Lyons: Jesus Christ – 'the second Adam'

The most developed Christology during the second century comes from Irenaeus of Lyons. Challenged by his *Gnostic adversaries who, as in the case of the *Valentinians, shared a docetic view of Christ, Irenaeus produced one of the most advanced theories. This theory encompassed his views on participation in the life of the true Church as well as on growth in spiritual maturity towards perfection. Although Irenaeus was a biblical theologian, not a philosopher like Justin Martyr or Clement of Alexandria, his theology included various aspects of his views on the Church, sacraments, salvation and eschatology. In the centre of that rich outlook was Irenaeus' view of Christ, the Saviour of all, who was 'the second Adam'. The foundation of Irenaeus' understanding of the whole scenario of salvation was the notion of 'recapitulation', (Lat. *recapitulatio*), which suggested repetition of some past events, but with opposite outcome.[3]

> 'Recapitulation', or 'summing up' (Lat. *caput* – 'head', which is Christ's title, see Eph. 1.10): one of the most important Patristic doctrines elaborated by Irenaeus of Lyons. As a theory of salvation, it highlights the central role of Jesus Christ, the 'head'. Jesus' life 'summed up' and fulfilled the true meaning of all revelations in the history of salvation and finally established the communion between God and humanity.

> Therefore the Lord calls himself 'the Son of Man', because he recapitulates in himself the first man [Adam – P. A.-S.] who was the source of the human race formed according to its mother [Eve – P. A.-S.]. As through the defeat of the first man our race descended into death, so through the victory of the Man we may ascend towards life.
>
> Irenaeus of Lyons, *AH* 5.21.1, trans. P. A.-S.

Irenaeus' vision offers an insight into God's all-embracing process of redemption, which includes creation, the fall, the incarnation, resurrection and eschatological hope. In the centre of this panoramic perspective is Jesus Christ. In Irenaeus' view, Logos/Christ repeated the circumstances of Adam's life, but with the opposite result. Where the first Adam failed to be faithful to God, the second 'Adam', Christ, became the archetype of the perfect obedience.

Jesus' earthly life was the example to all and the 'path' of salvation leading through various stages and events, such as temptations in the desert, suffering, death, finally resurrection and ascension. According to this theory, the first Adam's defeat was repaired by the second Adam's victory and the first Adam's humiliation led to the second Adam's glorification. Evil powers lost the battle and were conquered by the human and divine Saviour. Christ's life, death and resurrection as the human existence of the divine Son brought all humanity back to its Father and Creator. The relationship broken by human disobedience in Eden was reintroduced by Jesus Christ. It is thus the Son of God who, as divine and human at the same time, is the unique 'bridge' between humanity and God. Furthermore, Christ is the ultimate 'channel' and Mediator of salvation through whom divine grace comes down to human beings, and by whom men and women can be elevated to their original place in God's kingdom.

> Unless Man had triumphed over the adversary of humanity, this adversary would not have been ultimately defeated. On the other hand, unless it had been God who gave us salvation, we would not have possessed it permanently. Unless the Man had been united with God, it would not have been possible for us to share in God's incorruptibility. Truly, the Mediator between God and humanity, by his relationship with both, had to gather both together in friendship and unity, and bring humanity back to God, while at the same time revealing God to all men and women.
>
> Irenaeus of Lyons, *AH* 3.18.7, trans. P. A.-S.

Thus, the history of salvation reaches its climax and full realization 'in Christ' as he restores the original unity broken by the human act of disobedience and accomplishes God's redemption. It is quite clear that in order to perform this act of 'recapitulation' the main character, that is the Saviour himself, must have been fully divine and fully human. Otherwise, neither would humanity be penetrated by God's grace and might, nor would the noblest human hero and the most holy saints reach the divine realm. To bring together two realms, the divine and human, eternal and created, the Saviour had in his nature both elements. Irenaeus' theory of salvation can be summed up by one of his theological slogans, the so-called 'exchange formula', which was later repeated by Athanasius of Alexandria in his dispute against the Arians:[4] the Son of God by nature became a man in order that human beings may become the adopted sons of God.[5] This attractive theory established Christology as one of the pillars of Christian doctrine, faith and hope. The mystery of the incarnation clearly played an essential role in his approach to salvation. Although Irenaeus' theory was promoted as a response to the Gnostic questioning, it provided the Church with an imaginative vision of the meaning of history of salvation in centuries to come.

The Redeemer: Alternative Christian Views

Irenaeus' opponents, the so-called Gnostics, did not represent one unanimous and united ecclesiastical party. On the contrary, there is a convincing body of evidence from their documents that there existed a diversity of Gnostic schools and theologies, including a diversity of Gnostic views on the Redeemer's nature and mission. As the outspoken adversary of those alternative opinions, the Bishop of Lyons stated that his opponents were like the 'many-headed hydra of Greek myths'.[6] That theological polyphony formed not just one, easily defined Christology, such as the docetic tendency, but rather it developed a great number of models, which were loosely connected or even exclusive.

In order to present a sketch of the Gnostic views of Christ, it is necessary to note three aspects of the Gnostic Redeemer. These aspects are: (1) the Redeemer's origin, (2) his nature and (3) the meaning of his descent to this world. This brief presentation must stress that the Gnostic use of titles such as 'Christ', 'Logos', 'the Son of God', 'the Lord', 'the Son of Man' and even 'God' and 'Saviour' differed radically from their use by the authors of the Church. Gnostic Christologies emphasized the nature of the Redeemer, which remained hidden, spiritual and alien to this world and therefore escaping from all human categories, images and intellectual concepts.

> Straightway, [while I was contemplating these things,] behold, the [heavens opened and] the whole creation [which is] below heaven shone, and [the world] was shaken. [I was afraid, and behold I] saw in the light [a youth who stood] by me. While I looked [at him, he became] like an old man. And he [changed his] likeness (again), becoming like a servant. There was not a plurality before me, but there was a [likeness] with multiple forms in the light, and the [likenesses] appeared through each other, and the likeness had three forms. He said to me, 'John, John, why do you doubt, or why [are you] afraid? You are not unfamiliar with this image, are you? – that is, do not [be] timid! – I am the one who is [with you (pl.)] always. I am [the Father], I am the Mother, I am the Son. I am the undefiled and incorruptible one. Now [I have come to teach you] what is [and what was] and what will come to [pass], that [you may know the] things which are not revealed [and

those which are revealed, and to teach you] concerning [the unwaver-
ing race] of the perfect [Man]. Now, therefore, [lift up] your face, that
you may [receive] the things that [I shall teach you] today, [and] may
tell [them to your] fellow spirits who [are from] the [unwavering] race
of the perfect Man.'
>> The Nag Hammadi Library, *ApJ* 2.1.30—2.25, trans. F. Wisse

Still, both groups, Irenaeus' Catholic fellow-believers and their rivals, such
as the Valentinians, assumed a planned ordering of salvation. However, the latter group excluded the flesh and ignorance from their plan of salvation. Many
documents from the Coptic *Nag Hammadi Library provided various dramatic
settings of the prehistorical catastrophe, which caused the fall of all spiritual
elements ('particles of light') into the current world ('body/prison'), where they
mixed with the material element. Gnostic literature also offered a number of
different scenarios of the ultimate redemption and the ascent to the original
homeland.[7] As in the case of the apologists, Gnostic narratives gave a detailed
account of the original tragedy, which then led to the appearance of the current
experience of 'exile'. Nonetheless, the same documents provide support for the
human desire for liberation and redemption. As in the Catholic interpretation,
so for the Gnostic authors, the role of Redeemer/Christ is at the centre of this
process. Some of these narratives portrayed the role of the divine Redeemer as
the one who came down to provide those fallen sparks of light with illumination,
awakening and knowledge of their true nature and destiny. This crucial function
of the Redeemer/Instructor meant that he freed his people from their ignorance
('sleep', 'drunkenness') about the condition of their lives and the status of this
temporary universe. The Redeemer was sending the 'call' to those who could
hear[8] and understand. From this role, it is evident that the Redeemer must have a
special status and power. The general conviction among those Christians was that
the Saviour was a part of the divine assembly, that is, the first group of emanated
divine beings. As the Ultimate God was unattainable, these beings represent the
highest divinities, the 'household of the Father of truth'.[9] Therefore he emanated
from the Father – the Absolute; he was 'the light' from the power of the true
God, 'the spotless mirror' of his Source and the reflection of the goodness of the
Absolute.[10] These alternative Christologies located the origin of the Redeemer
in the divine realm, or even his generation from the Father/Mother, while some

of them amplified the axiom that his nature could not combine with a material body. As the divine/spiritual element is incompatible with the material/animal flesh, the Redeemer, although 'heard' and 'seen' by some, was not a 'man in the flesh'. Consequently, he did not suffer and die on the cross, as the bloody and grotesque interpretation promoted by the Catholics tried to portray (see chapter 4). To Irenaeus and many other apologists, this serious disregard was a direct assault on the core belief in Jesus' human and divine natures and as such was rejected in many polemical treatises and in the statements of the ancient Creeds.

Clement of Alexandria: the Logos – the Revealer

Clement of Alexandria and Origen continued and enriched the Logos theology, this time elaborated in the light of Christian revelation. Clement's contribution can be summarized in two points. He reaffirms that the essence of God is unutterable and incapable of being circumscribed.[11] Therefore the divine Logos becomes the only revealer of his Father. In the light of Christian revelation, Clement's view emphasizes his role as a personal 'teacher', 'instructor', 'physician', 'bridegroom'; in brief, he is more than just a perfect divine principle. Unlike his Valentinian and other opponents, Clement's theology of the Logos emphasizes his real incarnation,[12] although the historical and factual details of the Logos/Christ's life are peripheral in his theology. Yet Clement of Alexandria left many problems unresolved. For example, he seemed to accept two stages of the origin of the Logos' existence before and after the creation of the world, but the scholar does not elaborate on the origin of the Logos, as the Mind of God co-exists with God,[13] as his Son proceeds from the Father,[14] as divine Wisdom is created first of all.[15] Among all these and many more ambiguities, one aspect of his status as the divine being is certain: the Logos is subordinate to his Father in status and function.

Origen: the Logos – the Second Divine

Origen's contribution to theology of the Logos is highly important. However, it is also complex and contains some unfinished thoughts. The Logos holds the central place in Origen's theology of salvation. As Origen emphasized the transcendence of God (see chapter 1), the Logos is the mediator between God and the rest of creatures. It is through the mediation of the divine Logos, as God's agent, that creation and redemption took place. The Logos who directly contemplates his Father is also the ultimate Revealer of God's will to humanity. Even from this synopsis it is possible to note that the Logos, whom Origen identified with Jesus of Nazareth, is a real being, different from his Father. It is also possible to observe that the Logos must have existed before the creation of the world, or even that the Logos is co-eternal with his Father. However, as the Father's agent, the Logos holds 'second place' among the three divine beings. The exact way of generating the Logos by his Father still leaves some room in Origen's theory for further investigation; nonetheless, the Son proceeds from the Father like 'light from light'. However, Origen's own creative and speculative theology of the Logos also developed as a response to some erroneous theories, which the great theologian wished to refute.

As has been pointed out in the previous chapter, Origen's polemic against Modalism prompted him to emphasize what is really different among the three divine persons, rather than their unity or what they share. In his polemic against a pagan philosopher Celsus, Origen seems to address a much bigger issue than just philosophical criticism of Christian belief in Jesus as God's messenger. On that occasion Origen affirms his understanding of God as three distinct real beings (Gr. *hypostases*),[16] although existing as one (Gr. *hen*) in the harmony (Gr. *symphonia*).

It may seem that Celsus' criticism contains something plausible: 'If these people worshipped no other God but one, they would perhaps have a good argument against their critics. But they worship a man who has recently come to this world, and they believe that there is no offence against their God if they worship his servant too.' The reply to this accusation is simple. If Celsus had known Jesus' saying, 'I and My Father are one' [John 10.30], and the words said in prayer by the Son of God, 'As You and I are one' [John 17.22], he would not have supposed that we worship any other besides the Supreme God. Christ said, 'My Father is in me, and I in the Father' [John 14.11]. However, if anybody fears by these words that we share the views

> of heretics who deny that the Father and the Son are two beings [Gr. *hypostases*], let him consider this passage: 'the whole group of those who believed were of one heart and soul' [Acts 4.32], that he may understand the meaning of the statements: 'I and my Father are one' [John 10.30].
>
> Origen, *AC* 8.12, trans. P. A.-S.

Origen's intention was to protect the three distinct divine <u>persons</u> (Gr. plur. *prosopa*) against certain erroneous interpretations (Monarchianism or Modalism).

> '**Person**' (Gr. *prosopon*): alternative term to *hypostasis* (see chapter 1) as it put emphasis on the individual, real existence of a (divine) person. The Greek term and its notion translated into Latin as *persona*. This term includes that 'a person' has knowledge, free will, performs actions and can enter into relationship with other beings. In the case of each divine person, these characteristics denote their ultimate perfection and unceasing (eternal) existence.

Origen rejected the tendency to see God as one divine substance/being which emerges at different stages of the history of salvation with a different 'face' and personality. This kind of divine amalgam diluted what in Origen's view was the crucial part of Christian revelation, namely, the triune nature of God and the person of the Son of God and 'our Lord'. Consequently, for Origen, God exists as the Father, the Son and the Holy Spirit eternally, that is independently of the stages of revelation and salvation.[17] As the Father 'never became' Father, but always was, it is possible to say the same about his Son. Nonetheless, his status is not equal with his source of being, as the Son is begotten, while the Father is the one who begets.[18] Origen's Christological legacy secured the real difference of the divine persons, while at the same time it emphasized a rather hierarchical, inner, 'structure' of the divine. But what truly caused some problems in the next generation of Alexandrian theologians was that Origen's authority did not leave much proof that the Father and the Son shared <u>the same substance</u> (Gr. *homoousios*).

'The same substance' or 'consubstantial' (Gr. *homoousios*), therefore of the same nature: the term appeared originally in Valentinian theology, denoting a common essence shared by the human element ('spirit', 'mind' or 'spark') with the divine Saviour. The term was applied by Paul of Samosata (third century CE) to God the Father and the Son in a Modalist way: the divine unity of the substance excluded any real difference between two persons. While some theologians had a problem with the ambiguity and affiliation of the term *homoousios* and proposed the use of *homoiousios* ('being of like substance') in relation to the Son, the theological contribution of Athanasius, Basil of Caesarea (East) and Hilary of Poitiers (West) clarified and secured the correct meaning of the term. The pro-Nicene use of the term highlighted the numerical identity of essence between first the two, soon the three persons of the Trinity, stating that the 'substance' of each one of them is the same.

The Arian Controversy: Created or Begotten?

Logos theology was one of the strongest characteristics of Alexandrian Christology. *Arius, the Alexandrian presbyter and theologian, was a child of that tradition and milieu. His 'conservative' theological attitude was faithful to 'the letter and to the spirit' of this tradition and consequently it opened one of the most significant conflicts in the Patristic era. Arius was not the *enfant terrible* of Logos theology, but rather its radical and relentless exponent. The dispute over Arius' view broke out around 320, when he was asked by his bishop Alexander, soon his first opponent, to comment on the nature of Wisdom in the context of a scriptural passage (Prov. 8.22–5). Biblical exegesis seemed to support his theological stance: that the genuine, correct Christian view proclaims only one God, while in the case of the so-called 'Son' of God, we should use only respectful, allegorical titles. The Logos was called to existence as the only mediator between the ineffable God and his creatures. As such, he was the first creation (i.e. not co-eternal) and he did not participate in any way in God's nature.

> But we are persecuted because we have said, 'The Son has a begin-
> ning, but God is without beginning.' We are also persecuted because
> we have said, 'He is made from nothing.' But we have so said because
> he is not a part of God or made from any thing previously existent.
> Arius, *The Letter to Eusebius of Nicomedia*, in Epiphanius, *Chest* 69.7,
> trans. F. Williams

Hierarchically, the Logos was much lower than God and, finally, he was changeable as God's creation. According to Arius' logic, God cannot 'beget' as this notion would suggest some form of reproduction and even a common nature between the divine parent and his offspring, therefore it would be anthropomorphic. The daring assumption of 'sharing the same nature' (Gr. *homoousios*) implies a materialistic division or extension of the divine and, in the context of Christology, leads to a neologism. Jesus Christ, as embodiment of the Wisdom, was created before time/world for the sake of the history of salvation. He was also created not of the substance of his divine origin, but out of nothing (see chapter 1). Therefore Christianity is still a monotheistic religion, faithful to Jesus' teaching about himself as not equal to the Father (e.g. John 14.28). The pro-Arian theologians protected in their view the original Christian belief from any 'modernization' either by non-scriptural terminology (Gr. *homoousios*) or by polytheistic inclination (more than one God). The Logos, as the Alexandrian tradition established, performed crucial functions in the history of salvation, but he was only God's Revealer and Administrator; he exists from his beginning on a lower level than his divine Creator, the only true God. The evident subordination of the Logos to his Creator is one of the most distinctive features of the Christology presented by the group known as 'Arians'.[19]

Arius and his supporters found in Athanasius of Alexandria, who succeeded Bishop Alexander after his death (328), one of the most uncompromising adversaries. Two interesting facts call for our attention. First, Athanasius did not intend to argue with Arius only on the basis of the Scriptures, although he examined a number of passages referring to the relationship between God the Father and his divine Son.[20] Rather, by analogy with, for instance, 'radiance' and 'light' or 'stream' and 'the fountain', it is possible to comprehend two elements in the same nature.

Again the Father is in the Son, while giving his essence to the Son, like the essence of the sun is passed on to its rays, as the mind is present in a word, and as the spring is present in the stream, therefore the one who contemplates the Son contemplates also the essence of the Father and is able to understand that the Father is in the Son. The Father's essence and divinity is indeed the same as the Son's [. . .]. For they are one; not as one thing divided into two parts, although it remains still one; nor as in the case of a person who may be called by one name, while another time by another; in a sense that sometimes the Father can be called 'Father', while another time, he is called the Son [. . .]. But they are two persons [Gr. *hypostases*], because the Father is the Father and not the Son; and the Son is the Son and not the Father, but the essence is one and the same.

Athanasius, *OrAA* 3.3–4, trans. P. A.-S.

Second, if Arius can be defeated, one does not thereby reject the Alexandrian legacy as a whole, but rather selects its valuable assets and strengthens with them the new and correct project of Christology.

To achieve the first purpose, Athanasius' theory brought to light an important notion of salvation, which had already been mentioned by Irenaeus of Lyons. The crucial notion that directed Athanasius' approach to Christology was his understanding of salvation. Between God and humanity there is such a enormous gulf that only a person representing both realities, that is divine and human at the same time, can bring together and reconcile these two. It is thus Jesus of Nazareth, affirmed by orthodox, correct faith as the Son of God and 'our Lord', that is 'our Saviour' who is able to cross over that ontological chasm. No mere human being can reach the divine, that was the first axiom of Athanasius' theology of salvation, but only the divine can descend to the human realm and then bring back humanity to God. That was his conclusion. As God the Father did not descend, it was his only Son, begotten of the Father, 'from the substance of the Father' who descended in order to reconcile men and women with their Creator. As the Logos/Christ was born of his Father, in nature he was equal to him, neither 'mixed'[21] with him nor separated, as extreme subordinationism suggested. Athanasius did not hesitate to assimilate the non-biblical term co-substantial (Gr. *homoousios*) in order to bring more clarity into the divine relationship between the Father and the Son.[22] From now on, this term will have its unquestionable place in Catholic Christology.

With regard to the second purpose, Athanasius himself was the heir of the Alexandrian theology of the Logos, but he seems to emphasize the ineffability of God's substance as such, while the term 'Father' points to the nature of the divine Father (begetting) and similarly, the notion of the Son is correlated with the essence of the second person of the Trinity (begotten).[23] As the heir of this tradition, he knew that Christians, unlike Gentiles, should worship the only true God, not a semi-divine Arian Christ, but the Father, the Son and the Holy Spirit. Athanasius' position brings together the theory of salvation, Christology and spirituality in such a way that Christ as the only mediator remains also the only natural offspring of his divine Father.[24] After years of personal, but also ecclesiastical and political disarray, the local synod at Antioch (325) promoted a specific statement of 'Catholic faith' against the Arians. It was based on a text provided by Bishop Alexander of Alexandria. Then, later the same year, the doctrine which claimed 'consubstantiality' of the Son with the divine Father received more authority by its promulgation at the *First Ecumenical Council of Nicaea (325) with clear terminology denoting the Son as 'only-begotten from the substance of the Father'.

> The Creed of Nicaea (325)
> We believe in one God, the Father almighty, maker of all things, both visible and invisible; and in one Lord Jesus Christ, the Son of God, begotten of the Father, only-begotten; that is, from the substance of the Father, God from God, light from light, true God from true God, begotten, not made, of one substance (Gr. *homoousios*) with the Father.

The confusion related to Arius' teaching did not end with the promulgation of the Nicene formula of faith or with the political support of the pro-Nicene emperors or even with the strong emphasis of the *Second Ecumenical Council of Constantinople (381) on the authority of the Nicene confession of faith. It still caused anxieties in various parts of Christendom after Arius' and Athanasius' death. One of the casualties of that ultra-sensitivity was one of Athanasius' oldest friends, *Apollinarius the bishop of Laodicea in Asia Minor (Turkey). Apollinarius cultivated biblical learning, with his admiration of Jerome and classical culture, even possibly Greek philosophy. Apollinarius' view on human being was both Platonic as well as Pauline, with the same tripartite distinction of the elements: body, mind and spirit. His extreme reaction to Arianism and his passionate defence of the pro-Nicene Christology led him to believe that the divine Logos in his incarnation replaced the human mind/soul. Christ was a heavenly man as his human flesh was inhabited by the divine mind. This theory may sound peculiar to a modern reader. Yet in the Platonic context of an anthropology in which a human being consists of three elements, the incarnation was seen by Apollinarius and his followers as a substitution of the human mind in Jesus by the divine mind of the Logos. By the replacement, Jesus' deity was protected by the divine mind (i.e. <u>impassible</u>), while his humanity was fully accepted by his soul and body (i.e. fallible and changeable).

> **Impassibility** of God: a view which claims that God is not able to experience any kind of suffering or change as any increase or diminution in knowledge and experience would undermine his divine, perfect and unchanged nature. In relation to Jesus Christ, this doctrine claims that Jesus as the divine being was incapable of sharing any human experience such as pain and limited knowledge. See also the term *apatheia* in chapter 6.

This modification of Christology maintained the unity of the two natures in Christ; however, its lack of the human mind points to an incompleteness of the incarnation. Soon, Catholic critics highlighted that the fact that Apollinarius' theory endorsed an incomplete humanity in Christ and consequently this 'imperfect' human/divine Saviour redeemed only some parts of human nature, but not all. Apollinarianism was condemned as a heresy, first by the synods in Rome (374–80) and then at the Council of Constantinople (381).

Antiochene Christology

The next crucial debate broke out when two more opponents crossed swords in the following century. One of the features of Patristic theology is that it was strongly related to the academic milieu and to a city and region. In the early

Church the most significant position was held by the churches established by the apostles, at least according to religious legends. In the western part of Christianity the leading role was held by Rome (Peter and Paul), while in the eastern part they included Jerusalem, Antioch (Peter), Ephesus (John) and Alexandria (Mark). So far Alexandria has been at the centre of our attention, but now another two places make their mark on the map of the Patristic world: Antioch, city and region in Syria (Turkey), and Constantinople. Unlike the city of Constantinople, founded by the Emperor Constantine the Great in 330 by the picturesque Bosporus, the city of Antioch already had a long history of affiliation with Christian origins and an established position among other Christian metropolises. The theological position of the city/region was reaffirmed by a number of illustrious theologians and exegetes, beginning with Theophilus of Antioch and then at the end of the fourth and in the early fifth century with Diodore of Tarsus, *John Chrysostom, *Theodore of Mopsuestia and *Theodoret of Cyrrhus. Those eminent thinkers and leaders contributed to the specific trajectory of exegesis which became known as the Antiochene 'school'. This tradition was opposed to the Alexandrian approach, which overemphasized the role of allegory. In brief, it is right to say that the Antiochene approach aimed to bring some balance to Alexandrian radical allegorical–spiritual exegesis by the further development of textual criticism, advanced philological studies and an emphasis on the historical context of Christian literature. In addition, the Antiochene tradition elaborated with great attention Christ's human experience and existence. While accepting the post-Nicene agreement about Christ's two natures, the key scholars from the Antiochene point of view commented on Jesus' human nature, the reality of his incarnation and his human soul and moral choices. At the same time Alexandrian exegesis, while commenting on the scriptural narratives and Christological motifs, put more emphasis on the divinity of Christ, so well defended by Athanasius, by now the champion of orthodoxy, as the harmonious co-existence of the two natures of Christ. In this context, Constantinople during the fifth century was an extension of the Antiochene spirit. As in the case of Arius, the whole conflict began with exegesis of the Scriptures, but soon also engaged political competition between leading Christian cities, this time between Alexandria and Constantinople.

Nestorius' Concerns

In April 428 *Nestorius, a monk from Antioch, was appointed as the bishop of Constantinople and the successor of an outstanding but controversial preacher, John Chrysostom. Nestorius believed in the two natures of Christ: the human and the divine. In his view, since the divine, eternal element is totally different from the created human one, these two natures 'existed' in Christ in a parallel way after his incarnation. Consequently, while noticing a growing devotion to Mary, the Mother of Christ, Nestorius expressed his opposition to the title 'Mother of God' or 'God-bearing' (Gr. *Theotokos*), since as a human being she could give birth only to Jesus' humanity (see chapter 3). It would be correct, according to Nestorius, to call Mary 'the Mother of the man – Jesus' or 'Christ-bearing' (Gr. *Christotokos*). This radical distinction in Christology between the divine and human natures, as well as undermining popular piety, not to mention other much more political and personal reasons, drew attention to Nestorius from *Cyril, the bishop of Alexandria. At the end of the same year (428), Cyril vigorously attacked Nestorius' doctrine. In 430 Cyril sent a dogmatic letter to his opponent demanding that he renounce his views and accept *the Twelve Anathemas.* The negative response from Nestorius unleashed one of the greatest Christological controversies in the early Church. Cyril's theology won the acceptance of the members of the *Third Ecumenical Council of Ephesus (431), which condemned Nestorius and his followers; in turn, they continued to exist as the Nestorian churches in the Syriac East and further east towards central Asia.[25] Cyril's Christology was accepted by the members of the Council as they also confirmed the maternity of Mary as the mother of the divine Christ. This conflict emphasized the role and meaning of an important theological idiom commonly known in its Latin expression as 'interchange of the properties' (Lat. *communicatio idiomatum*).[26]

Interchange of the properties (Lat. *communicatio idiomatum*): a theory about the way of attaching the properties of one of Christ's natures to the other on the basis of the unity of the person. Therefore *idiomata* ('properties') of his humanity (such as hunger) can be predicated of his divinity, while *idiomata* of his divinity (e.g. infinite power) also denote his humanity.

SCM STUDYGUIDE TO EARLY CHRISTIAN DOCTRINE

In Cyril's adaptation, interchange of properties explained what Nestorius could not comprehend in his view, that all properties of the divine Logos are applicable to the human Jesus; therefore, *Theotokos* was a correct and precious title. In addition, the divine Logos, ineffably born of the Father, while bodily of a woman, suffered, died and was raised from the dead.[27] But the final stage of the development of Christology in the Patristic period included yet another radical theologian: *Eutyches. His zeal to support Cyril of Alexandria and defend orthodoxy against Nestorius' heresy led him to amalgamate the two natures of Christ into one (Gr. *monos* – 'one' and *physis* – 'nature'). In brief, while Nestorius' radical distinction separated the two natures, at least from the orthodox point of view, Eutyches bound them so tightly that both became one mixture. His famous phrase expressed that belief in the following way:

> I believe that the Lord was 'from two natures' before the union, but after the union I acknowledge only 'one nature'.
>
> *Acta Conciliorum Oecumenicorum*, 1927–32, ed. E. Schwartz, Argentorati–Berolini–Lipsiae, 143, trans. P. A.-S.

The Monophysites, who held a strong position in monastic communities and the imperial court of Constantinople, tried to promote their views as orthodox at the 'Robber Synod' of Ephesus (449). Soon, thanks to the significant role of Leo the Great, the bishop of Rome (who made a political alliance with Pulcheria, the elder sister of the Emperor Theodosius II and a very powerful, learned, devout and ambitious woman), the theory of 'one-nature' was rejected. The ultimate definition of the union of 'two natures in one person' was established at the *Fourth Council of Chalcedon (451).

> Following the holy Fathers, we all with one voice declare the confession of one and the same Son, our Lord Jesus Christ, who is the same perfect in divinity as in humanity, the same truly God and truly man, of a rational soul and a body; consubstantial [Gr. *homoousios*] with regards to his divinity, and the same consubstantial [Gr. *homoousios*] with us as to his humanity; he is like us in all things except for sin; begotten of his Father before the ages as regards his divinity; and in recent days

the same for us and for our salvation, from Mary the Virgin the God-bearer [Gr. *Theotokos*] as regards his humanity. This one and the same Christ, Son, Lord, the only-begotten Son known in two natures, which are without confusion, without change, without division, without separation; at no point was the difference of the natures taken away by the union, but rather the properties of both are preserved, and are united in one person [Gr. *prosopon*] and a single subsistent being [Gr. *hypostasis*], who is not parted or divided into two persons [Gr. *prosopa*], but who is one and the same Son, the only-begotten, God, the Word, the Lord Jesus Christ, as the prophets taught in ancient times about him, and as the Lord Jesus Christ himself revealed and as the creed of the Fathers passed on to us.

The Chalcedonian Definition, trans. P. A.-S.

The Council proclaimed as the Catholic faith belief in the co-existence of two natures affirmed as 'without confusion, without change, without division, without separation'. The grammar of this pronouncement unveils the Chalcedonian agreement as negative. It excluded ('without') certain concepts as erroneous, while its positive, correct affirmation remained somehow unfinished and controversial: Jesus is declared 'in two natures', human and divine, but what does it mean in the context of Jesus' human and divine experience that 'the properties of both are preserved, and are united'? Did Jesus know more about hunger and suffering after incarnation than before? Although it strengthened the doctrinal unity between Eastern and Western Churches, the Council of Chalcedon also excluded other Christians, such as those in Syria and Egypt who did not accept and still cannot accept the 'two natures' definition. Although the present summary has to stop at this point, Christology still had a fascinating future in, for instance, its Coptic and early Byzantine development. There, with the input of such luminous theologians such as *John of Damascus, it entered a new phase of development, which then found its continuation in early medieval theology.

Conclusion

This brief summary of the development of Christology in the Patristic period confirms its irreplaceable value in the Christian doctrine of the Son of God. During this period more happened in this field of theological investigation than in many centuries to come. Even if a number of those ancient notions and ideas call for a new evaluation, their status as 'classical' Christological notions remains unquestioned.

Questions for Discussion

- Which Christological debate do you find the most relevant to modern views on Jesus Christ?
- What kind of Christology is promoted by contemporary cinematography?
- Which aspects of the Patristic, Gnostic, Arian and Nestorian views do you find most attractive?

Further Reading

For beginners

R. A. Burridge and G. Gould, 2004, *Jesus Now and Then*, Grand Rapids, MI: Eerdmans.

A. Spence, 2008, *Christology: A Guide for the Perplexed*, Edinburgh: T&T Clark.

J. Astley, D. Brown and A. Loades (eds), 2009, *Christology: Key Readings in Christian Thought*, London: SPCK.

For more advanced readers

J. Court and P. R. Carrell, 2005, *Jesus and the Angels: Angelology and the Christology of the Apocalypse of John*, Cambridge: Cambridge University Press.

P. B. Clayton, 2007, *The Christology of Theodoret of Cyrus: Antiochene Christology from the Council of Ephesus (431) to the Council of Chalcedon (451)*, Oxford: Oxford University Press.

S. J. Davis, 2008, *Coptic Christology in Practice: Incarnation and Divine Participation in Late Antique and Medieval Egypt*, Oxford: Oxford University Press.

M. Franzmann, 1996, *Jesus in the Nag Hammadi Writings*, Edinburgh: T&T Clark.

C. A. Gieschen, 1998, *Angelomorphic Christology: Antecedents and Early Evidence*, Leiden: Brill, pp. 187–346.

J. McGuckin, 2004, *Saint Cyril of Alexandria and the Christological Controversy*, Crestwood, NY: St Vladimir's Seminary Press.

G. O'Collins, 2009, *Christology: A Biblical, Historical and Systematic Study of Jesus*, Oxford: Oxford University Press.

Internet Resources

Arius (Geographical distribution of bishops who supported Arius)
    http://www.fourthcentury.com/notwppages/arius-supporters-map.htm

Christological controversy
    http://www.monachos.net/library/Christological_Controversy_Study_Area

Nestorius and Nestorianism
    http://www.nestorian.org

Notes

1 See, for example, *Odes of Solomon* 7 and 15 with the crucial notion of 'illumination' as the synonym of baptism (Heb. 6.4).

2 Cf. Tertullian, *Flesh* 14.

3 More in E. Osborn, 2005, *Irenaeus of Lyons*, Cambridge: Cambridge University Press, pp. 97–140.

4 *IncarnationL* 54.3.

5 *AH* 3.19.1; 5 preface.

6 *AH* 1.30.15.

7 For example *BThC* 7.139.28–30.

8 Cf. Eph. 5.14 and *CGP* 6.4.39.33—40.5.

9 For example *STGS* 50.7–13.

10 For these and many more titles, see *TS*, 112.33–5; 37–113.7.

11 Cf. *Strom.* 6.39.1–3.

12 For example, *Exhortation* 7.1.

13 For example, *Strom.* 4.155.2.

14 For example, *Strom.* 5.16.3.

15 For example, *Strom.* 7.7.4.

16 *ComGJ* 2.10.75.

17 *Princ.* 1.2.2.

18 *Princ.* 1.2.4–5.

19 More in L. Ayres, 2006, *Nicaea and its Legacy: An Approach to Fourth-Century Trinitarian Theology*, Oxford: Oxford University Press, pp. 105–30.

20 For example, *OrAA* 2.5.

21 *OrAA* 3.4.

22 *Dec.* 19–23.

23 *Dec.* 22.

24 For more, see V. Burrus, 2000, 'Fathering the Word: Athanasius of Alexandria', in her *'Begotten not Made': Conceiving Manhood in Late Antiquity*, Stanford: Stanford University Press, pp. 37–79.

25 It is interesting, at least as an anecdote, that the first form of Christian faith that arrived in China was Nestorianism, a century before Marco Polo.

26 Origen was already using this method to emphasize the reality of the incarnation of the Logos, cf. *Princ.* 1.2.6. It was, however, rather an intuition about the core meaning of this theory. The *communicatio* in its full form appeared in the later Patristic period (sixth century CE).

27 Cyril, *Incarnation* 97.200.

3

Incarnation: the Holy Spirit and the Virgin Mary

See also chapters 1, 2, 4, 6, 7, 8, 11.

Consider this Task

Find some ancient iconographical representations of the Virgin Mary and describe the characteristics of the woman represented by these images. What kind of theology and piety emerge from those representations of Mary?

Introduction

This article of faith binds together the Holy Spirit (divine) and the Virgin Mary (human) as the two principal factors which allowed the incarnation of God's Son to happen. It is remarkable that this divine–human co-operation was re-affirmed in Patristic theology not once but on several occasions. This examination points out the main circumstances in which this belief was of primary importance to the early Church as pronounced in various Creeds. In addition, as Patristic theology was inseparably interwoven with spirituality and often with Marian devotion, this chapter notes some examples of that devotion to Christ's mother, which shaped a significant part of theology of the Church.

I would like to emphasize the difference between Jesus' miraculous conception (that is, without the participation of a male partner) and the belief that Mary herself was without sin when she was conceived. The second belief was much later formalized as the idea of the 'Immaculate Conception' of Mary (not Jesus!) and accepted by the Roman Catholic Church. These two notions are sometimes confused. In the latter view, Mary was conceived and born free from the taint of original sin in order that she might become the mother of Christ. But it is quite hard to find any serious early Patristic evidence supporting this view before the emergence of the doctrine of original sin (*Pelagius versus *Augustine, see chapter 9). The former opinion on the virginal conception and virginal birth of Jesus was rather common among the Patristic authors.

Opening Question

Is it possible to accept Christ's divinity without the miraculous conception and then the virgin birth? Explore the possible answers and support them with theological arguments.

Development of the Argument

The present credal statement unites the Holy Spirit (first) and the Virgin Mary (second) by a simple conjunction: 'and' (Gr. *kai*). But behind this grammatical construction lies a complex history of multilevel exegesis combined with intellectual discernment and, last but not least, great devotion to the 'Mother of Christ'. The nature of the Holy Spirit is discussed in chapter 7, and for that reason I limit myself in this place to a brief note that the credal statements of the early Church assume his divine nature. My attention turns here to the second subject of the statement: the Virgin Mary and her role in the incarnation.

To many readers it may be surprising how few New Testament passages refer directly to the mother of Christ, and in contrast, how enormous is the Patristic literature commenting on her role in the incarnation. While the New Testament documents, mainly the four 'canonical' Gospels, noted Mary *en passant*, the *apologists and Christian apocrypha soon began to pay a great deal of attention to her role in God's plan of salvation. One of the first theologians who emphasized Mary's role was *Ignatius of Antioch.

Ignatius: Mary, the vital Witness against Docetism

The Bishop defended the reality of Christ's incarnation against Docetism (see chapter 2), which as a 'heretical' doctrine he encountered in Asia (Antioch). Docetism was also noted and rejected by the author of the first letter of John (4.2–3), showing that this view was widespread among various Christians in Asia. Against this kind of theological opposition, Ignatius, in his ardent apology for the reality of Christ's flesh, amplified the participation of a human mother in his factual, not phantom-like, incarnation.

> There is only one physician, who is both in the body and the spirit, born and unborn, God present in men, true life in death, born from Mary and from God, first who suffered and now who suffers no more, Jesus Christ our Lord.
>
> Ignatius of Antioch, *Eph*. 7.2, trans. P. A.-S.

> Our God, Jesus the Christ, was conceived by Mary according to God's plan from the seed of David and the Holy Spirit.
>
> Ignatius of Antioch, *Eph.* 18.2, trans. P. A.-S.

In another passage from Ignatius' letter, the author linked 'three greatest mysteries': Mary's virginity,[1] Jesus' conception and his death. These mysteries, in his view, represented three crucial stages in the recent history of salvation.[2] All three events underlined the positive value of the flesh in no way separated from salvation, as his opponents seemed to believe. The Bishop's correspondence contained the core of the credal declaration. Ignatius' theological intuition led him to see in Mary the Mother of God not just the mother of a man called Jesus. In this way, the Bishop of Antioch was one of the first theologians who clearly and much more openly than, for instance, Paul the Apostle, recognized the divine motherhood of Mary. In Ignatius' polemic we encounter the origin of a very important tradition, which made Mary irreplaceable in the history of salvation, while at the same time his theology inspired even more Christian devotional attachment to the Virgin.

Irenaeus of Lyons: Mary versus Eve

In the next example, the theory of salvation elaborated by *Irenaeus of Lyons, Mary received even more attention, and her co-operation with the Holy Spirit plays an exemplary role for all Christians. As has been noted, the crucial origin, dynamic and direction of Irenaeus' theology came from his theory of recapitulation (see also chapter 2). First, Irenaeus' imaginative pedagogy puts together pairs of characters, where one represents the archetype of a sinner, while the second denotes the model saint. This construction offers a vivid contrast: just after the first pair: Adam – Christ, there is the second pair: Eve – Mary. Irenaeus eulogizes Mary's obedience by means of which she counterbalances Eve's transgression. Soon the contrast highlighted by Irenaeus played a further role in the rhetoric used by the Church fathers, as Eve became a synonym for heresy, and the Virgin Mary for orthodoxy (for both terms see chapter 1).[3]

In accordance with this purpose, Mary the Virgin was found obedient, saying, 'Behold the handmaid of the Lord; be it unto me according to thy word.' [Luke 1.38] But Eve was disobedient; for she did not obey when she was a virgin. And even as she, having indeed a husband, Adam, but being nevertheless as yet a virgin [. . .] having become disobedient, was made the cause of death, both to herself and to the entire human race; so also did Mary, having a man betrothed [to her], and being nevertheless a virgin, by yielding obedience, became the cause of salvation, both to herself and the whole human race. [. . .] And thus also it was that the knot of Eve's disobedience was loosed by the obedience of Mary. For what the virgin Eve had bound fast through unbelief, this did the virgin Mary set free through faith.

Irenaeus, *AH* 3.22.4,[4] trans. P. A.-S.

In brief, Mary was triumphant where Eve had failed. This straightforward typology hints at Irenaeus' effort to support the evident example of faithfulness to God. This pedagogy counter-attacked what the Bishop saw as the greatest threat among his flock: disobedience and the mythological speculations of his rivals. Second, against the docetic tendency encountered by Irenaeus, Mary was elevated to the role of the main witness of Christ's real (literal) incarnation. Her motherhood and physical intimacy with her offspring guaranteed that the Saviour had human flesh.[5] In addition, Mary and her humanity constituted a direct link between her Son, the 'second Adam', and the first man.[6] Mary was not a passive channel of the descent of the Saviour, and her womb was not 'a pipe through which the Saviour descended like water' as some of Irenaeus' adversaries seemed to believe.[7] Furthermore, Christ's mission did not begin with his baptism in the river Jordan, as other Christians thought.[8] In Irenaeus' theory of recapitulation it was Mary, the Mother of Christ, who began the whole process of spiritual regeneration of humanity by giving birth to the 'new Adam'.[9] In consequence, Mary is also the spiritual Mother of the new life of Christians. Irenaeus' elaboration leaves an opening for the place of Mary in Christian worship, as she is united with Christ's first coming, which initiated the process of redemption. It is clear that Irenaeus' theology and devotion set Mary as the exemplar of Christian submission to God, the Father and his Church.

Tertullian: the Virgin and the Holy Woman

The third example of special attention given to Mary with a particular purpose comes from a lay theologian from North Africa. *Tertullian's polemics, again opposing docetic theology, parallel Ignatius' and Irenaeus' criticisms. It gives evidence of the strength as well as the geographical spread of this alternative view of Christ's nature. In his fierce rhetorical attack on *Marcion, Tertullian rejected the view that Christ's body was a mere phantom, and he discarded any compromise with Docetism as well as any divergence from the view that Christ was 'in the flesh'.[10] The theological confusion caused by docetic opinions was so serious that Tertullian decided to write a special treatise defending Jesus' human body. That work is known as *On the Flesh of Christ*, confirming that the incarnation includes flesh, as Jesus was conceived and begotten in the flesh.[11] With this emphasis Tertullian highlighted the role of the Virgin Mary. Furthermore, the theologian of Carthage was anxious to elaborate on Mary's virginity before she conceived her baby (Lat. *ante partum*). However, unlike many Patristic authors, Tertullian did not accept Mary's virginity 'during' (Lat. *in partu*) and 'after' (Lat. *post partum*) the birth of her Son.[12] In Tertullian's theology, Mary and the virgin birth were central parts of the divine economy of salvation. Both Mary and Christ's birth introduced the Saviour into human reality, which reached its climax in his death and bodily resurrection/ascension. Still, Tertullian's view on Mary's virginity revealed much more. It gave witness to the crucial correspondence between human sexuality, highly valued sexual self-control and the participation of these two aspects in achieving Christian perfection. No doubt, for the Latin, Greek and soon Coptic and Syriac theologians, the Virgin Mary becomes an ideal of that integration. So far both bishops (Ignatius, Irenaeus) and a lay theologian (Tertullian) magnified the role of Mary in order to find a proper 'model' and 'a reliable witness' for their followers against a common threat. Their approach calls for a brief encounter with their adversaries and their view on Mary.

Mary and Jesus – the Voices of Gnostic Christians

Turning our attention to other ancient documents, it is important to acknowledge that, for instance, docetic views were by no means held by all representatives of *Gnosticism. The vibrant collection of theologies and spiritualities from the Coptic documents preserved in the *Nag Hammadi Library contains more than just one, dominant Christology. Within this mosaic of colours and shapes there are some which echo pro-Catholic criticism. However, there are also others which do not have much in common with the charge made by the representatives of the Church. Among pro-docetic theologies, which rejected any possibility of the real flesh of the Saviour, there were voices expressing disbelief that the divine could 'mix' with the human element and the spiritual could be contained in the material. Consequently, the Saviour only 'passed through the Virgin's womb',[13] and adopted the human man Jesus of Nazareth.[14] In another version, the divine Redeemer only 'took on' the flesh as a temporary garment[15] in order to cheat and conquer the evil powers,[16] which dwell in this material world.

Other Gnostic documents, such as *the Gospel of Philip*, saw the Virgin Mary together with the divine aeon Sophia/Wisdom and the Holy Spirit as one of the three most faithful female companions of the Saviour.[17] Mary is openly called his 'virgin' mother.[18] Yet the theological tradition that underpinned this narrative with the strong female characteristics of the Holy Spirit (see chapter 6) excluded any possibility of conceiving the child 'by' the Spirit, as Mary and the Holy Spirit were both female.[19] The *Gospel of Philip* confirms Mary's virginity, but it adds a rather unusual interpretation of her status.

> Some said, 'Mary conceived by the Holy Spirit.' They are in error. They do not know what they are saying. When did a woman ever conceive by a woman? Mary is the virgin whom no power defiled. She is a great anathema to the Hebrews, who are the apostles and [the] apostolic men.
>
> GPh. 55.20–30, trans. W. W. Isenberg

Mary conceived as a virgin not because she did not have sexual relationship with Joseph, as the Catholic sources claimed, but because she was free from defilement by demons.[20] Joseph was the natural father of Jesus of Nazareth.[21] Mary's freedom from defilement had a rather different significance than just exemption from pollution by a sexual act. She was unpolluted by evil powers, as the Mother of the Saviour. Together with the Holy Spirit, Mary was the co-mother of Jesus. Nonetheless, it was the divine Spirit who was Christ's true *Genetrix*.[22] In this way the Saviour's first birth took place in the divine realm, while the second, for the salvation of the Gnostics, took place through the Virgin Mary. In a metaphorical way, the Christian Gnostic is also Mary's and Jesus' child since they as parents provide him or her with a divine and human pedigree. In this elaboration Mary is removed from a literal scriptural context as the exclusive, biological mother of Jesus, and she becomes together with her son the source of the 'spirituals' (Gr. *pneumatikoi*), the most advanced Christians. As it may be concluded, this version of Christianity accepted the double generation of Christ as well as the double generation of the Gnostic. It is correct to assume that for some of the Church fathers this adaptation of the figure of Mary and her role was yet another form of the Gnostics' dangerous heretical corruption of the gospel and its collapse into mythology.

The Virgin and Apocrypha

In this early stage yet another development has to be briefly noted. So far it is possible to see that the role of the Virgin Mary was focused on witnessing Christ's full humanity. But very soon, among various groups of Christians, we may observe more devout and emotional attachment to the Virgin Mary. Although not divine, Mary was placed by Christian piety, at least in some circles, near the divine, or directly, closest to her divine Son. Mary the Virgin gradually lost her Jewish, human characteristics as a woman, and was portrayed by devotional literature written by men as the embodiment of angelic purity. In order to retrace one of the sources of this imagery, we have to introduce an important document, the apocryphal Gospel known as the *Protoevangelium of James*.

Apocryphal Gospels (Gr. *ta apokrypha* – 'the [things] hidden'): religious literature written for devotional purposes, which was not included in the canon of the New Testament.

This poetic, colourful narrative portrayed the Virgin Mary sheltered within the sacred interior of the Jerusalem Temple, separated from the world and protected by God from any form of pollution.[23]

> She was pure in her body and her soul, she never put her face outside the doors of the Temple, she never looked at a strange man, and she never moved herself to gaze upon the face of a young man. Her appeal was dainty. Her tunic came down over her seal; her headcloth came down over her eyes [. . .] She never craved for a large quantity of food, neither did she walk about in the market-place of her city [. . .] There was no limit to her beauty, and the Temple was wont to be filled with angels because of her sweet odour, and they used to come and visit her for the sake of conversation.
>
> *Protoevangelium of James*, trans. E. A. W. Budge

Mary lives a life totally dedicated to God, pure in her body, mind and spirit. Mary, the icon of holiness, is alone, submerged in contemplation and prayer, removed from the company of other women. The narrative presents her as the embodiment of the most holy Virgin. Mary is infiltrated by the divine presence, and she is ready to respond to God's will. This over-spiritualized picture of Mary, who gave birth to the Saviour while retaining her virginity, originated a unique way of thinking about the Mother of Christ. Mary has much more in common with the holy spirits and the divine than with other women, their menstruation and suffering the pain of giving birth to a child or children. Mary, the ideal woman and the Virgin-Mother, appears in some traditions of Patristic theology in a unique position, highly elevated by Christian piety and supported by Catholic theology, where she fulfils a specific role against different theological opponents, mainly giving witness to the real incarnation and human flesh of the Saviour. Soon this ideal and perfect Virgin overshadowed the real woman, the mother of Jesus of Nazareth. If Patristic theology grew in the context of a continuous doctrinal battle in which the centre was Christology, the Virgin Mary was one of the most visible banners of the Church.

To sum up this pre-Nicene phase of theology, I wish to point out that the role of the Virgin Mary and the Holy Spirit in its credal expression safeguarded the crucial theological data: the reality and physical aspect of the incarnation. As has been noted above, this belief not only protected the involvement of divine and human elements in the incarnation. It also emphasized the reality of the Son as a person against various forms of Monarchianism and adoptionist Christologies (see chapter 2); but first and foremost it strengthened the faith in the double origins of the Saviour and his two natures. Although opposition to this belief changes around the beginning of the fourth century, the same crucial connection between the Holy Spirit and the Virgin Mary is still upheld and receives further clarification.

The Mother of God and Conflict with Arianism

The conflict with *Arianism, which began as a local exegetical dispute between Bishop Alexander and his presbyter *Arius (see chapter 2), soon stirred up the minds and emotions of many leading theologians outside Alexandria and Egypt. It is not surprising that when the divinity of Christ had been so seriously undermined by the supporters of Arian Christology, both Alexander and Athanasius used the title 'Mother of God' or 'God-bearer' (Gr. *Theotokos*) as a theological, visible label, which summed up his stance as opposed to the teaching of his opponents.

> 'God – birth-giver' (Gr. *Theotokos*; where Gr. *theos* means 'God' and Gr. *tokos* refers to a woman who gives birth to her offspring): the term was translated into Latin as *Dei Genetrix*. The direct English translation is rather awkward; therefore the preferred translation is 'Mother of God'. However, it must be noted that the original Greek word *tokos* highlights 'giving birth', whereas the English word 'mother' includes the act of giving birth and implies being a parent throughout the life of the child.

Alexander and Athanasius highlighted this title in order to defend and promote their views on the two natures of Christ. As in the case of Irenaeus, so now among Alexandrian defenders of the correct faith, Mary and Marian piety become a theological and political weapon against Arians. This mixture of theology and politics, although in this case focused on the correct use of the title

Theotokos, was one of the important characteristics of Patristic theology. Bishop Alexander first used the new and controversial title in his epistle against the Arians (324).[24] Then his successor, *Athanasius, in the spirit of Irenaeus' interchange of properties (see chapter 2), endorsed this explicit title as the most appropriate to Mary.[25] For Athanasius, this theological tradition, elevating the role and status of the Virgin Mary, served as yet another argument in his defence of Christ's divinity. If the Blessed Virgin was revered as the Mother of the Saviour by some established theological authorities from previous centuries, and because she was venerated as such by many ordinary people, it follows that the divinity of her Son must be commonly accepted. In Athanasius' theology, Mary, her divine Son and the incarnation were three columns of the most ancient and genuine faith which held the whole architecture of the Church. Undermining one of them meant destabilizing the whole structure of salvation. Alexandrian pro-Nicene Christology, together with the growth of Marian piety accommodated the *Theotokos* as one of the most remarkable and valuable expressions of Mary's unique role as the Mother of the divine and human Saviour. This combination of devotion with theology produced one of the most ancient prayers to the Virgin Mary, known under its Latin title as *Sum Tuum Praesidium*.[26] It shows that, at least in Egypt, in the period before the Council of Ephesus, Mary was given the title *Theotokos*. This title highlighted her divine maternity as well as her personal, exceptional holiness and status. It shows also that the prayer was a part of the liturgy and inspired Christian imagination with a specific bond between Mary, the Holy Mother of God and Jesus Christ: divine and human Saviour. This connection was one of the most significant features of post-Nicene Alexandrian, or even Egyptian theology and piety, which were interwoven with politics of the Church.

Towards the Dogma

The spiritual heirs of this Alexandrian ethos were the *Cappadocians, such as *Gregory of Nazianzus. He saw in this particular expression a benchmark of orthodoxy.[27] In his view, Mary was purified at the annunciation by the Holy Spirit in anticipation of becoming the dwelling of the divine Son.[28] *Gregory of Nyssa shed some light on yet another aspect of Mary's motherhood. He returned to the idea of the exchange formula, which we have already noted in

Irenaeus and Athanasius (see chapter 2), and he affirmed that the Logos, as the divine, spiritual being, took flesh from the Virgin Mary in order to give spirituality and divine grace to the human body, as the Saviour participated in our human nature.[29] Again, the direct connection between Christ's incarnation thanks to the Virgin Mary and elevation of human nature to the divine is expressed by Gregory of Nyssa as the epitome of the Christian hope.[30] The Cappadocian fathers confirmed the irreplaceable role of Mary as not only the witness of Christ's incarnation and his deed of salvation, but also the greatest example of a human being totally sanctified by the might and grace of the Holy Spirit. Mary, a real Jewish woman, as she was in her historical existence, from now on becomes the pure and holy Mother of Christ, the most noble and blessed ideal of Christian perfection.

Ambrose of Milan: Mary the Icon

Before we discuss the final stage of development of Marian theology and piety, I wish to note one important example of Latin reflection on the Virgin Mary and her contribution to salvation. It was *Ambrose, the bishop of Milan,[31] who by joining together exegesis, a theological agenda and personal devotion advanced a highly idealized picture of the Virgin Mary. His ardent admiration of Mary made her not only the embodiment of female holiness, dedication to God and purity, but also an example to all Christian women, especially virgins. Ambrose stressed that the Blessed Virgin did not pass on any 'stain' to her son. The righteous Jesus Christ was conceived, unlike all other human beings and even the most holy men and women, by an act without iniquity or shadow of sin. Christ was born of the Holy Spirit from a Virgin. Thus far Ambrose's theology and preaching followed the mainstream Christian lineage. But he also magnified Mary's personal purity as her human origin was protected by miraculous conception.[32] As I have noted, this bold step had significant theological implications as the pure, immaculate, sinless Virgin Mary, unlike all other people, was not marked by original sin and therefore, she did not die like all other descendants of Adam and Eve. With the controversy caused by Pelagius' theology, one of the issues was the theory of original sin (see chapter 9). Augustine of Hippo addressed Mary's freedom from original sin and opened a new stage of Patristic speculation.[33] In his view, although procreation is good, the transmission of original sin took place through the sexual act from which a child was created. As a result, in order to avoid participation in that natural transmission, it was necessary that the sinless Christ had a sinless mother and was conceived in a way that did not contain any pollution. As a result, the act of conceiving Jesus Christ had to be a miracle (i.e. not natural). Although the Greek theologians remained less enthusiastic about this method of defending Mary from original sin, they put the emphasis on the end of her earthly life. The picturesque motif of 'assumption', or the bodily elevation of Mary to heaven, appeared first in preaching, for instance by Andrew of Crete (d. *c*.740) and subsequently it was accommodated in the liturgy. Latin and Byzantine churches celebrated the feast of the 'Assumption of the Virgin Mary into heaven' (Gr. *koimesis*, Lat. *dormitio*, 'sleep') from the seventh century.

Piety and Dogma

The ultimate affirmation of Mary's role at the incarnation, as the Mother of a Son who was at once divine and human, came during the confrontation between *Cyril of Alexandria and *Nestorius in the fifth century (see chapter 2). Nestorius' theological, exegetical and cultural background was deeply rooted in the Antiochene tradition. Antiochene Christology recognized the two natures of Jesus Christ, but saw them in clear distinction as parallel.

For example, for *Theodore of Mopsuestia, one of the leading exponents of this tradition, because the human and divine cannot mingle together or amalgamate, the natures of Christ are separable. Consequently, Theodore avoided some confusing expressions such as 'incarnate God' or even 'God-bearing' as Mary's title.[34] However, he accepted that the Virgin Mary was the natural mother of Christ's humanity. Theodore's careful language and theology was a response to *Apollinarius' challenge, later heresy (see chapter 2). From Theodore's perspective, Apollinarius' theory that the divine Logos replaced the mind of the human Jesus simply introduced confusion. In addition, Apollinarius claimed that the title 'Mother of God' and the Virgin birth of Christ were among the most important Christian articles of faith, as truly the blessed Mary gave birth to Jesus, the man with the divine mind. It is not surprising that in those circumstances the title *Theotokos* was a symptom, to Theodore and later to Nestorius, of dangerous theological errors to be avoided at any price.

Nestorius' dogmatic purity found a challenger in Cyril of Alexandria, for whom, according to the Alexandrian tradition, this very title emphasized a profound theological truth and devotion. It pointed towards the mystery of Christ's incarnation and expressed devotion to the Holy Mother of God. For Cyril, as an Alexandrian theologian, the divine Logos descended to this world, which was a part of his 'self-emptying' (Gr. *kenosis*), an act which involved being born of Mary.[35]

> '**Self-emptying**' (Gr. *kenosis*) of the divine Son in the act of the incarnation: the original concept comes from Philippians 2.7, ('he emptied himself, taking on the form of a slave'). Soon, however, it was interpreted in terms of God's mighty love that made Christ descend and accept the condition of a human being and the humblest servant of salvation.

It is through Mary, her positive response to God's call, then through her body, that the Saviour was conceived (biologically) and formed (ontologically) within the human race. Mary, in Cyril's theology, was not a symbolic means of expression of Christ's humanity, but the real donor of his physical, biological, nature, and in spiritual terms, she was the 'Container of the Uncontainable'.

> As the Holy Virgin gave birth to God who is substantially united with flesh according to nature, therefore we call her God-bearer [Gr. *Theotokos*]. It is not because we assume that the nature of the Logos had the beginning of its existence from the flesh, for the Word was at the beginning and the Word was God, and the Word was with God [John 1.1.], and the Word himself is the Maker of the ages, co-eternal with the Father, and Creator of all. But as we have already acknowledged, the Word united himself substantially with the human nature in her womb, he was born with a human body.
>
> Cyril of Alexandria, *3 EpN* 11, trans. P. A.-S.

This strong Marian interpretation of salvation did not allow any room for weakening Mary's position. Therefore Nestorius' challenge found in Cyril the most ardent challenger. Cyril's great personal devotion to the Virgin Mary added yet another reason for rebuking Nestorius' blasphemy.

> Hail, Mary Mother of God, the world's holy treasury, the unfailing light, the glory of virginity, the mirror of true faith, the indestructible temple, the place whom no place can hold, the Mother and the Virgin through whom the 'blessed one' comes 'in the name of the Lord!' Hail, holy Mary, who received into your virginal womb the immense and incomprehensible God! Through you the Trinity is glorified and worshipped; through you the priceless Christ is celebrated and adored throughout the world, through you the angels and archangels rejoice, evil spirits are put to flight and Satan falls from heaven. Through you the fallen humanity is taken into heaven, creation rejects idolatry and knows the truth, believers receive baptism with the oil of gladness, churches are everywhere established, and the nations come to penitence. What can we say more? Through you God's only-begotten Son came as light to 'those in darkness and the shadow of death', the Apostles preach his salvation, the dead are raised to new life, and kings exercise their authority under the guidance of the Holy Spirit. Therefore joy spread through all creation. May we reverence and adore the undivided Trinity and praise Mary, the Virgin and the temple of God, together with her Son and Spouse for ever and ever. Amen.
> Cyril of Alexandria, *Homily at the Council of Ephesus* 4, trans. P. A.-S.

Confrontation between more than just the individual views of Cyril and Nestorius led first to the decrees of the *Third Ecumenical Council of Ephesus (431) condemning Nestorius and defending the use of the title 'God-bearer', then to the *Fourth Ecumenical Council of Chalcedon (451), which ultimately reaffirmed that the Virgin Mary was the mother of the divine and human Jesus Christ.

> 1. Whoever does not confess that Emmanuel [Isa. 7.14, Matt. 1.23] is truly God, and therefore that the holy Virgin is the God-bearer [Gr. *Theotokos*] (for she gave birth in flesh to the Word of God who become flesh), let him be condemned [Gal. 1.8, 9].

> 2. Whoever does not confess that the Word of God the Father has been substantially united with the flesh and is one Christ with his own flesh, that is therefore the same God and the human being together, let him be condemned.
>
> 3. Whoever divides the persons in the one Christ after their union, joining them only by a conjunction of dignity or authority or power, instead of a combination according to a union by natures, let him be condemned.
>
> Cyril of Alexandria, *The Twelve Anathemas,* trans. P. A.-S.

In summary, I would like to emphasize that the development of the doctrine of the incarnation between the Council of *Nicaea (325) and the Council of *Chalcedon (451) went through a phase when one of the main questions was about the specific character of the union between the two natures of Christ. While this question had primary importance, the character and role of the Virgin Mary and a growing awareness of the specific nature of the Holy Spirit as a divine person safeguarded the crucial intuition on Christ's double origin. Dogmatic statements came as an outcome of a clear response to theological questioning of Christ's being and reaffirmed that earlier intuition. Christian iconography and prayers begin to address the mystery of the incarnation, as first the dialogue of Mary with God, represented by the angelic messenger, then as a Mother with a child, which after the Arian crisis is portrayed with a halo showing him to be divine. Christian imagery from this time on is marked by the image of a holy Mother-Virgin with the holy child.[36]

The Symbol of Virginity and Asceticism

The early baptismal Creeds already show that the idea of the virginal conception, quite problematic in the canonical Gospels, found its place in Christian doctrine. Similarly, early rules of faith, as we know from Tertullian's evidence, emphasized the virginity of Christ's mother.[37] On the way, the scriptural narrative received a strong apostolic interpretation which suited well the more Christological, polemic purposes in their confrontation with some alternative theologies such as Adoptionism and Docetism. Further, the important connection between the Virgin Mary and Christian life, at least in the context of the Church, had been strengthened by the appearance and growing value of Christian asceticism. The sexual chastity of Jesus[38] and his Mother became the paradigm for the highest Christian ethical norm. *Imitatio Christi*, which appeared to be a call for some Christian men and women, easily encompassed the example of Mary. In the rather extreme, certainly ascetical interpretation of *Jerome, Mary, thanks to her virginity, becomes the Mother of the Saviour.[39] This was one of many examples that encouraged virginity as the embodiment of the true and holy Christian life. While marriage and the act of procreation produces potential saints and virgins, still virginity as a choice of imitating Christ and his Mother was promoted as the noblest form of Christian life. As noted by some feminist scholars, the ascetic life of virginity offered Christian women a unique possibility to escape from the constraints of socially and sexually established roles. The Virgin Mary might have been seen then as the 'liberating' example of that freedom. On the other hand, with the increasing authority of religious literature and Patristic authors, such as Athanasius *On Virginity*[40] (Greek, later Coptic milieu) and a work of Ambrose of Milan[41] (Latin milieu), Mary was portrayed as the ideal for the consecrated virgins, and the eulogizing of virginity was one of the most recognizable features of Patristic theology.[42]

Conclusion

Patristic theology provides us with a fascinating story about Mary, Christ's mother, and her relationship with God. As in the Gospels, when she appeared in the crucial moments of Jesus' life, so too in the Patristic period she emerged in the fundamental moments when the Christology of the Church was constructed. Unlike the few scriptural statements about her, in Patristic narratives she takes much more space and time, stirring up emotions and influencing fervent theological debates. The Virgin Mary and the Holy Spirit are the principal guardians of Christ's real, double, divine and human origins. Depreciating the role of Mary would lead to undermining Christ's humanity, while diminishing the role of the Holy Spirit would reduce the Saviour to a charismatic miracle-maker. This credal article gives evidence of Patristic logic. It also unveils that this logic did not appear in an emotional vacuum, but was inspired by devotion.

Questions for Discussion

- Why did Christian piety need to enhance the role of Mary as the mediator between the Christians and her divine Son (e.g. the prayer *Sub Tuum Praesidium*)?
- Does the need of Mary's participation in Christ's incarnation limit God's omnipotence?
- How do you assess the connection between the Patristic presentations of Mary as the ideal Woman and the later development of the ascetic ideal of virginity?
- What does the image of the Virgin Mary mean for women's sexuality?

Further Reading

For beginners

L. Gambero, 2004, *Mary and the Fathers of the Church: The Blessed Virgin Mary in Patristic Thought*, trans. T. Buffer, San Francisco: Ignatius Press.

A. J. Levine and M. M. Robbins (eds), 2005, *A Feminist Companion to Mariology*, London and New York: T&T Clark.

E. Osborn, 1997, *Tertullian, First Theologian of the West*, Cambridge: Cambridge University Press, pp. 88–115.

For more advanced readers

S. J. Boss, 2000, *Empress and Handmaid: On Nature and Gender in the Cult of the Virgin Mary*, London and New York: Cassell.

P. Brown, 1988, *The Body and Society: Men, Women and Sexual Renunciation in Early Christianity*, London: Faber & Faber, pp. 348–9.

E. A. Castelli, 2008, 'Virginity and its meaning for Women's Sexuality in Early Christianity', in A. J. Levine and M. M. Robins (eds), *A Feminist Companion to Patristic Literature*, London: T&T Clark, pp. 72–100.

G. Cloke, 1995, *This Female Man of God: Women and Spiritual Power in the Patristic Age, AD 350–450*, London and New York: Routledge.

B. E. Daley, 1998, *On the Dormition of Mary: Early Patristic Homilies*, Crestwood, NY: St Vladimir's Seminary Press.

S. Elm, 1996, *Virgins of God: The Making of Asceticism in Late Antiquity*, Oxford: Clarendon Press.

S. S. Shoemaker, 2002, *The Ancient Traditions of the Virgin Mary's Dormition and Assumption*, Oxford: Oxford University Press.

T. M. Show, 2008, 'The Virgin and Charioteer and the Bride of Christ: Gender and the Passions in Later Ancient Ethics and Early Christian Writings on Virginity', in A. J. Levine and M. M. Robins (eds), *A Feminist Companion to Patristic Literature*, London: T&T Clark, pp. 193–210.

F. Young, 2003, '*Theotokos*: Mary and the Pattern of Fall and Redemption in the Theology of Cyril of Alexandria', in T. G. Weinandy and D. A. Keating (eds), *The Theology of St Cyril of Alexandria*, London and New York: T&T Clark, pp. 55–74.

Internet Resources

E. Kidd. 'The Virgin Desert: Gender Transformation in Fourth Century Christian Asceticism':

http://lyceumphilosophy.com/?q=node/73

Mary: Theotokos and the ever Virgin: selection of Patristic texts:

http://hagioipateres.wordpress.com/2006/12/02/mary-theotokos-aeiparthenos/

Notes

1 Mary's virginity (Lat. *ante partum*, *in partu* and *post partum*) had its supporters among the majority of Greek and Latin Fathers, and it was proclaimed by the oldest Creeds, such as the Roman Creed. Mary's perpetual virginity was declared by the Fifth Ecumenical Council of Constantinople (553), canon 2. It highlighted Mary's status as the 'ever virgin'.

2 *Eph.* 19.1.

3 On Eve as the archetype of 'heresy', see more in V. Burrus, 1991, 'The Heretical Woman as Symbol in Alexander, Athanasius, Epiphanius and Jerome', *HTR*, 83.3, pp. 229–48.

4 Cf. *Proof* 33.

5 *AH* 3.22.1.

6 *AH* 3.21.10; 3.22.3.

7 *AH* 1.7.2.

8 *AH* 1.21.3.

9 *AH* 4.33.4 and 11.

10 *AM* 3.8; 4.10; 5.14.

11 *Flesh* 18.5.

12 *Flesh* 24; *Mon.* 82; *OVV* 6.3.

13 For example, *TTruth*, 45.14–15;

14 For example, *GE* III.63.5–25; III.64.2–3/IV.75.16–17.

15 For example, *TP* 47.16–18; 49.12–13; 49.15–16; 49.17–18; 49.18–19; *2 ApJames* 56.5–15.

16 For example, *EPP* 136.20–2.

17 Cf. *GPh.* 59.6–11.

18 *GPh.* 55.27–8.

19 *GPh.* 55.23–31.

20 *GPh.* 55.31.

21 *GPh.* 55.33–6; 73.10.

22 *GPh.* 71.5.18.

23 More in P. W. Van Der Horst, 2005, 'Sex, Birth, Purity and Asceticism in the *Protoevangelium Jacobi*', in A. J. Levine and M. M. Robbins (eds), 2005, *A Feminist Companion to Mariology*, London and New York: T&T Clark, pp. 56–66 and M. F. Foskett, 'Virginity as Purity in the *Protoevangelium of James*', in Levine and Robbins, *A Feminist Companion to Mariology*, pp. 67–76.

24 Alexander of Alexandria, *Ep.* 54.

25 For example *OrAA* 3.29.

26 The Rylands Papyrus 470 containing this prayer comes from the third century and was found in Egypt. Cf. C. H. Roberts, 1938, *Catalogue of the Greek and Latin Papyri in the John Rylands Library*, III 'Theological and Literary Texts', Manchester, pp. 46–7.

27 *Ep.* 101.

28 *Or.* 38.

29 *AE* 3.2.54; *CO* 5.

30 *AApp.* 53.54

31 *ExPs.* 37.5.

32 *ExPs.* 117.

33 The beginning of the new debate about the status of Mary's conception can be traced to Augustine's polemical work *Against Julian*. However, this treatise should not be taken as the first Patristic evidence of a new doctrine.

34 *CH* 8.5, 16; 6.3.

35 *ExpIsa.* 7.14–16.

36 As one of many early Christian representations, see the fragmentary leaf of the Alexandrian Chronicle, with the Mother of God carrying the Child, in A. Grabar, 1980, *Christian Iconography: A Study of Its Origin*, London: Routledge & Kegan Paul, illustration 64.

37 For example, *OVV* 1.3.

38 *Virgins* 1.5.

39 *Ep.* 22.38. In this context I would like to mention Jerome's fervent dispute with Helvidius (fl. *c.*400), Jovinian (*c.*405) and Vigilantius (fl. *c.*400). The first opponent

denied the belief in perpetual virginity of Mary on the basis of the Scriptures, that is the references to Jesus' brothers and sisters as well as some traditions, for instance, *Tertullian. Next, Jovinian held the opinion that 'in God's view' virginity had no higher status than marriage. Finally, Vigilantius undermined the ascetic and monastic ideal of life promoted by Jerome. All three opponents received, or rather became the subjects of Jerome's polemic.

40 *OV* and *Letter to the Virgins.*

41 *Virgins* 2.2. Ambrose was also the author of *On Virginity*, *An Instruction for a Virgin* and *Praise of Virginity.*

42 See, for example, Methodius of Olympus, *On Virginity*, 7, 3, 157–8 and more in Tertullian, *On the Veiling of the Virgins*, Cyprian of Carthage, *On the Dress of the Virgins*, Ambrose, *On Virgins to sister Marcellina*, Augustine, *On Holy Virginity*, John Chrysostom, *On Virginity*, Gregory of Nyssa, *On Virginity*. Cf. G. Clark, 2004, 'Body and soul', in her *Christianity and Roman Society*, Cambridge: Cambridge University Press, pp. 60–77.

4

Pontius Pilate: Jesus' Crucifixion and Death

See also chapters 2, 3, 5, 6.

Consider this Task

Try to find out more about the details of Jesus' trial and punishment. Why was Jesus condemned to die on the cross, rather than, for example, to be stoned like Stephen (Acts 7.59) or beheaded like Paul (later Christian tradition)?

Introduction

This credal pronouncement attests Jesus Christ's physical death, which concluded his earthly life. It is, however, intriguing that from the earliest days various Christian narratives pointed to a foreigner, the Roman <u>Prefect</u>, Pontius Pilate, as a witness of the climax of Jesus' dramatic death.[1]

Prefect (Lat. *praefectus*, 'the man put in charge of': the public office which combined military, financial and judicial authority in a specific area of the Roman Empire.

As may be concluded from the scriptural evidence, Pilate's role in Jesus' trial was ambiguous, but it was he who delivered the final verdict indicating the way of Jesus' death: crucifixion. However, with the *Arian controversy, Christ's crucifixion received another significant interpretation, and the interest of Catholic theologians in the value of this statement was amended. Later Christological debates explored further consequences of this article of Christian faith. Alongside this development, Pilate's role and character received a new and much warmer welcome in Christian catechesis.

Opening Question

Find prophecies in the Hebrew Scriptures which refer to circumstances of the Messiah's death. Do they suggest any specific kind of death?

Development of the Argument

The earliest Christologies expressed more as an intuition than as a systematic doctrine belief in Jesus of Nazareth's divine and human origin. The early theologians who shared that view were opposed to two radical theories, which either overemphasized the divinity of the Saviour, thus alienating him from human nature, or rejected his divinity and stressed his merely human origin. The apostolic core belief found its proclamation in the form of a summary that Jesus died 'under Pontius Pilate' in the most ancient Creeds[2] and pastoral correspondence,[3] bringing together the historical figure of the Roman Prefect of Judea (26–36 CE) with the context of Jesus' factual death.

> Be deaf therefore when they speak to you apart from Jesus Christ of David's family, the son of Mary; who really was born, who ate and drank; was really persecuted under Pontius Pilate, and then was really crucified and died.
>
> Ignatius of Antioch, *Tral.* 9.1, trans. P. A.-S.

No doubt this association served various theological and catechetical purposes, but in the present context, it emphasized the real death of the divine–human Saviour. The bishop writing these words and letters as his legacy highlighted Jesus' ultimate self-sacrifice so that his readers might identify their faith with the central event of Christ's life: his death and then resurrection. Ignatius seemed to say there was only one true story (that is the gospel) about Jesus Christ, and his real death on the cross verifies whether or not various Christian teachers teach and represent the true and genuine apostolic legacy.

The proclamation of Christ's crucifixion with special reference to Pontius Pilate faced two sources of criticism in the earliest phase of the development of the doctrine: first, outside the Church from pagans and Jews; second, inside Christianity from the Gnostics, especially those with docetic views. It was the last group who challenged the belief in Jesus' real death most radically. While Jews and pagan polemicists did not question the facts relating to the end of Jesus' life, they expressed more suspicion about the claim of Jesus' resurrection and divinity.[4] However, among some Christians the idea of the death of what was divine and immortal was seriously contested. To exemplify the earliest teaching of this belief, I will turn to its greatest Christian apologists. Chronologically, we will recall the witness of *Justin Martyr – against the Jews; *Origen – against pagan intellectuals; and *Irenaeus of Lyons – against the Gnostics. Then, with Tertullian, we shall see some light shed on a rather surprising change of tune about the role of Pontius Pilate.

Justin Martyr and the Jews' Critique

In a polemic against Jewish opponents, whose voice we may find in Trypho, Justin highlighted the value of Christ's redemptive death and resurrection. As an exegete of the Hebrew Scriptures, Justin tried to convince his Jewish interlocutor that all Hebrew prophecies about the Messiah's life found their realization in Jesus of Nazareth. Using a number of references to prophetic statements, Justin aimed to prove that they all referred to Jesus of Nazareth and his death on the cross. For instance, Moses' way of prayer with outstretched arms symbolized Jesus' crucifixion,[5] the bronze serpent lifted up on the pole was another prefiguration (Gr. *typos*) of the cross.[6] But first and foremost, in Justin's exegesis Jesus was the sacrificial 'lamb of God' whose innocent blood cleansed believers.[7] These kinds of argument aimed to convince his opponent that the crucified Christ is the central figure of the prophecies in the Hebrew Scriptures and that the death of the Crucified One brought salvation to all. Jesus, 'the Paschal Lamb', takes the curse of all humankind and then his death saves for eternity. Christ's crucifixion is the centre of salvation.[8] The cross is the new pole on which the Saviour has been hung and from which he brought deliverance from the 'bites of the serpent'.[9] Justin was able to link together his theory of salvation with Christology and the event with the liturgical life of Christians, where all these aspects were focused on the mystery of the cross. Jesus' death on the cross became the source of the new creation and new relationship with God. In this context of salvation, the role of Pilate takes on a special significance. The Roman Prefect takes part in the fulfilment of the prophecies (Hos. 10.6, cf. *Dial.* 103) about the detail of Jesus' death.

And in yet another passage, David speaks of the suffering and the cross using this allegory: 'They pierce my hands and my feet; they counted all my bones. They stare and gloat over me. They divided my clothes among themselves and cast lots for my garments' [Psalm 22.16–18]. When they crucified him, by nailing him, they pierced his hands and feet. Those who did it divided his garments among themselves, each one of them cast lots for what he wished to have and they received according to lots. And if you [i.e. Trypho – P. A.-S.] say that this Psalm does not refer to Christ, you must be completely blind. Also you cannot comprehend that nobody among your race that was called 'King-Messiah' has ever had his hands and feet pierced when he was still alive, or even that he died in this unique way, except Jesus alone.

Justin, *Dial.* 97.3–4, trans. P. A.-S.

Pontius Pilate was a part of the drama foretold by the Hebrew prophets, and therefore his name became connected with Christ's redemptive death. In Justin's interpretation, Pilate became the irreplaceable facilitator of Jesus' death specifically by crucifixion. This kind of death fulfilled yet another prophecy about the wounds of the Messiah's body.[10] Consequently, Pontius Pilate is included in Justin's credal formulas. It did not matter whether Justin addressed the Jewish audience or the pagan authority: Christ's crucifixion 'under Pontius Pilate' was already for him the vital theological idiom and concept. It proved, at least to him, the fundamental connection between the history of salvation, which is the 'old covenant' with the Jews, and the very recent events in Palestine, which opened a new era and 'new covenant' with all humanity.

Origen and Pagan Mockery

The Roman view of Jesus' crucifixion was totally different from the Jewish perspective. However, it expressed a similar mistrust in the stories about Jesus of Nazareth, his life and death. First, the Roman historian Tacitus, while recording the great fire of Rome (July 64 CE) and the subsequent persecution of Christians by Nero, noted that:

Christus, from whom the name had its origin, suffered extreme penalty during the reign of Tiberius at the hands of one of our procurators,

> Pontius Pilatus, and a deadly superstition, thus checked for the moment, again broke out not only in Judea, the source of the evil, but also in Rome.
>
> Tacitus, *Annals* 25.44.2–8, trans. J. Stevenson, 1987, *A New Eusebius: Documents Illustrating the History of the Church to AD 337*, London: SPCK, p. 2.

Christianity is described as 'a superstition' (Lat. *superstitio*), not as a religion. 'Superstition' meant for Romans an irrational obscure cult of a new deity, and they viewed Christianity as dangerous to the status quo of Roman society and culture. To Tacitus and many other Roman intellectuals the new cult originated with the life of 'Christus', a Jew who was punished under Pontius Pilatus, 'one of our procurators'. It must be noted that in this view Christianity, although a treacherous cult, was not based on some oriental mythology, but was related to factual events in a shadowy corner of the Roman Empire. Still, 'Christus' and his followers were pitiful people. The popular ridicule of Christianity is preserved by a graffito scratched on a stone on Palatine Hill, near the Circus Maximus in Rome. It presents a man with the head of an ass hanging on a cross. A bystander raises his hand, possibly as a gesture of respect or salutation, and the inscription below it reads:

> Alexamenos worships his god.
>
> H. Solin and M. Itkonen-Kaila, 1966, *Graffiti del Palatino, vol. 1 Paedagogium*, IRF, Helsinki, pp. 209–12.

Although previously Romans accused the Jews of worshiping an ass, this denigration has been now attributed to Christians, seen as 'a Jewish sect'. Yet, this caricature reveals that for pagan observers, the essential belief of the new cult was about the crucified man who Alexamenos 'worshipped as god'. The most serious attack on Christian belief came in the second century from a certain Platonic philosopher *Celsus, in his treatise, *True Doctrine*. This work is lost, but Origen's reply and defence of Christian doctrine in *Against Celsus* contains a substantial amount of quotations and summaries from the original work. Celsus criticized and ridiculed many Christian beliefs and particularly the

ΑΛΕ
ΞΑΜΕΝΟΣ
ΣΕΒΕΤΕ
ΘΕΟ

central ones such as faith in the incarnation of God's Son, the resurrection of the dead and Christian worship of a crucified God–Jesus. He argued that Jesus as a mere magician was not worthy of any honour and that Christians should choose other brave men, such as Jonah or Daniel, both victorious heroes.[11] Celsus states that the crucified God–Jesus would be an anticlimax for any rational religion: Jesus was a synonym for failure. Thus *apologists faced unsympathetic pagan critics to whom the central event of Christ's death under Pontius Pilate was yet another example of a bizarre set of beliefs. However, the genius of theologians such as Origen matched well the intelligence of their intellectual opponents. Against Celsus, who undermined Jesus' status and teaching, Origen replied that even with the cross Christ can be compared to the greatest teachers of humanity, such as Socrates. The ancient philosopher died as a consequence of his faithfulness to his teaching. But unlike Socrates, who was unable to prove that he did not commit any evil, it was impossible to point out any evil act performed by Jesus.[12] The disgraceful manner of Jesus' death was not unique in the history of civilizations, as Origen noted,[13] but Jesus' intention and mission were exceptional in human history.

Surprising Gnostic Scenario

The third and the strongest opposition to the idea of the Saviour's death came from the docetic tendencies within Christian *Gnosticism. As we have seen while discussing the notion of the incarnation (see chapter 2) this specific Christology claimed the divine Saviour only took Jesus' human form as a temporary dwelling place, 'an envelope' for the duration of his mission. Then the Redeemer left Jesus on the cross, and this very moment was recorded as Jesus' cry: 'My God why have you forsaken me?' (Matt. 27.46; Mark 15.34)[14] In another variation of the docetic scenario, it was not Jesus who died on the cross, but Simon of Cyrene.[15]

> Yes, they [the adversaries of the Redeemer – P. A.-S.] saw me; they punished me. It was another, their father, who drank the gall and the vinegar; it was not I. They struck me with the reed; it was another, Simon, who bore the cross in his shoulder. It was another upon whom they placed the crown of thorns. But I was rejoicing in the height over all the wealth of the archons and the offspring of their error, of their empty glory. And I was laughing at their ignorance.
> STGS 56.5–20, trans. R. G. Bullard and J. A. Gibbons

Again the divine Redeemer took this appearance to mislead the evil spirits and the ignorant crowd. The death of a substitute only confirms the spiritual blindness of the persecutors who were not able to see the divine Redeemer, as they did not participate in his status and nature. This interpretation of the events assumes that people learn and perceive according to the rules of similarity, where only like can recognize like (Gr. *homoion homoio* – 'like to like'). Therefore as long as they live in ignorance, or have only literal understanding of reality based on their senses, they are neither able to recognize nor value the spiritual, which is identified with the divine Saviour. Apart from that, theologically, it is rather evident that human beings cannot 'wound' or 'kill' the divine being.

Irenaeus' Eulogy of the Reality of the Execution

Irenaeus of Lyons was aware of those alternative views of Jesus' suffering and death. Against certain alternative interpretations, Irenaeus proclaimed Jesus Christ's death under Pontius Pilate as boldly as his predecessor, Ignatius of Antioch.[16] In Irenaeus' elaboration, Pontius Pilate receives the role of 'a chronological signpost', and he reaffirms the historicity of the events as contrary to the Gnostic predisposition to see them as a purely allegorical pattern of salvation. The Bishop of Lyons put a strong emphasis on their factual and real nature, because Pontius Pilate was a real Roman official who sentenced Jesus Christ to real death by crucifixion on a real wooden cross. It is thus the reality of the cross and the empirical suffering of Jesus Christ which Irenaeus magnified against the allegorical inclination of Gnostic, including docetic, adversaries. For Irenaeus, the Christian faith is based on the very paradox that God was killed on the cross by human beings, and the instrument of humiliation became the sign of glory.[17] Irenaeus lauds Christ's humiliation on the cross, his suffering and death in the flesh, as the lowest point in the history of salvation and at the same time the turning point leading towards glorification of the Risen Lord. Again, by his theory of recapitulation, this very moment of Christ's real death on the cross as ordered by Pontius Pilate inaugurates a new humanity and a new era. For Irenaeus, the crucified Saviour represents at the same time the glorious Lord at his very moment of triumph in his disfigured body.[18] Christ's crucifixion was, for Irenaeus, the fullest epiphany of his mission: love and salvation for all.

> Likewise the same objection applies to those who claim that he suffered only in appearance. For if he did not really suffer, no thanks to him, there was no suffering at all; and when we shall actually suffer, he will seem as leading us astray, exhorting us to be beaten, and to turn the other cheek [Matt. 5.39], if he did not himself before us in reality suffer the same. He would also mislead them [i.e. the Docetists – P. A.-S.] by seeming what he was not; even more would he mislead us, by exhorting us to endure what he did not experience himself. [In the case of persecution – P. A.-S.] we would be even above our Master,

because we suffer and experience what our Master never suffered and experienced. But as our Lord is the only true Master, so the Son of God is truly good and patient, the Word of God the Father having been made the Son of man. He fought and became victorious.

Irenaeus of Lyons, *AH* 3.18.6, trans. P. A.-S.

Irenaeus tried to counterbalance docetic interpretations of salvation, by commenting on the events known from the Gospels and recognized by the Church,[19] as the factual documents within his principal theory of 'recapitulation' (see chapter 2). But his theology of the suffering and crucified Lord served yet another purpose: to show those who were confused the way to the true Church. Pontius Pilate and the faith in crucifixion were one of many indicators. For Irenaeus, God's creation of the visible world, Christ's birth from the Virgin, his suffering and death under Pontius Pilate, then his resurrection, ascension and the last judgement are stages in the one divine economy of salvation. From these events he constructed his creed.[20]

Tertullian: Pontius Pilate the Friend of Christians

In the pre-Nicene period, yet another theologian should be mentioned, as he either initiated or highlighted certain ideas and terminology, which shaped Christian understanding of Christ's death in centuries to come. *Tertullian plays a very important role in the history of Christian doctrine. Even the embarrassing fact that he ended his life as a fervent supporter of <u>Montanism</u> does not change his reputation.

Montanism: a fervent apocalyptic movement (second century CE) with strong ascetic inclination. Montanists believed in the immanent and overwhelming presence of the Holy Spirit in the Church, which has been already experienced by the ecstatic prophecy of its leaders: *Montanus and his female companions Prisca and Maximilla. Montanists proclaimed very rigid ethics with, for instance, prohibition of second marriage, extension of fasting as well as disallowing flight from persecution. Tertullian encountered Montanism in North Africa and joined the group.

There are three main reasons, at least in the context of the present article of faith, why Tertullian deserves special attention. First, it was Tertullian whose comment on Christ's death as 'satisfaction' has strengthened for good or ill an important understanding of Jesus' execution in the history of Christianity. Second, Tertullian's polemic against the theory which claimed that the Father rather than the Son was crucified (i.e. *Patripassianism; see chapter 1), reaffirmed the real death of the second person of the Trinity. Third, Tertullian's reinterpretation of the role of Pontius Pilate in Jesus' crucifixion offered a new outlook on the co-existence of the Empire and Christianity. All three points, which appeared as intuitions in various earlier authors, with Tertullian's sharp intellect, rhetorical zeal and influence gained a new brightness and capacity to inspire later generations of theologians.

Christian apologists tried to give a convincing answer to the crucial question: 'Why did Jesus die on the cross?' In the case of Justin, the answer lay within the scriptural prophecies, because Jesus' life and death fulfilled the teaching of the Hebrew prophets inspired by the Spirit. Irenaeus of Lyons understood that for Christ's public, the most humiliating execution was the greatest triumph of the Son of God, who by this very act offered new life to humanity and redirected the history of salvation towards its final conclusion. Origen, at least in his work against the pagan philosopher Celsus, proclaimed Christ's death as the most dignified self-sacrifice of the most innocent man that ever existed, the Son of God whose love for humanity called from him the greatest act of self-sacrifice. As such it provided Christians with the model to imitate.

Tertullian's theology of Christ's death amplified a very important theory of salvation. It was Tertullian who introduced the word and the theme 'satisfaction' (Lat. *satisfactio*) to Christian theology, although the significance of that introduction was discovered much later, particularly by medieval theologians such as Anselm of Canterbury (*c*.1033–1109). Tertullian's juristic background and career are still discussed, because his theological theory is clearly based on a legalistic assumption that each offence calls for reparation. In Tertullian's view, Christ's death on the cross under Pontius Pilate brought satisfaction to God the

Father for the sin of the first people.[21] Christ's death was a ransom offered to God for the offence committed and as such it brought justice. It was an act of reparation done by somebody whose dignity and innocence were able to match God's perfection and divinity.

> Who has redeemed another's death by his own, but the Son of God alone? For even in His very passion He set the robber free [Luke 23.39–43]. For to this end had He come, that, being Himself pure from sin [1 John 3.5], and in all respects holy [Heb. 7.26—8.21], He might undergo death on behalf of sinners [1 Peter 3.18].
>
> Tertullian, *Mod*. 22.4, trans. S. Thelwall

The whole purpose of the incarnation was to pay this heavy <u>ransom</u>.[22]

> Theory of '**Ransom**' (Gr. *lytron*) or 'substitution': there are several Patristic variations, but the basic model can be summarized as follows. When the first people sinned, they passed into the power of the devil. God permitted this. However, he immediately promised the Saviour who would pay the 'ransom' with his own sacrifice in order to liberate the captives. Because the first people sinned, they were under the curse. Then the curse and death were transferred on to the righteous. The Saviour's sacrifice had a surpassing efficacy and it saved all humanity but also conquered the devil's might. The model was based on yet another version of the 'exchange formula' and had a strong emphasis on justice, which has to be done in the case of an offence. As a general model, this theory highlighted that the ultimate sacrifice had to be done *by* God, not *to* God.

Christ's death was sacrificial as he died for the sins of all.[23] The idea of ransom paid by the Saviour to Satan was not new,[24] and it was expressed by Tertullian in a rather unsystematic way; nevertheless, he drew attention to the fact that human beings have to make satisfaction to God for their sins, and the most perfect satisfaction can be made only by God's Son. Second, Tertullian's attack on Praxeas' theology delivered not only severe criticism of *Monarchianism as a theory of God, but, in a positive way, introduced a number of significant distinctions, terms and ideas, which became the foundation of Latin theology of the Trinity. *Against Praxeas,* as a theological work, combines exegesis and logical argument and produces a coherent theology of God, where the Son and the Father are presented as two different divine beings (Lat. *personae*), while they share the same nature (Lat. *substantia*). However, it was the Son who stood in front of Pontius Pilate,[25] and then was crucified.[26]

Before we introduce the third point, it must be noted that already the canonical Gospels portrayed Pontius Pilate as someone who acted under pressure from the aggressive Jewish crowd and as an outcome of a plot prepared by Jewish authorities. This, if not sympathetic, certainly not hostile appearance in the Gospels contradicts other ancient, Jewish sources about the character of the Roman Procurator.[27] According to the historians *Philo of Alexandria and Flavius Josephus, Pilate was a violent man, and his governance included the whole repertoire of provocations and executions without trial. It is possible that the earliest Christian records wished to contrast the hostility of the Jewish establishment of Jerusalem towards Jesus with the more compassionate approach of the pagan and certainly his wife.[28] This discrepancy in attitude towards the Jewish authorities and pagan Prefect is further explored by Tertullian. His *Apology* presents a new portrait of Pontius Pilate painted by the Christian apologists. Unlike previous Patristic accounts of the role of Pontius Pilate in the crucifixion of the innocent Jesus Christ, Tertullian showed a great deal of sympathy to this representative of Roman law and order. Pilate is, according to Tertullian, pressed by the Jews to sentence Jesus to death.[29] It looks as if, unlike the Jews, Pilate is on Jesus' side and becomes the adversary of the Jews, which for Tertullian is a welcome sign.[30] Pilate is in favour of Jesus' teaching, but he is not strong enough to resist yet another Jewish plot. In Tertullian's view, it was Pilate himself who told the story about Jesus to the emperor in Rome.[31] That colourful redecoration of Pilate's image by Tertullian hints at the possibility of reconciliation between Christianity and the Roman Empire. In this setting Pontius Pilate represents the potential of accepting Jesus' teaching, which may lead to the end of animosity towards Christians and the end of persecution. We do not know how many read or even heard about Tertullian's bold project, but if the idea was broadcast through his treatise, it may have reached Roman candidates for conversion, at least among the upper classes in Carthage. Tertullian, like many apologists before him, tried to present the new system of belief as respectable and acceptable to a Roman audience. Tertullian illustrates very well the effort of some Christians expressed in the apocrypha, to 'christen' Pontius Pilate and make him the first

pagan follower of Jesus or even a saint. Some churches, following that ancient tradition, canonized Pilate. It is quite remarkable how Pontius Pilate began to inspire Christian imagination; while disappearing from the common history,[32] he had a long life in Christian legends and iconography.[33]

Pontius Pilate and later Patristic Theology

The second phase of theological debate around the significance of Christ's death started in the fourth century. The appearance of the *crux invicta* to Constantine[34] and his famous victory over Maxentius (312 CE) made Tertullian's dream come true. The religion which proclaimed that the crucified Jesus was the Saviour of the world became tolerated, then supported, by the authorities of the Empire. The gospel was preached to the family and friends of the emperor, while his army accepted the *chi-rho* sign, which is the sign of Christ, as their symbol.[35] In addition, Helena, the mother of the emperor, rediscovered the cross, which as an event can be seen as a metaphor, a new stage of the development of the doctrine of Christ's passion. This new stage, sometimes characterized as 'imperial' or 'triumphalist' Christology, changed Christian comprehension of this article of faith irrevocably. In the period between Nicaea and Chalcedon, while reciting one of the existing pro- or anti-Nicene Creeds, one acute question returned almost with every generation of Christians. When Jesus was crucified 'under Pontius Pilate', who was actually crucified? Was it the humanity of Jesus which suffered death? Or was it perhaps possible for human beings to kill Christ's divine nature too?

Athanasius of Alexandria

Athanasius' defence of Christ's full divinity and humanity led him to believe that Christ's humanity and divinity died on the cross, when Jesus gave up his spirit to his Father. The Word of God took a human body, which was not different from any other human flesh,[36] and with it he also took human corruption and death. Being fully human, the Logos offered humanity to his divine Father. This fundamental act of redemption centred on the cross achieved two purposes. Christ united with all humanity in his flesh fulfilled the sentence of the ultimate punishment and death as declared by God for the original transgression. Therefore that 'sentence of death' was put on Christ who on behalf of all transgressors died on the cross. But his death provided all men and women with his own eternal life and incorruptibility because he is the divine Son of God.

And thus taking the body like ours, since we all were liable to the corruption of death, and surrendering it to death on behalf of all, he offered it to the Father. And this he did in his loving kindness in order that, as all die in him, the law concerning corruption in men might be abolished – since its power was concluded in the Lord's body and it would never again have influence over men who are like him – and in order that, as men had turned to corruption, he might turn them back again in incorruption and might give them life for death, in that he had made the body his own, and by the grace of the resurrection had rid them of death as straw is destroyed by fire.

Athanasius, *IncarnationL* 8.4, trans. R. W. Thomson

Athanasius' theology of Christ's death, based on his axiom about the human and divine nature of the Son of God, offers a coherent interpretation of Christ's crucifixion and death as the one redemptive act by which humanity is completely redeemed, because the Redeemer not only represents, but by his nature is, fully human and divine. Christ's cross, like a bridge, joined together the divine and the human, and now men and women can approach the divine, while the divine can pour its grace directly on the human. Athanasius' theory of salvation, it may be noted, contains the idea of 'sacrificial offering' and ransom paid by the innocent Jesus to redeem sinful and corruptible humanity.[37] In conclusion, Athanasius argued, Christ's crucifixion highlighted his bond with human flesh and the human condition after the fall; therefore, it emphasized the purpose of the incarnation. Second, by the most real encounter with death, the Word of God, the true life, destroyed the dominion of death over humanity. Christ's death liberated all from existence in the shadow of death, while at the same time elevating human nature to the realm of eternal existence with God.

Cyril of Alexandria

In the next generation, *Cyril of Alexandria, yet another great champion of orthodoxy, 'a saint and sinner',[38] called attention to the death of both natures united in the same person of Jesus as the most perfect *satisfaction* in his polemic against *Nestorius. On the cross and under Pontius Pilate, it was Jesus who suffered and then ended his life; the death on the cross was, in other words, the death of the divine Logos. In his interpretation of Christ's death, the *leitmotif* of ransom reappears again with strong emphasis on the Saviour's redemptive act as a recompense for human disobedience.[39] The only-begotten Son of God was submitted to suffering and death on behalf of evildoers,[40] and in consequence he died on the cross. While applying the theory of 'interchange of the properties', Cyril maintained not only that Christ suffered and died in his humanity, but also that his divine nature went through the same experience.

> This is what we mean when we say he suffered and rose again; not that God the Word suffered blows, nail-piercing or other wounds in his own nature (the divine is impassible because incorporeal), but what

is said is that since his own created body suffered these things he himself 'suffered' for our sake, the point being that within the suffering body was the impassible. We interpret his dying along exactly comparable lines. The Word of God is by nature immortal and incorruptible, is life and life-giving, but since, again, his own body 'tasted death for every men' [Heb. 2.9], as Paul says, 'by the grace of God', he himself suffered death for our sake, not as though he had experience of death with respect to his nature (to assert or imagine that is lunacy) but because his flesh, as I have just said, tasted death.

Cyril of Alexandria, *2 EpN* 4, trans. P. A.-S.

Cyril's theology was deeply rooted in Alexandrian Christology,[41] and as such his view of Christ's death pointed to the ultimate glory of the crucified Logos: divine and human.

For the later Alexandrian theologians, whose Christology fully assimilated the theory of interchange of the properties, Jesus' death on the cross included his divine and human natures. We may even observe that as long as this theory was applied to Christ, the Latin and Greek fathers unanimously proclaimed Christ's real death. At the same time the emphasis on Pilate's role becomes less significant, as the crucial event which allowed the crucifixion and therefore redemption was Jesus' incarnation through the Virgin Mary. This trajectory in the development of the doctrine originated with Irenaeus of Lyons' theology. Then, Tertullian drew attention to various analogies with juristic notions, but it truly flourished under Athanasius' elaboration as a theological weapon against the Arians. In the case of Cyril of Alexandria, the same theory was still useful to strengthen orthodoxy against Nestorius and his followers. To understand the alternative view which culminated with Nestorius' teaching, we have to turn to a crucial intuition of the Antiochene tradition. As an example of that reservation, we may point to *Theodore of Mopsuestia.

Theodore of Mopsuestia

Theodore was a theologian whose main concern was to protect the correct faith against any deformation and pollution with error. As an exegete, he was very unsympathetic to the Alexandrian allegorical interpretation of the Scriptures. Naturally, this allegorical exegesis led to further theological constructions, including a highly spiritualizing Christology. Also, as a theologian, Theodore was aware of the distinction between theology originating in careful exegesis, which takes into account a factual context (Gr. *to historikon*), and popular piety, which relies upon emotional expression of faith. For example, he accepted rhetorical expressions such as 'incarnated God', 'God-bearing' and 'God died on the cross', but as a theologian he was convinced that divinity could not mingle with humanity and that certainly divinity is immortal. As a pro-Nicene bishop and intellectual, he believed and defended the notion that Jesus Christ was fully divine and human, but Christ's humanity and his experience of life in the flesh took priority in his reflection on salvation. Considering the co-existence of the two natures in Jesus after his incarnation, while approaching the mystery of the cross, Theodore was careful not to confuse the reaction of the Christian emotions with the stance of Christian reason. He feared that transcendence of God and the divinity of Christ might be compromised for the sake of our human perception of Jesus' death. Theodore knew about the Alexandrian theory of interchange of properties (see chapter 2), but again he was cautious to apply this theory each time when speaking about Jesus, especially in the context of his suffering and death. His Christology endorsed the idea of Christ's two natures, which remained neither 'amalgamated' nor in a state where the divine nature could undermine Christ's real humanity.

> Neither he was God alone, nor man, but he has both natures: divine and human: God the Word, the one assuming and man who assumed. [. . .] The one assuming is of the divine nature, which did everything for our salvation, while the one assumed is the human nature. This was assumed on behalf of all of humanity and is united to the divine in a union beyond words which will never cease to exist.
>
> Theodore of Mopseustia, *CH* 8.1, trans. P. A.-S.

Consequently, any linguistic or theological projection of characteristics of the human nature on the divine must have clear limits, in his view, if one wishes to avoid complete confusion and paradox: immortal/mortal or impassible/suffering at the same time. When Christ uttered the famous words during his passion on the cross: 'My God why have you forsaken me?' he referred to the similar experience of David. In brief, for Theodore, it was impossible to kill divinity in Christ, therefore to protect the coherence of his Christology he affirmed that the son of God remained in Christ until the very end of his earthly life.[42]

Doctrinal Proclamation

The Council of Chalcedon (451) confirmed that the dramatic events on Golgotha ended Christ's earthly life: the Son of God died. In the view of the Church fathers, Christ's death was not a metaphor, but had a literal and factual meaning as life was taken away from the person of Christ, and both his natures 'tasted' death. But Jesus' death, even if it was only a phase in God's economy of salvation, was an extreme way of paying a 'ransom' to God, literal humiliation, a very personal and painful means of restoring humanity to full communion with its Creator. This crucified God was needed by us, as Gregory of Nazianzus expressed in his *Oration*. His blood offered eternal life to human beings, and at the same time united all the redeemed in one, universal family.

> We needed God incarnate and then crucified so that we may live. We were put to death with him in order that we may live and we died with him that we may be purified. As we died with him, we also rose to life with him. Then, as we rose from death with him, we were glorified with him. There were many miracles at that time. When God was crucified, the sun darkened and then lighted up as it was proper for the creatures to participate in suffering as their Creator. When blood and water poured from his side, the veil [in the Temple – P. A.-S.] was torn apart. Blood appeared, as he was truly a human being, water poured out, as he was killed on behalf of human beings. The earth shook and the rocks were split on behalf of the Rock. Dead were raised as the assurance of the final common resurrection; the sign appeared at the tomb and after the tomb, and who may be worthy to glorify [these wonders]? However, nothing compares to the wonder of my salvation! A few drops of blood recreated the entire world and they became like rennet in milk, uniting and bringing together all of us in one.
>
> Gregory of Nazianzus, *Or* 45.28–9, trans. P. A.-S.

Conclusion

This specific credal statement has a double life. First in the pre-Nicene phase, it served to amplify specific claims of the early Patristic authors against their pagan, Jewish and Gnostic opponents, while in the second period of Patristic theology, from Nicaea to Chalcedon, it approached Christ's death on the cross with a new agenda and interests. However, both periods promoted the image of Christ as the victor over sin, Satan and death. The gravity of Arius' challenge permanently reshaped the theological landscape. The important models of salvation which appeared in polemic with Arianism, after some modification, were applied again in new contexts and new challenges. The position of Pontius Pilate appeared to be more commemorative in the earlier Creeds, then it gained a new role, while Christ's death affirmed his full participation in human nature and posed new problems to comprehend the union of that humanity with his assumed divinity.

Questions for Discussion

- In the light of Patristic theology, if human transgression destroyed the original relationship with God, why could the divine justice not be satisfied with a recompense made by a human being, a saint, for example?
- Present the theological arguments which support the theory of ransom and some counter-arguments. Which ones prevail in your view?
- What is the difference between the docetic interpretation of Christ's crucifixion and the approach of the Antiochene tradition?
- If Christ died on the cross and experienced death, does this kind of 'knowledge' impact on his divine compassion towards the suffering of men and women before his incarnation?

Further Reading

For beginners

E. Fergusson, 2003, *Backgrounds of Early Christianity,* 3rd edition, Grand Rapids, MI: Eerdmans, pp. 416–19.

For more advanced readers

H. K. Bond, 1998, *Pontius Pilate in History and Interpretation*, Cambridge: Cambridge University Press.

V. Brümmer, 2005, *Atonement, Christology and the Trinity: Making Sense of Christian Doctrine*, Aldershot: Ashgate.

D. Chapman, 2008, *Ancient Jewish and Christian Perceptions of Crucifixion*, Tübingen: Mohr Siebeck.

S. M. Heim, 2006, *Saved from Sacrifice: A Theology of the Cross*, Grand Rapids, MI: Eerdmans.

R. E. Heine, 2004, 'The beginning of Latin Christian Literature', in F. Young, L. Ayres and A. Louth (eds), *Christian Literature*, Cambridge: Cambridge University Press, pp. 131–41.

Internet Resources

Pontius Pilate (from the Ecole Initiative)
http://ecole.evansville.edu/articles/pilate.html
Atonement (Stanford Encyclopaedia of Philosophy)
http://www.science.uva.nl/~seop/entries/christiantheology-philosophy/#Ato

Notes

1 A fragment of inscribed stone found in Caesarea in 1961 confirms Pontius Pilate's official Latin title as the *praefectus*, that is, the governor of Judea.

2 For example, in the Old Roman Creed as preserved by Rufinus Tyrannius (*c.*345–411): 'who under Pontius Pilate was crucified and buried' (Lat. *qui sub Pontio Pilato crucifixus est et sepultus*). Another Creed from the third century, this time representing Greek Christianity, is preserved by Marcellus of Ancyra in Cappadocia: 'who under Pontius Pilate was crucified and was put to the grave'. Similarly, the baptismal Creed in Hippolytus' *Apostolic Tradition* (third century CE) refers to Jesus' crucifixion under Pontius Pilate.

3 Ignatius, *Smyr.* 1.1–2.

4 For example, see the reaction of Celsus in Origen, *AC* 2.55 and Trypho's problem with the same notion in *Dial.* 36.1 and 63.1.

5 *Dial.* 90.

6 *Dial.* 92; 94.

7 *Dial.* 13; 40; 54.

8 *Dial.* 86.

9 *Dial.* 91; 111–12 and Isa. 27.1.

10 *1 Apol.* 13; *1 Apol.* 61; *Dial.* 85.2.

11 *AC* 7.53.

12 *AC* 2.40–1.

13 *AC* 7.56.

14 See Irenaeus, *AH* 1.26.1.

15 See also *ApPeter* 81.10–11.

16 For example *Proof* 74; 77; 79.

17 *Proof* 48.

18 *Proof* 56.

19 *AH* 3.11.11.

20 *AH* 3.4.2.

21 *Pen.* 5.

22 *Flesh* 6. Some scholars suggest that it was not Tertullian, but Hilary of Poitiers (*c.*315–67/8) who applied this very meaning directly to Christ's death. However, my intention is to name Tertullian as the provider of the notion itself.

23 *AJ* 13.

24 The first theologian who mentioned the idea of 'ransom' as a theory of atonement was *Irenaeus of Lyons, *AH* 5.1.1. Soon it appeared in other authors, such as *Clement of Alexandria, *Tutor* 1.5.23; 1.11.97; 3.12.98, *Origen, *ComGMat.* 16.8; *ComGJ* 6.274; *Athanasius, *IncarnationL* 9 and 25; *Gregory of Nazianzus, *Or.* 45.22; *Gregory of Nyssa, *AE* 6; *Basil of Caesarea, *HomPs.* 7.2; *Ambrose, *ExLk* 4.7; *Pelagius, *ExRom.* 3.25; *Augustine, *Trin.* 13.19; *Theodoret of Cyrrhus, *ExRom.* 3.24, *Cyril of Jerusalem, *CL* 13.2.

25 *AP* 16.6.

26 *AP* 28.4; 29.3–4; 30.

27 For example *Philo of Alexandria, *Embassy,* 301–2; *Josephus, *JW* 2.169–77; *JA* 18.55–9, 62.

28 Matt. 27.19. Pontius' wife had a surprising career in Patristic literature. In the fourth century CE in the apocryphal *Acts of Pilate*, she is named as Procula. Some Christian traditions, such as that of the Ethiopian Orthodox Church, recognize her as a saint, and together with her husband she is commemorated on 25 June.

29 *Apology* 21.18.

30 *AJ* 8.18.

31 *Apology* 21.24

32 Eusebius of Caesarea suggests that Pontius Pilate was deposed and sent to Rome (36 CE) in order to justify his governance, and then he committed suicide. Cf. *EH* 2.7.

33 The first known iconography of Pontius Pilate comes from the fourth century, and it is no coincidence that at this period Pontius becomes a very popular motif in

Christian apocrypha (see chapter 3). As for the ancient documents presenting Pontius Pilate in a new, Christian light, see the *Gospel of Peter* (*c.*200), which claims Pilate's innocence and attributes the full responsibility for Jesus' death to the Jews and Herod. The *Gospel of Nicodemus*, the first chapters of which are known under another title as the *Acts of Pilate*, comes from the beginning of the fifth century. Again, this document introduces Pontius Pilate as Christ's supporter against the Jews. For an example of iconography, see the illustration from the *Rossano Gospels* (sixth century CE), http://www.calabria.org.uk/calabria/arte-cultura/CodexPurpureusRossanensis/codex13.htm

34 Eusebius, *LC* 1.28.

35 Lactantius, *DP* 44.5. More in A. Cameron, 2006, 'Constantine and the "peace of the church"', in M. M. Mitchell and F. M. Young (eds), *Christianity: Origins to Constantine*, Cambridge: Cambridge University Press, pp. 538–51. See here: http://www.jesuswalk.com/christian-symbols/chi-rho.htm

36 *IncarnationL*, for example, 8.2; 10.4; 37.2.

37 More on Athanasius' theory of redemption in T. G. Weinandy, 2007, *Athanasius: A Theological Introduction*, Aldershot: Ashgate, pp. 27–48.

38 Cf. F. M. Young, 1983, *From Nicaea to Chalcedon: A Guide to the Literature and its Background*, London: SCM Press, p. 242, more 240–65.

39 *OTF* 2.7.

40 *Worship* 3.

41 By this term I understand an Alexandrian approach to the incarnation, which saw in Jesus of Nazareth the divine Logos who descended and fully dwelt in human nature in order to sanctify it. The Logos' dwelling in human flesh was an exact union between both natures.

42 *CH* 5.6.

5

Descent to Hell

See also chapters 2, 3, 4, 6, 9, 10, 11.

Consider this Task

Search for the earliest Christian examples of iconography of Christ's descent to the underworld. Find out more about their historical background, didactical function and theological message.

Introduction

At the centre of Christian claims about Jesus of Nazareth is the belief in his resurrection. This most mysterious event expresses the apex of the Messiah's redemptive mission. Another significant theological theme emerged in relation to the idea of resurrection. The Church fathers, as commentators on the Scriptures, encountered the enigmatic theme of Jesus' 'descent to hell'. This motif expressed the belief in Christ's victory over evil and death, which as a triumph extends its consequences to the 'underworld'. Chronologically, between Christ's death on the cross (the 'day before the Sabbath day') and his appearance to his disciples ('on the first day of the week') he went down and liberated those departed who were imprisoned in the underworld. Christ's descent liberated those inhabitants of the lowest sphere to become fully included in Jesus' salvation. Thus, 'descent' implies the ultimate extension of Christ's coming down from heaven (incarnation) to reach the departed. The Patristic teaching about the universality of salvation in Jesus Christ encompassed those who were dead by the time of Christ's

1. Waters above the firmament
2. Storehouses of snows
3. Storehouses for hail
4. Chambers of winds
5. Firmament
6. Windows of heaven
7. Pillars of the sky
8. Pillars of the earth
9. Fountain of the deep
10. Navel of the earth
11. Waters under the earth
12. Rivers of the nether world

advent, but who still were and are God's children, unforgotten either by their Father or by his Son: the Saviour of the world. Although later Latin authors such as *Rufinus of Aquileia elaborated on this specific doctrine, it never entered the Creeds accepted by the Orthodox Churches, nor did it become a <u>dogma</u>; nonetheless, it attracted theological and iconographical attention among Eastern Christians.

Dogma (Gr. *dogma*, 'the opinion, which seems (Gr. *dokei*) to be right'): in the Patristic context, the term denoted the view which was in agreement with the authority of the Scriptures, later Councils and the Catholic Church. Among the apostolic authors, the apologists and later also Origen, this term referred to the correct understanding and teaching of Christian faith as well as doctrine. Later fathers, for example Basil of Caesarea, saw a dogma as sacred and yet another characteristic of the holiness of the Christian orthodoxy. Some Latin theologians, such as Augustine, used this term as a negative description of an erroneous opinion.

The 'descent to Hell' did not appear in credal statements until the fourth century. It is found in the Fourth Creed of Sirmium (359), Nike and Constantinople (360), and then, expressed by the Creed used at Aquilea and Rome, gained greater importance later on with the Apostles' Creed. Among the Greek confessions, the so-called 'Athanasian' Creed (381–428) professes faith in Christ's descent into Hades.

Opening Question

What are the main characteristics of the underworld/Hades in the New Testament documents?

Development of the Argument

The theological effort to promote this belief faced many tests, which gradually and naturally changed together with the membership of the Church. While the core of this belief has been retained to the present day, its precise theological meaning and interpretation has shifted together with the pastoral needs of Christians and even with the social and ethnic membership of the Church. For example, the early Christian apologist *Justin Martyr, while addressing the Jews represented in the *Dialogue* by Trypho, referred to the Hebrew Scriptures in order to convince them about Jesus' life as the life of the Messiah. At this early stage, many Christians were acquainted with the Jewish narratives and symbols that elaborated on a mysterious descent of the Righteous One into the under-world. Soon, the Christian exegetes and rhetoricians elaborated on Jesus' death, and then shed some light on the destiny of all those departed in relation to Christ's mission, which embraced all spheres of the universe. In the early Jewish-Christian context, the belief in 'descent to Hell' also expresses a concern that the saints of 'the Old Covenant', or the Hebrew Scriptures, would be included in Christ's salvation.[1] Among authors such as *Clement of Alexandria, the scrip-tural passages about Christ's descent to Hades only confirmed God's mercy and desire to proclaim the gospel to all people.[2]

Jewish-Christian Imagery

As a part of the introduction to the Patristic interpretation of the descent into Hades/Sheol, which is interwoven into the story about Jesus' resurrection, it must be said that the motif of the Righteous One's journey into the realm of departed souls was an important part of Jewish theories of salvation. These literary sources later inspired the authors of the New Testament documents (for example, Acts 2.24–31; Rom. 10.7; Eph. 4.8–9, 1 Pet. 3.18–20) and Jewish-Christian literature.[3]

> Sheol saw me and was shattered, and Death ejected me and many with me.
> I have been vinegar and bitterness to it, and I went down with it as far as its depth.
> Then the feet and the head it released, because it was not able to endure my face.
> And I made a congregation of living among his dead; and I spoke with them by living lips; in order that my word may not be unprofitable.

> And those who had died ran towards me; and they cried out and said, 'Son of God, have pity on us.
>
> And deal with us according to your kindness, and bring us out from the bonds of darkness.
>
> And open for us the door by which we may come out to you; for we perceive that our death does not touch you.
>
> May we also be saved with you, because you are our Saviour.'
>
> Then I heard their voice, and placed their faith in my heart.
>
> And I placed my name upon their head, because they are free and they are mine.
>
> *Odes of Solomon* 42.15–26, trans. J. Charlesworth, modified P. A.-S.

The journey or descent to the underworld was an important part of theological folklore, which nurtured the hope that all good people would not only be remembered by God, but also, somehow, brought back to life and his presence. In this context, the passionate interest in the underworld and speculation about its nature, which characterized the Jewish and Jewish-Christian theology of the period, created a convenient setting for the development of this article of faith.

The Apologists: More Than Just Another Myth

When, however, Christian apologists addressed a pagan audience, not only critics, but also potential converts, they aimed to promote the conviction in Jesus' resurrection in a way that would not be confused with mythologies about the afterlife of the Hellenic heroes. They attempted to show that Christ's descent to the underworld had nothing in common with those mythologies but fulfilled a totally different theological purpose.

> **Mythologies** (Gr. *mythos* – 'story' – Gr. *logos* – 'teaching'): a collection of myths which although describing ancient events in historical terms aimed to convey an important religious and philosophical teaching.

The third line of interpretation of the belief appeared during the struggle with docetic Christology. At this time the same pronouncement was used to highlight two important points: first, that Christ's resurrection was physical and real, as opposed to purely allegorical, and 'in flesh' as opposed to 'in spirit'. Second, the same belief amplified the point that the salvation was inclusive and open to all, including 'those who were asleep', as opposed to the idea of salvation limited to 'a pre-selected elite'.

The phrase 'the third day' was an additional confirmation of Christ's own prophecy about the extent of his absence from this world, which did not suggest any kind of annihilation or decomposition but rather a continuation of the same mission commissioned by his Father, though this time in a different world. Since Jesus is the universal Lord and Saviour, his death gave him access to the world of the departed where virtuous men and women could also be reconciled with God and brought to his kingdom. This belief not only provided the Church with a strong argument about Christ's unique victory over death, but also affirmed that there was no limit to Christ's salvation and reign and that he is the Saviour of the living and the dead. This dual function highlights the fact that the rhetorical and pedagogical efforts of the Church often had a number of theological motivations.

The belief also hints at the classical cosmological and religious division of the world into three spheres, in which the centre of the afterlife is 'under' the current world of the living. In this way the movement of 'descent' presupposes Christ's 'ascent', or at least the first stage of this 'ascent' – the ultimate phase took place with the return of Christ to his Father. Thus, the statement under discussion is the literary 'pivot' of the Creed, which recounts a turning point in God's economy of salvation. The statements that follow this one focus on the glorification of Jesus Christ, and extend the meaning of salvation, ecclesiology and eschatology.

Justin Martyr: The Importance of the Descent to Sheol

One of the earliest references to Christ's descent to the underworld can be found in Justin's polemic against a Jewish theologian, Trypho. The Christian apologist

accuses the Jews, represented here by Trypho, of tailoring the scriptural prophecies about the Messiah in a way that veils their direct connection with the events
of Jesus' life. In a brief statement Justin hints that the ancient Hebrew prophecies
about the Messiah included his descent to 'the graves' in order to preach to the
departed Jews the message of salvation.

Again, they [i.e. the Jews – P. A.-S.] have removed these words from
Jeremiah's prophecy: 'the Lord God, the Holy of Israel remembered his
dead, who had fallen asleep in the graves, and he descended to them
in order to proclaim his salvation.'

Justin Martyr, *Dial.* 72.4, trans. P. A.-S.

In this line of interpretation, Christ's descent to the underworld is a natural
phase of a number of events (death, descent, resurrection) which lead to his
re-emergence as the Risen Lord and Saviour and proclamation of his victory
to all creation. In his polemic against Trypho, the Christian apologist refers to
the evidence of the Scriptures in order to persuade his listeners and readers
that what was more or less openly predicted in the Hebrew Scriptures about
the Messiah was fully realized in Jesus' life. This rhetoric aimed to convince
Jewish opponents, first, that Jesus was the promised Messiah as the Scriptures
and the historical events 'proved it', and second, that the living Jews should
take their lead from the departed Jews and accept Christ's message. In this
context, belief in Christ's descent to the dead, as well as his resurrection, represented the natural, predicted and expected climax of the history of salvation,
which started with the creation of the world and ended with the redemption
of all who accept God's might expressed by Jesus' resurrection from the dead.
The first day of creation and the new day of salvation conclude the whole
economy of salvation. It must be noted that the Jewish-Christian literature[4]
of this period provided a number of images of Sheol, where the souls of the
dead were guarded by either God's angels or evil spirits. This kind of literary
and symbolic background helped to endorse the new Christian message about
the universal salvation given by Christ's resurrection and his final victory over
evil spirits.

Clement of Alexandria: the Logos and the Underworld

Confronting pagan and philosophically oriented potential converts, the same belief about Christ's resurrection and descent to Hades acquired another significant colour. A good example can be found in Clement of Alexandria's adaptation of the motif. First, while persuading his Hellenic or Hellenized listeners, among whom many were familiar with Greek mythology and various forms of mysteries, Clement ridiculed the story of Dionysus' adventurous descent to Hades,[5] which in Clement's interpretation originated the idolatrous worship of Dionysus. The Christian scholar did not deny the actual descent to Hades, but rather the legendary account of the journey to the underworld and its significance. However, in a different context, though probably to the same audience, Clement of Alexandria used the motif of descent to Hades as an example or even proof of the universal proclamation of the gospel, which has been announced even to the dead.

> Therefore the Lord preached the gospel to those in Hades [1 Pet. 3.19]. Thus the Scripture says: 'Hades says to destruction: we have not seen his form, but we have heard his voice [Deut. 4.12].' But it was not 'the place' which heard the voice – as the words have just said, but those who have been put in Hades, and have abandoned themselves to destruction, as persons who have thrown themselves of their own free will from a ship into the sea. Those people are the ones who heard of the divine power and the voice. Who in his common sense can assume that the souls of the righteous and the sinners may be in the same place of condemnation? Who would dare to charge Providence with this kind of injustice? Do not the Scriptures show that the Lord proclaimed the gospel to those that perished in the flood, and those who had been chained or kept 'in prison' [1 Pet. 3.19]?
>
> Clement of Alexandria, *Strom.* 6.45.1–2, trans. P. A.-S.

Clement's adaptation of the motif underlines that while the incarnation of the divine Logos made his message accessible to those among the Greeks and the Jews who lived during and after Jesus' mission, Christ's descent after his death allowed those who were dead but righteous to receive his word. Incarnation and descent seem to be a part of the same process of salvation and God's economy towards the whole universe, which before God does not have any divisions (upper/underworld), limitations (alive/dead) or hidden places (Hades). However, in Clement's view, the departed must have been free from idolatry – that is, anything which would disturb contemplation of God – in order to understand Christ's message. Thus freedom from idolatry is a necessary preparation for souls to hear the gospel of the divine Logos. This implies that those pagans who followed, for example, the teaching of Plato or Pythagoras were open to salvation, while participants in religious cults were not.

Irenaeus of Lyons: Jesus' Descent in Flesh

The third kind of opponents challenged by the proposition under discussion were groups of Christian *Gnostics, particularly those who embraced docetic theology or those who limited redemption to only the most perfected Christians. Two testimonies are particularly important in the present context. First, according to *Irenaeus of Lyons, Christ has risen 'in flesh', and his bodily resurrection is a paradigm of the eschatological resurrection of all.

> In the same way, as Christ was raised with his body and showed to his disciples the marks of the nails as well as the wound in his side [John 20.2] (and these are the indications of the body risen from the dead), so 'shall he also', it is said, 'raise us up by his own power' [1 Cor. 6.14]. And again to the Romans he says, 'But if the Spirit of him that raised up Jesus from the dead dwells in you, he that raised up Christ from the dead will also give life to your mortal bodies [Rom. 8.11].'
> Irenaeus of Lyons, *AH* 5.7.1, trans. P. A.-S.

Christ's risen body is not a phantom, but carries the marks of his passion. This is a direct polemic against those Christians who showed some inclination towards docetic theology. To Irenaeus, Christ's resurrection was intrinsically connected with his physical body, or rather his physical body was at the centre of this spiritual event. Similarly, this strong link appears in the situation of the resurrection of all (see also chapter 10). God's might, which raised Christ from the dead, will also raise all the departed with their bodies. This Patristic interpretation based on the analogy between Christ and humanity reaffirms another crucial theme of Irenaeus' theology: the motif of Christ as the 'second Adam'. The Son of God, in order to save all people, imitated the first man, Adam, although unlike him Christ responded to God's will with perfect obedience. As a result Christ assimilated himself to man in his life and death.[6] After death Christ followed the path of Adam and descended to Hades, to the place of the dead. This act was a necessary stage of Christ's mission. Irenaeus' theology concludes with the statement that Christ fought for all humanity and won freedom for all, not just for the most perfect Christians. Christ liberated the captives from all forms of slavery, including eternal death in Hades, where the Saviour also conquered its power, bringing salvation to the whole creation.[7] Christ's death, descent to Hades and his resurrection in flesh are stages of the process of redemption which expressed Irenaeus' idea of 'recapitulation' (see chapter 2). This is the truly cosmic victory of Christ in which all spheres of the universe regain their natural connection with God. To Irenaeus of Lyons, as previously to Justin Martyr and Clement of Alexandria, Christ's triumph over evil and death means bringing a new life and opening a new chapter in history which includes all dimensions, sectors and levels of the architecture of the visible and invisible world.

A Gnostic Interpretation of Hades

So far we have introduced only some commentaries representing the mainstream of Christianity. But it is important to bring in at least one variation of the same motif from the Gnostic tradition. In this case, *The Testimony of Truth* offers another revision of the scriptural revelation, combined with other sources,[8] to give the motif a distinctive Gnostic flavour.

For the Son of [Man] clothed himself with their first-fruits; he went down to Hades and performed many mighty works. He raised the dead therein; and the world-rulers of darkness became envious of him, for they did not find sin in him. But he also destroyed their works from among men, so that the lame, the blind, the paralytic, the dumb, [and] the demon-possessed were granted healing.

TTruth 32.22—33.8, trans. S. Giversen and B. A. Pearson

In this account, the Saviour goes down to Hades 'undercover', that is, clothed with 'first-born of the powers' (32.23–4) in order to perform 'many mighty works' (32.25) and continue his fight against the multiple evil powers, which dominate this sphere of the world. The descent to Hades and confrontation with the spirits of darkness 'in their territory' continues the mission of liberation realized by the Saviour. He achieves victory over different 'world-rulers of darkness' – here the Gnostic document includes the conquest of the realm of death that was under 'control' of those enemies. There, in the heart of the realm of death, the Redeemer performs many miracles (32.26—33.25), which bring life to it; for example, he raises the dead who are in this sphere (32.26–7). Interestingly, the details of the Saviour's mighty deeds in Hades resemble the miracles of Jesus from the 'Catholic' narratives as performed in this present world. But this possible parallel is not surprising, as 'the whole Hades' might be understood by this school of Gnosticism as a metaphor for visible reality and the act of descent as an analogy to the 'Catholic' doctrine of incarnation. To this kind of Gnostic thought, the current material world has many features of 'Hades' from the original or classical typology. Therefore, the Saviour's descent to Hades has some similarities with the descent of the Saviour to this world, as pictured by the narratives of the Church. Of course, this parallel may pose some questions about the events in the Gnostic upper-world which led to descent, that is, coming to this world, but the Gnostic cosmogony did not aim to mirror the Catholic model of cosmology. It reinterpreted similar scriptural references with great creativity according to its own pedagogical aims. Also, in the light of this document, the main focus is on the dramatic battle of the Saviour with the rulers of Hades, therefore liberation of the departed from their 'prison' is not discussed in detail. For this reason, the notion of determinism as a common amnesty versus liberation of the few predestined, possibly the elite, is left unanswered. However, other Gnostic schools had much clearer concepts of liberation from Hades. According to Irenaeus' observation,[9] the disciples of Saturninus believed that the Saviour descended to the underworld to upset evil people and the spiritual powers supporting them, and to liberate only the righteous. This kind of theory of salvation hints at the possibility of predestination.

As can be seen, all these ancient documents enjoy very much the idea of Christ's *descent* to Hades/Sheol, later 'Hell', which is conceived as an act of liberation/salvation of all or a few carried out by the Saviour before his resurrection.

However, the Gnostic narratives are less interested in further details of Christ's resurrection either as 'a spirit' or 'in flesh' as his appearance to the most perfect disciples has a mainly spiritual character. Christ's resurrection 'in flesh', so central to the Catholic faith, seems to have been treated by the Gnostics as a naïve, literal and erroneous understanding of a purely spiritual event.

Later Patristic Proclamation: John Chrysostom

The theology which underpinned the belief in the pre-Nicene period found other interests and inspirations in later phases as it addressed new audiences and controversies. The first example comes from *John Chrysostom's *The Paschal Homily*. This homily, also known as *The Catechetical Homily*, is still used in a liturgical context and read in every Orthodox church on Easter morning.

> Let no one grieve over sins; for forgiveness has dawned from the tomb. Let no one fear death; for the Death of our Saviour has set us free. He had destroyed it by enduring it. He despoiled Hades, when He descended thereto. He embittered it, having tasted of his flesh. Isaiah foretold this when he cried out: 'You, O Hades, have been embittered by encountering him below'. It was embittered – for it was abolished. It was embittered – for it was mocked. It was embittered – for it was slain. It was embittered – for it was annihilated. It was embittered – for it is now made captive. It took a body, and, lo, it discovered God. It took earth and behold, it encountered Heaven. It took what it saw, and was overcome by what it could not see. O death where is your sting? O Hades where is your victory? Christ is risen and you are annihilated.
>
> A fragment of John Chrysostom's *Paschal Homily*, from *Greek Orthodox Holy Week and Easter Services: A New English Translation*, 2003, South Daytona, FL: Patmos Press, p. 482.

This hymn describes Christ's descent to Hades as an important prelude to his glorious resurrection. The two events – or rather two stages of the same event – are theologically interconnected, as the first episode declares Christ's total (universal or cosmological) triumph over his and his people's greatest enemy, symbolized here by 'Hades'. In this rhetorical narrative Christ's conquest of Hades acquires anthropological characteristics such as frustration or fury in response to Christ's victory. Hades is also a metaphor for sin, alienation and remoteness from life and light. Hades is thus the opposite pole of God's realm or kingdom. Although this is only a brief liturgical and lyrical story, it contains some significant theological insights into this belief. Christ's death and bodily descent to the underworld highlight for Patristic authors the material reality of Hades. Certainly, John Chrysostom highlights the reality of Christ's death, which encompasses both his natures united in one person. John's Christology, although formed just before the outbreak of the debate between *Cyril of Alexandria (d.444) and *Nestorius (d.451), hints at his strong conviction about Christ's divine and human natures. Here, in the context of Christ's descent to Hades, John proclaims what was to become the orthodox understanding of Christ's mystery as one person of two natures. The Antiochene school, to which John Chrysostom belonged, did not treat the motif as an allegorical multilayered symbol, but as a real event which destroyed or seriously weakened the power of evil over the Christian departed. Christ's arrival in the underworld, which was previously dominated by death and darkness, changed its nature, opened 'the door' and gave freedom from paralysing sin. John Chrysostom does not suggest the abolition of hell or death as the result of Christ's triumph but rather implies the new hope offered to Christians: a limitation of the influence of the underworld, death and evil. Christians are encouraged to participate in the Saviour's victory, proclaimed as the new 'V-Day'.

Basil of Caesarea: the Saviour's Ultimate Triumph

The second example of elaboration of the motif of Christ's descent to Hades comes from *Basil of Caesarea. His famous and controversial treatise, *On the Holy Spirit* (see chapter 8), written around 375 CE, took up the scriptural motif, yet with a new emphasis. In his pedagogical interpretation, Christ's descent represented the experience of every Christian who, following the Saviour, in the water of baptism, is called to descend to Hell, as a synonym for death. In Basil's interpretation the enigmatic scriptural motif received quite clear, comprehensive and convincing comment. It became a model of Christian's descent/ascent in the act of baptism, which includes both renunciation of sin (i.e. descent to Hades) and purification from distracting, unnecessary, often sinful inclinations towards worldly values. The second aspect points to 'ascent/resurrection from death', represented here by 'Hades'.

> If we wish to transform our life, death must conclude our past and mark the beginning of a new life. But how can we die? By imitating Christ's burial through our baptism as we descend into Hell. The bodies of those who are baptized are buried in the water. Therefore baptism is a symbol of renunciation of the sins of our fallen nature. [. . .] In baptism the soul is purified and delivered from the impurity of worldly thoughts and desires. Baptism is the image of Christ's death and resurrection by which the world is saved.
>
> Basil of Caesarea, *OHS* 15.35, trans. P. A.-S.

Events in Christ's life, including the Saviour's death and resurrection, serve as the paradigms of Christian life. In Christian life, these two crucial moments are denoted by 'death to sin' and 'new life' given by the Holy Spirit. Basil's treatise emphasizes the role of the Holy Spirit in the metamorphosis which takes place in the current existence, with the centrality of baptism which symbolizes 'death' and 'resurrection'. Basil's explanation does not refer to any early motifs and highlights the seriousness of the present, Christian existential choice of opening a new stage of life under the guidance of the Holy Spirit. This new phase of spiritual growth 'buries' old habits and inclinations: their place is in 'Hades', in the realm of shadows, as now the soul is enlightened with a divine knowledge and spiritual light.[10]

Gospel of Nicodemus: Faith and Imagination

The third example of the appearance of this belief and its specific pedagogical and catechetical function comes from the apocryphal *Gospel of Nicodemus* (fifth century CE). The third part (17—27) of this work, entitled 'Christ's descent to Hell' (Lat. *Descensus Christi ad inferos*), includes a colourful reinterpretation of the episode.

> 21.1 And as Satan the prince, and Hell, spoke this together, suddenly there came a voice as of thunder and a spiritual cry: 'Remove, O princes, your gates, and lift up everlasting doors, and the King of glory shall come in.' [Ps. 24.7] When Hell heard that he said to Satan the prince: 'Depart from me and go out of mine abode: if you are a mighty warrior, fight against the King of glory. But what have you got to do with him?' And Hell cast Satan forth out of his dwelling. [. . .] 21.4. But when all the multitude of the saints heard it, they spoke with a voice of rebuking to Hell: 'Open your gates that the King of glory may come in.' [. . .] 22.8 Then the King of glory in his majesty trampled upon death, and laid hold on Satan the prince and delivered him unto the power of Hell, and drew Adam to him unto his own brightness. [. . .] 24.1 And the Lord stretching forth his hand, said: 'Come to me, all of you, my saints which bear mine image and my likeness. You, who by the tree and the devil and death were condemned, behold now the devil and death condemned by the tree.' And forthwith all the saints were gathered in one under the hand of the Lord. And the Lord holding the right hand of Adam, said unto him: 'May peace be with you and with all your children that are my righteous ones.' But Adam, casting himself at the knees of the Lord pleaded him with tears and beseeching, and said with a loud voice: 'I will magnify you, O Lord, for you have set me up and not made my foes to triumph over me: O Lord my God I cried to you and you have healed me; Lord, you have brought my soul out of hell, you have delivered me from them that go down to the pit.

Sing praises to the Lord all of his saints, and give thanks to him for the remembrance of his holiness. For there is wrath in his indignation and life is in his good pleasure.' In like manner all the saints of God kneeled and cast themselves at the feet of the Lord, saying with one voice: 'You are the Saviour of the world, you are foretold by the law and by your prophets. You have accomplished your deeds. You have redeemed the living by your cross, and by the death of the cross you have come down to us to save us out of hell and death through your majesty. O Lord, in the same way as you have set the name of your glory in the heavens and set up your cross as a symbol of redemption on the earth, so, Lord, set up the sign of the victory of your cross in hell, that death may have no more power.'

Fragments from the *Gospel of Nicodemus*, from *The Apocryphal New Testament*, 1924, trans. M. R. James, Oxford: Clarendon Press, 1924, modified P. A.-S.

This imaginative, creative story interwoven with references to the Old and New Testaments begins with a dialogue between Satan and Hell, as the prince of darkness warns his companion against the forthcoming visit of Christ. The whole spectacular episode is conceived like a break-in to a prison in order to liberate its captives. The drama clearly identifies all the characters of the plot; the emotions of the reader are immediately attached to the 'good' types, while the 'bad' are punished with loss and suffering. The value of this last document lies in the way that it engages the imagination and feelings of the reader in order to inspire faith rather than simply relying on theological arguments designed to persuade through reason. It represents a new stage of the belief, which had an important influence on Christian art and folklore.

Conclusion

Christ's descent to Hades/Sheol is an idea that has proved remarkably adaptable to changing theological contexts. Its origin was closely related to the Jewish-Christian hope of salvation of the righteous forefathers, and it evolved together with Patristic theology, its new generations of contributors and new audiences.

The key implication of belief in the descent of the Saviour and its later modifications was that the theologically crucial triad, death – descent – resurrection, expressed one act of salvation with three interrelated aspects. These aspects in turn highlighted Christ's humanity, divinity and solidarity with (all) the departed.

Questions for Discussion

- How do you assess the connection between Christ's death, descent to the underworld and resurrection?
- Which theological elements of the Patristic concept of Christ's descent have continuing relevance in contemporary Christianity?
- How does the sequence of death, descent and resurrection enlighten your view of the divine and human natures of Jesus?
- Why did Jesus need 'some time' to reveal himself to the departed? What could be the literal and allegorical meaning of this belief?

Further Reading

For beginners
J. Pelikan, 2003, *Credo: Historical and Theological Guide to Creeds and Confessions of Faith in the Christian Tradition*, New Haven and London: Yale University Press.

For more advanced readers
A. Y. Collins, 2000, *Cosmology and Eschatology in Jewish and Christian Apocalypticism*, Leiden: Brill.
A. L. Pitstick, 2007, *Light in Darkness: Hans Urs von Balthasar and the Catholic Doctrine of Christ's Descent into Hell*, Grand Rapids, MI: Eerdmans.
J. A. Trumbower, 2001, *Rescue for the Dead: The Posthumous Salvation of Non-Christians in Early Christianity*, New York: Oxford University Press.
P. S. Johnston, 2002, *Shades of Sheol: Death and Afterlife in the Old Testament*, Downers Grove, IL: InterVarsity Press.

Internet Resources

The article by J. A. Tvedtness, 'The Baptism for the Dead and the Coptic Rationale':
http://www.fairlds.org/Misc/Baptism_for_the_Dead_the_Coptic_Rationale.html

Notes

1 Hermas, *Par.* 9.16.3; *Odes of Solomon* 42.6–20.
2 *Strom.* 6.6.48.
3 Cf. *EpAp.* 26—7.
4 For example *AI* 10.8–10; *TTP/The Testament of Dan* 5.10–11; *SO* 9.16–17.
5 *Exhortation* 34.3–5.
6 *AH* 5.16.2–3.
7 *AH* 3.18.6.
8 *AI* 10; *EpAp.* 13.
9 *AH* 1.24.2.
10 *OHS* 15.35.

6

Resurrection – Ascension

See also chapters 2, 3, 4, 5, 8, 9, 10, 11.

Consider this Task

Reflect on and explain the consequences for the Christian theory of salvation of the following three possibilities:

1 The Risen Lord does not have the marks of the wounds on his body.
2 The Risen Lord has the marks of the wounds on his body.
3 The Risen Lord does not have a human body at all.

Introduction

Central to the Christian faith is belief in the bodily resurrection of Jesus from the dead. It is therefore not surprising that the resurrection also played a central part in the development of the ancient Creeds. Christ's new life and then return to his Father reaffirmed his identity as the Messiah and his mission as the Saviour of the world. Having accomplished his mission, he returns to the realm of God from where he came down. Therefore the present pronouncement is directly related to the two previous articles elaborating Christ's death and descent to Hades. Both Christ's death and resurrection were for the Church fathers essential parts of the same Paschal mystery, while the descent to Hades and glorification in heaven presented their theological extension. Development of the doctrine, although it emphasized various aspects of this mystery according

to current theological and pastoral needs, testifies to the way this specific article of faith was used and how it served to proclaim the Risen Lord as the sole Mediator between God and humanity. All this was accomplished without in any way compromising the value of the human body.

Opening Question

How do Christ's resurrection and ascension emphasize his humanity and divinity?

Development of the Argument

The present belief contains the core faith, which laid the foundation of the whole architecture of Christian doctrine. It appeared from the very beginning of the proclamation of the news of Jesus of Nazareth as the promised Messiah. In the earliest period, belief in Christ's resurrection/ascension had three rhetorical and catechetical functions. First, it reinforced the faith of Christian communities in Jesus, as God's Son, the Lord and the Saviour of all. Second, it announced to the 'outside' world the greatest miracle and sign of God's might, that Jesus of Nazareth was raised, is alive and has ascended to heaven. Third, this belief presented Christ's resurrection as an archetype of the final resurrection of all. In this chapter we shall explore the main characteristics of the first two kinds of proclamation, while the third will be discussed in chapter 10. It must be said that in the earliest period, for the Jewish Christian, this very belief had a different meaning from that held by those who were converts from paganism. Both groups, as they were part of the earliest sociological fabric of Christian communities, commented on this belief in specific but diverging ways that corresponded to their pedagogical and liturgical needs, which sometimes led to <u>controversy</u>.

Paschal controversy: debate in the early Church about whether Easter or the Christian Passover should be celebrated according to the Jewish calendar on a fixed day of the lunar month (14 Nisan), or always on the following Sunday. While the former was accepted by the churches in Asia Minor (Turkey), the latter was supported by the bishops of Rome. The view of the Church of Rome succeeded in the practice of the Church, while the opponents survived until the ninth century CE.

However, for both types of Christians, including moderate Gnostics who accepted Christ's death/suffering on the cross, the act of ascension fulfilled his previous descent/incarnation. The difference in the theological evaluation of the second act was the role Christ's body played in his final reunion with the divine realm.

Some Early Interpretations

Among Jewish Christians Christ's resurrection was overshadowed by their greater fascination with the motif of the exaltation of the Saviour.[1] In the Jewish-Christian tradition there are many visionary narratives describing the Lord ascending toward the highest heavens, often full of vivid imagery and frequently related to the Hebrew Scriptures.[2] Belief in Christ's ascension satisfied the personal fascination of the authors with the motif of re-establishing the primordial order of the universe based on the ascending hierarchy of the holy angels. Theologically, the resurrection and the ascension are two interwoven sides of the same magnificent event: the glorification of the Lord as finally 'he sits on his throne together with the Great Glory', that is God, and the angels of the Holy Spirit.[3] The Risen Lord ascends towards the realm of rest, above all heavens, through the seventh heaven,[4] and enters the eighth sphere of eternal peace. He is accompanied by the angels and the saints of the Old Covenant who were liberated by Christ's descent to Hades. It is understandable that for the Jewish Christian the hope of salvation given to their righteous ancestors was very encouraging.

> The Lord will indeed descend into the world in the last days, [he] who is to be called Christ after he has descended and become like you in form, and they will think that he is flesh and a man. And the god of that world will stretch out [his hand against the Son], and they will lay their hands upon him and hang him upon a tree, not knowing who he is. And thus his descent, as you will see, will be concealed even from the heavens so that it will not be known who he is. [. . .] And then many of the righteous will ascend with him, whose spirits do not receive [their] robes until the Lord Christ ascends and they ascend with him. Then indeed they will receive their robes and their thrones and their crowns, when he has ascended into the seventh heaven.
>
> *Ascension of Isaiah* 9.6–18, trans. M. A. Knibb

The imaginative picture of Christ's resurrection/ascent had a number of variations in Jewish Christian apocalyptic literature.

> **Apocalyptic** (Gr. *apokalypto* – 'to reveal'): literary genre flourishing close to Christian era (200 BCE – 200 CE) which claimed to unveil God's purpose behind the historical events.

This literature expressed the elementary hope that the triumph of the Risen Lord opened the heavens and everlasting life to all righteous Hebrew men and women from previous generations who are now with the Lord in his eternal glory. At the same time, those who were still making their journey to the final destination were encouraged to be faithful to their Christ-centred way of life. Through this commitment, they would join their forefathers with the Risen Lord. The Jewish-Christian concept of Christ's journey through heavens of various levels suggests a form of his return to his original 'angel-like' status as the messenger of God.[5]

Second, among non-Jewish Christians the same motif, but stressing resurrection more than ascension, unveiled other aspects of Christ's victory. To some extent under the influence of the religious and especially the philosophical dualism of the era, Jesus' resurrection proclaimed the ultimate victory over evil powers. Against some extreme ascetic tendencies and philosophical denigration of the material element, the belief amplified the value of the body.[6] Christ's life after death had nothing in common with the ideas known from the Greek and other mythologies about afterlife; nor was it a Christianization of the philosophical notion of reincarnation. Rather Christ's resurrection and ascension amplified yet another important theological theme: that he alone gave up his life voluntarily for the sake of all people and his life was given back to him by his divine Father.[7] Christ's death conquered the demons and their dominion, which were understood by the Christian *apologists as the sources of pagan idolatry.[8] Jesus' resurrection/ascension sealed off the defeat of evil and its servants, often seen as the true force behind the persecution of Christians. Death and demons lost their power,[9] although they were not ultimately destroyed. That final destruction must wait until the last judgement.[10] Yet the final salvation of humanity has begun through Jesus' resurrection. Therefore every follower of Christ was called by this rhetoric to follow the Lord's way of life, a way which led the Saviour to the cross and death. For those Christians too it signified possible persecution and death, but which would lead on to resurrection and life with God.

The Gnostic Threat

Anti-Gnostic polemic, as we see in the cases of *Irenaeus of Lyons and *Tertullian, highlighted yet another thread in the rich tapestry of the glorification of the Saviour. Both theologians anchored resurrection in the human, bodily element. The motif of Christ's resurrection/ascension, understood as a real, historical event and not a mere allegory, was well integrated into Irenaeus' theory of salvation and was a direct consequence of the incarnation. In this line of exegesis both Irenaeus and Tertullian belong to those theologians who endorsed the literal meaning of Christ's bodily resurrection. This event was not merely, as it was in some Gnostic documents, a metaphor for the liberation of 'the divine spark', mind or the spiritual element that dwelt in advanced Christians.[11] Certainly, the main pedagogical concern of theologians such as Irenaeus and Tertullian was to reassure their followers that Christ's resurrection and glorification was not a figure of speech for the 'awakening' of a Saviour asleep in the human mind/soul. These events were part of the history of salvation, factual but not natural episodes, the authenticity of which Catholic Christians can and should trust. Christ's resurrection and the following ascension, especially in Irenaeus, illustrate the whole process of the economy of salvation which raises the human element, that is the body, towards the divine. In the ascension, the human body received a special, positive evaluation as Christ's resurrection in the flesh became the paradigm for the resurrection of all people with their bodies.

In the same way as Christ rose in his body and then showed his disciples the marks of the nails and the wound in his side [John 20.25, 27], as these are the signs of the body which had risen from the dead, so 'he will rise up by his own power' [1 Cor. 6.14]. Again, in the Letter to the Romans it is written: 'But if the Spirit of him that raised up Jesus from the dead dwells in you, he that raised up Christ from the dead will also raise your mortal bodies' [Rom. 8.11]. What are mortal bodies? Are they souls? No, they are not, because souls are incorporeal when compared with mortal bodies. [. . .] What then remains, which maybe identified with 'the mortal body' apart from the flesh, which Scripture says was shaped and will be brought to life by God? This body dies and then falls apart but this does not happen to the soul or to the

> spirit. [. . .] We must conclude that death is mentioned in reference to the body as after the soul's departure the body is without breath and inanimate and decomposes gradually into those elements from which it was composed in the first place.
>
> Irenaeus of Lyons, AH 5.7.1, trans. P. A.-S.

The same connection between belief in Christ's resurrection/ascension and his body is clearly pronounced by Tertullian. However, the Latin theologian puts belief in Christ's resurrection at the centre of the paradox of Christian faith.

> I find no other grounds for shame, such as may prove that in contempt of dishonour I am nobly shameless and advantageously a fool. The Son of God was crucified: I am not ashamed – because it is shameful. The Son of God died: it is immediately credible – because it is silly. He was buried, and rose again: it is certain – because it is impossible.
>
> Tertullian, Flesh 5, trans. E. Evans

Tertullian's famous summary of Christian faith and attitude as 'credible because impossible' (Lat. *credo quia absurdum*) emerges in the direct context of proclamation against the Gnostics of the physical death and resurrection of the Son of God. The Latin orator is not ashamed of the most controversial event in Jesus' life. On the contrary, Tertullian proclaims 'the impossible' as the strongest argument that it was real, true and credible. The physical and brutal death of God's Son, followed by his mighty resurrection/ascension, only confirms, in Tertullian's view, that Christianity reveals what is otherwise inaccessible to the human mind. Tertullian does not promote 'irrational faith' or 'ridiculous belief', but rather against his opponents, he sees the source of true faith in what seems to be impossible from a purely human point of view. The sequence of events from Christ's life reaffirms the might of God and the strength of faith if only that faith is given and granted by the Holy Spirit. Second, against dualistic depreciation of the material element, Tertullian highlights that Christ's triumph encompasses, not excludes, the Saviour's glorified body.

Against another group of theological adversaries, Tertullian uses the same motif of resurrection/ascension to rebuke the *Monarchian claim that the

difference between the Father and the Son was an illusion, a claim which amalgamated the divine persons into one divine being. On the contrary, Tertullian magnifies the glory of the Risen Son who fulfils the task given him by
his divine Father. Against his opponent *Praxeas, Tertullian openly declared
that it was not God the Father who was crucified but the Son. Consequently,
at the ascension, it was not God the Father who returned to heaven, but Jesus
Christ, the Son, who from now on 'sits at the right hand of the Father, not the
Father at his own right hand'.[12] In both elaborations of the same theme, the
mystery of the incarnation finds its climax in the mystery of the resurrection,
particularly stressing that through Christ's coming to this world in flesh and
his Paschal sacrifice, human weakness and vulnerability was transformed into
divine perfection.

Origen: Ascension – Return to the Original Status

In this pre-Nicene period, we have to pay some, although very limited, attention to the illustrious Origen and his theory of resurrection. Christology was
central to Origen's theory of salvation, as it often was with the Church fathers,
but Origen began in a different place and ended with a different eschatological scenario. The motif of resurrection/ascension was treated by Origen with
yet another agenda. The divine Logos, through whom the visible and invisible
worlds were created, guides both realities to the fullness of time, which is salvation and reconciliation with his Father. Naturally in Origen's project, the Logos
is the pivot of salvation, and his incarnation and then his death on the cross are
two stages of the ultimate 'self-emptying' (Gr. *kenosis*)[13] (see chapter 3). With
Christ's resurrection the whole history of salvation reaches its turning point and
enters a new phase as perfection is given to the Church by this act.[14] But Origen
distinguishes three stages in the victorious event and triumphant liberation.
First, Christ's death and encounter with all the departed allowed him to free
them from the dominion of death.[15] The second act unveiled the Risen Lord to
his disciples, who were still in this world, and who decided to dedicate their lives
to proclaiming Christ's victory.[16] The third phase encompassed Christ's ascension, as he returned to his glory.

> The Word of God by descending to us and emptying himself of his proper status appeared among people. Then, it is said that he left this world and returned to his Father. In consequence, we see him in his perfection, returning from humiliation when he emptied himself [Phil. 2.7] in order to share our existence to his proper perfection [Col. 1.19; 2.9; Eph. 1.23]. If we accept him as our guide, we may also return from our present emptiness. Therefore, let us allow the Word of God to leave this world and go back to the One who sent him and let him go to his Father.
>
> Origen, *OP* 23.2, trans. P. A.-S.

However, though he is present in his Church in an invisible way, in the divine realm the Logos waits for the accomplishment of time.[17] Origen, like Irenaeus of Lyons before him, placed resurrection within the whole drama of salvation. Nonetheless Origen differed from Irenaeus by making bodily resurrection a little less important than other, greater themes in his theological symphony. Still, Origen's contribution to the development of the doctrine of Christ's resurrection/ascension was related to the strong emphasis on the Logos as the Mediator between the whole of humanity and God. By his death and then new life, the Logos elevates them as closely as possible to God.[18] Human beings can by participation access God's divinity through the Logos-Christ who is divine by nature and closest to his Father.

Athanasius of Alexandria: Christ's Ascent as an Example

How did the approval of the formula 'consubstantial with the Father' (Gr. *homoousion*) alter theological affirmation of the resurrection in the post-Nicene period? Again, Athanasius provides us with the classical model of the interpretation of the central motif, which was representative of pro-Nicene theology. Athanasius' theory of salvation is deeply rooted in and dependent upon his Christology. The crucial intuition that, in Jesus, Christ is entirely on the side of his divine Father (Lat. *consubstantialis Patri*) and at the same time, after his incarnation, entirely on the side of all human beings (Lat. *consubstantialis nobis*) was essentially hope to overcome the power of death. Christ's incarnation, then his death and resurrection/ascension, are parts of the same process of bringing humanity back to its original heavenly home.[19] Thanks to Christ's resurrection all humanity receives the gift of eternal life.[20] So for Athanasius the unity of the divine and human natures in Christ has the central role in theory of salvation, because it is by this unity that men and women ascend, with Christ, towards the divine. Christ's resurrection makes it possible, real and available to all who accept Jesus' gift of eternal life and are part of his Church. It is possible to summarize Athanasius' theology of resurrection and ascension as follows: by the incarnation, the divine Word made himself visible and performed all the acts necessary to redeem lost humanity. By his passion and death the divine Word descended to the darkest abyss of human experience and liberated human beings from death, 'expelling death from them like a straw from the fire'.[21] But then his resurrection provided the whole universe with new life, self-understanding and potential.

> For the Word spread himself everywhere, above and below and in the depth and in the breath: above, in creation; below, in the incarnation; in the depth, in hell; in breath, in the world. Everything is filled with the knowledge of God [Luke 19.10]. For this reason, not as soon as he came did he complete the sacrifice on behalf of all and deliver his body to death, and resurrecting it make himself invisible. But by means of it he rendered himself visible, remaining in it and completing such works and giving signs as made him known to be no longer a man but God the Word. For in this way our Saviour had compassion through the incarnation: he both rid us of death and renewed us; and also, although he is invisible and indiscernible, yet by his works he revealed and made himself known to be the Son of God and the Word of the Father, leader and king of the universe.
>
> Athanasius of Alexandria, *IncarnationL* 16.13–25,
> trans. R. W. Thomson

Athanasius' model of salvation is universal, in the sense that this central event not only transcends the human, visible and material reality, but is also 'the cosmic cross' of the Saviour. His resurrection, by its brightness, might and radiance penetrates all dimensions of the created universe. However, real death and real new life are central to it.

Ambrose of Milan: Jesus' Victory and Ours

Among Latin theologians of this period, Ambrose of Milan's contribution offers a new outlook on Christ's resurrection. Ambrose, a former political leader, became a major spiritual authority not only in Milan, but also in Western Christianity having, for example, a direct impact on Augustine's conversion. Ambrose's anti-Arian theology not only combined his philosophical interests with personal beliefs and commitment to pro-Nicene orthodoxy, but found its expression in the composition of a number of hymns and prayers, including possibly the *Exultet*[22] which is still sung as part of the Easter Vigil in many churches.[23]

Rejoice, heavenly powers! Sing, choirs of angels!
Exult, all creation around God's throne!
Jesus Christ, our King, is risen!
Sound the trumpet of salvation!
Rejoice, O earth, in shining splendour,
radiant in the brightness of your King!
Christ has conquered! Glory fills you!
Darkness vanishes for ever!
Rejoice, O Mother Church! Exult in glory!
The risen Saviour shines upon you!
Let this place resound with joy,
echoing the mighty song of all God's people!
My dearest friends,
standing with me in this holy light,
join me in asking God for mercy,
that he may give his unworthy minister
grace to sing his Easter praises. [. . .]
It is truly right
that with full hearts and minds and voices
we should praise the unseen God, the all-powerful Father,
and his only Son, our Lord Jesus Christ.
For Christ has ransomed us with his blood,
and paid for us the price of Adam's sin to our eternal Father!

Exultet, ascribed to Ambrose of Milan, from Roman Missal, modified P. A.-S.

While Athanasius' visionary outlook highlights the universal process of salvation which includes humanity, Ambrose's theology focused on Jesus Christ seems to be more personal, intimate and direct.[24] To Ambrose, the Risen Lord is not only 'the Saviour of all', the Lord God, the Creator and Redemptor, but he is also 'Christ for me', 'my closest Friend'.[25] The emphasis on that very personal relationship with Christ makes his resurrection/ascension the most joyful, welcome and precious news, which Christians wish to share with all. This very personal comprehension of salvation, as an act which first and foremost was done for the sake of people, also offers much space for human emotions and imagination to be involved in theological reflection. In Ambrose's personal and Christocentric spirituality, speculative theology and his theory of salvation become a more intimate encounter with the mystery of Christ's death and resurrection.

Augustine of Hippo: Against earlier Pessimism

Augustine of Hippo, certainly an attentive listener to Ambrose's homilies and like him a great admirer of Neoplatonic philosophy, approached the Paschal mystery with yet another interest. As a young, inquisitive person who had already read Cicero's dialogues, Augustine was attracted to Manichaeism for almost a decade.[26] Throughout this time he turned his attention not only to the search for the cause of evil, but also towards a radically dualistic view of the tension between the soul and the body.[27] Several elements combined to influence his theology of the resurrection and ascension: his Platonism aligned with a passionate personal faith; his dedication to the Church and rejection of Manichaeism. As for Ambrose, so too for Augustine Christ was a very personal authority, he was the universal way of salvation and the unique Mediator between God and humanity.[28] Augustine, like Athanasius before him, emphasized Christ's participation in divinity and humanity through both his natures as the human and divine Saviour. Christ's bodily resurrection was the climax of his work of salvation, which he fulfilled in responding to the will of his Father. Jesus' resurrection provided the Church with an example and the hope of resurrection of all.[29] The centrality of the divine–human Christ to salvation is upheld by the full force of

Augustine's anti-Arian vigour, but he also adds the following new characteristics to the unique position of Christ in salvation. As all humanity is deeply marked by original sin and its consequences, only Christ is the sinless, holy and perfect sacrifice whose death brought justification and necessary grace to all believers. He is also the Priest who offers the most holy sacrifice: himself[30] commemorated in the Catholic/Universal Church in the form of the Eucharist.[31] The essence of the act of salvation is Jesus' self-sacrifice and resurrection/ascension proclaimed by the Church.

> How is it that Christ is everywhere celebrated with such strong faith in his bodily ascension into heaven? [. . .] Truly, many miracles appeared as we cannot deny, to give evidence to that supreme miracle of salvation; the miracle of Christ's ascension into heaven in the body in which he rose from the dead.
>
> Augustine, CG 22.8, trans. P. A.-S.

As for Tertullian, so too for Augustine this belief was central to Christian faith. Both Latin theologians emphasized the bodily element in this miracle, although Tertullian did so against the Gnostics, while Augustine did so against the Manichaeans. Both theologians saw in this mystery the ultimate self-revelation of God in Jesus. To Augustine, Christ's resurrection/ascension in the flesh to the realm of God, reaffirmed the crucial role of Christ as the unique intermediary of God,[32] but it also named the Catholic Church as the unique heir of this faith.

Cyril and the Alexandrian legacy

As has been pointed out in previous chapters, *Cyril of Alexandria took over *Athanasius' basic model of salvation originating in Irenaeus' intuition of the 'exchange formula' as the central role of Christology. Therefore Cyril continued to develop the answer to the classical Patristic question, 'Why did God became man?' (Lat. *Cur Deus Homo?*), within the Alexandrian frame of understanding.[33] Cyril boldly put the idea of self-emptying (see chapter 3) at the centre of his theology of the cross and resurrection. The Logos' incarnation brought upon the divine Son human limitations and vulnerability, affecting the mind and soul, not just the body. In Cyril's view God-the-Logos entered into the human condition accepting its natural boundaries of the flesh and the experience of suffering as well as real death. Cyril emphasized that, by the act of the incarnation, the divine, impassible Logos came into the realm of human vulnerability and suffering in order to transform it and elevate it towards the divine. This act goes beyond the natural capacity of human nature.[34] Therefore Christ's death and resurrection in the human body delivered it from corruption and sanctified it. One important element of that theory must be noted. Christ's resurrection happened within a very obvious Trinitarian context: as the only-begotten became incarnate, then suffered and was killed in order to pay the ransom and bring humanity to his divine Father.[35] It was through the divine Spirit that Christ received his new life at his resurrection. The new life, post-Easter journey with Christ to God the Father is accomplished with the Holy Spirit.[36] In this process of transition from death to life, from existence in corruption to achievement of immortality, Christ's resurrection and ascension are examples of the might of the Spirit. They are also the key events, the signposts towards the final destiny of all human beings. Although Cyril of Alexandria found it difficult to combine the impassible nature of God with human vulnerability,[37] he stressed that Christ's passion and death were 'liable to destruction'.[38] This descent towards the ultimate abasement, followed by Christ's resurrection in the flesh, manifested the restoration to life of the whole Christ, not just his body. The mighty image of Christ's resurrection and then ascension, not only brought salvation to the human condition and the human flesh, but initiated a new process of deification of the human being. This new departure did not alienate men and women from their natural status as physical beings but encompassed the corporeal element in the same process.

By becoming the flesh of the Word, who gives life to all things, this flesh triumphs over the power of death and destruction; in the same way, no doubt, the soul, since it has become the soul of him who had no experience of doing wrong, has its state secured, immutable in all good, and incomparably stronger than the sin which before exercised dominion. For Christ is the first man who 'committed no sin and was convicted of no dishonesty' [1 Pet. 2.22]. He is so to speak, the root and the first fruits of those who are restored in the Spirit to newness of life, to immortality of the body, to certainty and security of divinity, so that he may transmit this condition to the whole of humanity by participation and an act of grace. Paul knew this, and was inspired to write 'As we have worn the likeness of the heavenly man' [1 Cor. 15.49]. By 'the likeness of the man of earth' (that is, of Christ), he means the steady course towards holiness, the rescue from death and destruction, the restoration to immortality and life. So we assert that the Word in his entirety has been united with man in entirety.

Cyril of Alexandria, *IncarnationOB*, trans. H. Bettenson

The Logos-Christ's resurrection changed the very condition of human flesh for good, as now it is able to ascend, like the flesh of the Logos, to the divine. The human body together with the soul is able now to participate in the life of the Holy Trinity. Two crucial stages of salvation which Athanasius identified as the incarnation and the resurrection are elevated by Cyril to be the parts of the same fundamental platform on which God sanctifies humanity in its totality: body, mind and spirit. Therefore from the act of creation nothing is lost, neglected or marginalized. Creation achieves its climax in the salvation of the whole human being. Indeed, Christ's bodily resurrection has established the human potential to access salvation in the body, not without it.[39] From this elaboration of the central motif of resurrection it is possible to see that Cyril's pedagogical concern was to reassure the believers that both natures of the Logos took part in death on the cross, as well as in resurrection and ascension. It was not, as *Nestorius would claim, that only Christ's humanity suffered, experienced death, rose and ascended to the realm of the divine. In Cyril's view, the congruence between both natures, which began at the incarnation, subjected them to the experience of death, resurrection and ascension.

Antiochene Exegesis and Christology

Antiochene theology of the resurrection and ascension seemed to elaborate more on the human experience of sin, change and ultimately mortality. These three commonly observable aspects were interconnected and reflect the destruction of the original triad: incorruptibility, impassibility and immortality. As death entered into human existence through sin and now dwells in every human being, so now our nature is vulnerable, weak and inclines towards further evil acts.[40] The human condition was taken on by Jesus Christ. However, the Saviour's bodily resurrection restored and renewed the original condition of the human being, as exemplified by Jesus Christ. Jesus, as the representative of all men and women and their condition, became the 'first fruit' of the new creation and new relationship with God in his post-Paschal risen life.[41]

Illustrating this, *Theodore of Mopsuestia, while holding to the theological axiom that the divine cannot be mixed with the human element and therefore Christ's divinity remained unattached to his humanity, yet emphasized Christ's resurrection in the body ('a human tabernacle'). It provided humanity with freedom from the power of sin, change and death as well as liberating us from the power of demons. Also to some extent sharing the Alexandrian fascination with the theme of deification, which was now achievable through the humanity of the divine Logos, Theodore stressed the value of 'filiation' of all Christians.[42] It was thus Christ's resurrection that restored an original relationship with the divine Father, which had been lost at the beginning of history, but was now found again through Christ. In both traditions Christ's resurrection is directly linked with salvation, and it has restored in men and women the original union with God, or at least renewed its potential.

The motifs of ascending with Christ towards the divine, becoming 'deified' or 'adopted' by the divine Father, all these outcomes of Christ's resurrection/ascension emerged with a new rhetorical power in the later Patristic teaching and preaching. This theme flourished as a powerful image and attractive narrative in various forms of catechesis, now including Christian iconography, mosaics and other artistic expressions. All these interpretations had at their centre the miracle and paradigm of the Christ's new life. But because they developed within the framework of anthropology, ethics and spirituality, not just a speculative Christology, they offered a very attractive and inspiring theme to all believers.

The Cappadocians

The *Cappadocian fathers, as they cherished and continued the Alexandrian tradition, valued this very theme in relation to their theories of salvation. The direct connection between Christ's resurrection and human immortality was fundamental to this pedagogical elaboration of the scriptural image, within the general project of the economy of salvation.[43] This project endorsed the Christian, ethical and spiritual metamorphosis from death to life, from existence in slavery to liberation from it, from the state of oppression by demons to the freedom of God's children. Christ's resurrection 'purified' human nature,[44] restored in it the state of impassibility (Gr. *apatheia*)[45] and pointed to the ultimate accomplishment of human destiny.

> 'Impassibility' (Gr. *apatheia*) in its human context denoted a result of ethical and spiritual activity which produces independence from bodily passions and desires. It refers to liberation from the disturbance of the senses, which is achieved by God's grace. (On God's impassibility, see p. 39.)

To the Cappadocian fathers the Paschal mystery, which unveiled the Risen Lord and then concluded with his glorious ascension, offered Christians a fascinating matrix of their spiritual progress; which turned them from life under the dominion of the senses towards a higher, more angelic existence focused on the contemplation of the realm to which Jesus ascended and where he waits for their arrival. This article of faith provided Christians with the base of their hope of eternal life with God (see chapter 11).

Conclusion

The resurrection and ascension of the Lord conclude the Paschal mystery. However, they did not conclude the Christological reflection which is preserved in the ancient Creeds. Still, Christ's second return and judgement of all creation, as well as the understanding of eternal life, caused serious controversies in the Early Church, as we shall see in the following chapters. Nonetheless, the vital understanding of the present pronouncement combining Christology and theology of salvation offered human beings, particularly the members of the Church, a certain hope of participation in the life of the Risen Lord. That forthcoming life encompassed their souls, minds and bodies. Throughout the whole Patristic period the scriptural, Pauline axiom (for example, 1 Cor. 15.12–23) that Christ's resurrection was the archetype of the common resurrection at the end of time was upheld unchanged and unchallenged. What did change through the first five centuries was the development of a more sophisticated comprehension of Christ's natures as a way of safeguarding the hope of bodily resurrection for all believers.

Questions for Discussion

- How much were the scriptural and then Patristic understanding of resurrection and ascension dependent on the cosmological models available to the ancient authors? If we free the Patristic narrative from this legacy, what important theological difference can we notice?
- If the risen Christ was free from the space–time dimension of this world, why is there a separation of his resurrection from his ascension in the Patristic documents?
- Can we understand Jesus' resurrection as the act of his resuscitation, not by his own agency but by God?

Further Reading

For beginners
R. Williams, 2002, *Resurrection: Interpreting the Easter Gospel*, London: Darton, Longman & Todd.

For more advanced readers
S. T. Davis, D. Kendall and G. O'Collins, 1999, *The Resurrection: An Interdisciplinary Symposium on the Resurrection of Jesus*, Oxford: Oxford University Press.
D. B. Farrow, 2004, *Ascension and Ecclesia*, London and New York: T&T Clark.
N. T. Wright, 2003, *The Resurrection of the Son of God: The Christian Origin and the Question of God*, London: SPCK.

Internet Resources

An interesting paper on 'The Post-Resurrection Appearances of Christ' to the holy women written by Polyvios Konis, which includes ancient iconography:
    http://www.rosetta.bham.ac.uk/Issue_01/Konis.htm

Later Roman ecclesiastical synthesis, illustration number 10 (*c.*400), Christ's resurrection and ascension:

http://www.hp.uab.edu/image_archive/ulg/ulgb.html

Notes

1 Cf. J. Daniélou, 1964, *The Theology of Jewish Christianity*, trans. J. A. Baker, London: Darton, Longman & Todd, pp. 248–63.

2 For instance, the ascension of Elijah (2 Kings 2.11–12) and the vision of the prophet Ezekiel with the chariot (Ezek. 1.4–21).

3 *AI* 11.31.

4 *AI* 3.16–20; 9.16–19.

5 See chapter 2, endnote 1.

6 Pseudo-Justin, *OR* 9.

7 Origen, *AC* 2.16. As may be seen from Origen's polemic against Celsus, the concept of the resurrection was incomprehensible in a culture influenced by Platonism, where the bodily element did not have the same value as the intellectual one (that is the mind) or spiritual (that is the soul). Platonism, like earlier Orphism, taught that there is a divine, eternal element in each human being, which needs to be cultivated and will remain indestructible after death. But the notion of life 'in the flesh' in the future intelligible world was highly unpalatable. This conviction was at odds with the Christian faith; first in Christ's bodily resurrection and ascension, as well as the ultimate resurrection of all.

8 For instance, Athenagoras of Athens, *Supplication* 26; Minucius Felix, *Oc.* 27.1; later Augustine, *CG* 8.22.

9 Melito, *HP* 54

10 Justin, *1 Apol.* 45.

11 For example *ApJ* 6.13 and Epiphanius, *Chest* 37.4.1–3.

12 *AP* 30.

13 For example, *Princ.* 2.6.1; 3.5.6.

14 *ComGJ* 10.35.229.

15 *AC* 2.66.

16 *AC* 2.56.

17 *AC* 2.65.

18 *Princ.* 2.6.1.

19 *IncarnationL* 11.

20 *IncarnationL* 10.

21 *IncarnationL* 8.

22 Tradition that attributes the authorship of the *Exultet*, the hymn sung during the Easter Vigil, to Ambrose of Milan is clearly noticeable in the twelfth and thirteenth centuries.

23 For example, *ExPs.* 45.11, 16; *ExLk* 2.1; 4.57.

24 For more information, see J. Moorhead, 1999, *Ambrose: Church and Society in the Late Roman World*, London: Longman, pp. 96–8.

25 *Ep.* 4.4; *Virgins* 16.99.

26 *Conf.* 4.1.

27 Augustine's change of view on the body appeared around the time of his ordination to the priesthood under the influence of Paul's teaching (Eph. 5.29). More in A. D. Fitzgerald, 1999, 'Body', in D. Fitzgerald (ed.), *Augustine through the Ages*, Grand Rapids, MI: Eerdmans, pp. 106–07.

28 *CG* 11.2; *Conf.* 10.43.

29 *CG* 22.12; 18.

30 *Conf.* 10.43.68–70.

31 *Trin.* 4.13.17; *CG* 10.20; *Conf.* 9.11.12. For a summary of Augustine's theory of the Eucharist as Christ's body, see J. Pelikan, 1975, 'Paradox of Grace', in his *The Emergence of the Catholic Tradition*, Chicago: University of Chicago Press, pp. 304–07.

32 *Conf.* 7.18.

33 Although Irenaeus, Athanasius and Cyril wrote in Greek, this question is well known in its Latin form as it became very popular in the medieval period through Anselm of Canterbury's treatise with this very title.

34 *ExGJ* 1.9. For more detail, see D. Keating, 2004, *The Appropriation of the Divine Life in Cyril of Alexandria*, Oxford: Oxford University Press.

35 *ExGJ* 1.29.

36 *ExGJ* 9.1.

37 Frances Young draws attention to Cyril's supposed docetic tendency ('he suffered without suffering') in her insightful comment on Cyril's theology. For more detail, see F. Young, 1983, 'Cyril of Alexandria', in her *From Nicaea to Chalcedon*, London: SCM Press, pp. 261–2.

38 *PH* 17.

39 *OTF* 2.7.

40 For example, Theodore of Mopsuestia, *CH* 12.8.

41 *ExEph.* 1.6.

42 For more information, see Keating, *Appropriation of the Divine Life*, pp. 206–27.

43 For example, Gregory of Nyssa, *AE* 3.10.36.

44 *CO* 35.7.

45 *OSR* (*Patrologia Graeca* 46.148).

7

The Holy Spirit

See also chapters 1, 2, 3, 8, 9, 10.

Consider this Task

Find out more about the chief names for the Holy Spirit in John's Gospel. Which of Jesus' statements identify the Spirit as 'a person' and not as an abstract divine power?

Introduction

This examination focuses on the most mysterious person of the Holy Trinity: the <u>Spirit</u>. It is important to highlight the natural limits of our language when we try to think of and then express the existence of the third divine person. It is equally important to be aware of our understanding of the term 'person' (see chapter 2) when we try to attach its content to the divine being.

> The English word 'Spirit' comes from the Latin word *spiro* and represents the act of 'breathing'. Originally it meant 'breath', and it was a synonym of 'air', 'wind', later becoming attached to the immaterial elements.

We have already encountered the Spirit while discussing various previous statements of the ancient Creeds. It may seem surprising that the structure of the early Creeds sets the statement on the Holy Spirit rather apart from the

direct connection with the sections on God the Father and the Son (chapters 1 and 2). Historically the debate about the nature of the Spirit was much later than the Christological controversies, and it provided the Church with a number of significant, helpful concepts as well as enlarging its theological vocabulary. This summary traces the main characteristics of the development of the doctrine of the Spirit from the original experience of the divine, sanctifying Power to a more elaborate understanding of the third person of the Trinity. It includes a note on the role attributed to the Holy Spirit in Christian achievement of holiness, since for the Patristic theologians growth in intellectual understanding was organically united with the quest for holiness.

Opening Question

How do you understand the difference between the incarnation of the Logos and the embodiment of the Spirit in a dove at Christ's baptism (Mark 1.10)?

Development of the Argument

The earliest Christian communities first and foremost experienced the overwhelming power of the Holy Spirit, enabling them to witness to their faith. For the first generation of Christians, who were still deeply influenced by Hebrew theology and imagery, the Holy Spirit was the same source of inspiration, the same descending 'Spirit of God' (Hebr. *Ruah Yahweh*) as for their Jewish forefathers: the patriarchs, prophets and leaders 'moved by' God.[1] This paradigm was soon accepted by non-Jewish Christians too.[2] However, the new element of that belief suggested that the Spirit of God was not merely an impersonal sanctifying might, but rather an entity, who has will (John 3.8) and rational faculty (John 14.26).[3] Christian revelation added a very important dimension and focus to the Hebrew background: the Spirit of God came down now on the new communities to continue Christ's mission and fulfil the history of salvation. The Spirit of God emerged in Christian interpretation as co-worker of the Lord Jesus, as the one who with Jesus Christ, and therefore with God the Father, is the source of the new life and the beginning of the new creation (cf. Matt. 28.18–19). In the apostolic period there were at least three main developments in the doctrine of the Spirit (Gr. *pneuma*, hence pneumatology).

The Holy Spirit is Always Active

First, the Spirit of God was the main author of the Hebrew Scriptures, and the ancient writers were influenced by this divine inspiration. This line of understanding defended the value of the Hebrew Scriptures against radical claims, like that of *Marcion, that Christianity should cut off all links with the Hebrew Scriptures and legacy, because this harmful heritage was a product of the evil, Jewish god/demiurge. In the apology of Christian faith against pagan critics the same argument regarding divine inspiration served another purpose, this time to strengthen the authority of scriptural revelation, because it had a divine origin.[4] In this polemical context, Catholic authors such as *Justin Martyr[5] promoted the idea of the divine, direct inspiration of the Hebrew authors and scriptural narratives.

Second, the Spirit of God was perceived as implicated not only in the Hebrew revelation, but more recently in the life and works of Jesus Christ. The Spirit was involved in the incarnation,[6] and the confirmation of Christ's authority and mission,[7] in Christ's resurrection/ascension as 'the servant of the God who suffers'.[8] Finally, the same Spirit is present and acting in the Church.[9] These points were elaborated by almost all Apostolic fathers, the apologists and other early theologians of the Church.[10]

Third, following Paul's intuition about the role of the Spirit in the sanctification of believers (Rom. 8.9–11), the Spirit of God was seen as the main source of holiness and regeneration of individual believers. He is the initiator of the process of divinization: 'participation in divinity'. This theological idea found particular attention among such authors as *Hermas,[11] *Irenaeus of Lyons,[12] *Origen,[13] *Athanasius of Alexandria,[14] *Cyril of Alexandria,[15] *Basil of Caesarea,[16] *Gregory of Nazianzus[17] and later *John of Damascus.[18]

In the early Christian efforts to comprehend the function of the Spirit it is possible to see that his divinity was rather commonly accepted. Less clear was the relationship between the Spirit and the Son,[19] or even the understanding of his nature as 'a divine person'. The 'place' or rather realm of the Spirit was with the Father and the Son, as illustrated by the Jewish-Christian apocrypha *Ascension of Isaiah*.[20] One of the earliest efforts to denote the origin of the Holy Spirit comes from *Athenagoras of Athens, who described the Spirit as 'emanation of the Father' (Gr. *aporria*), stressing his eternal existence and placing him between the Father and the Son.[21]

The First Questions about the Holy Spirit

The second century CE brought a number of challenges, which we have already noted in previous discussions (see chapters 1 and 2). *Monarchianism undermined any real existence of the 'Spirit' apart from being an expression of the divinity, while a less speculative and more empirical experience of the 'inspiration' by the Spirit, claimed by the apocalyptic movement known as *Montanism (see chapter 4), highlighted an outburst of charismatic gifts out of the control of the authorities of the Church. But it was Christian Gnosticism that originated discussion on the origin of the Holy Spirit – and highlighted her female character and function. This bold statement attracted the attention of the Church fathers.

The Holy Spirit and Gnosticism

According to the Coptic *Gospel of Thomas*, the Holy Spirit was the true Mother of Jesus,[22] and that identification gained its support from the nature of the Semitic language, where the noun 'spirit' (Hebr. *Ruah*) has feminine gender.[23] Gnostic mythologies pictured the Spirit as 'Wisdom' (Gr. *sophia*), emphasizing the feminine character of the divine. The Spirit was a divine Parent and Virgin at the same time, and Gnostic theologians had no problem with this paradox. Therefore, as suggested by yet another document, the *Gospel of Philip*, a true, mature Christian has the Logos as the 'father' and Spirit/Sophia as his or her mother.[24] The Christian Gnostic born of divine parents[25] receives a new dignity and is surrounded by divine protection from evil,[26] because his divine Mother dominates all powers.[27] Quite similar imagery and theology can be found in the New Testament apocrypha, the *Acts of Thomas*. Here, again, the mother Holy Spirit is named as the most intimate parent and revealer of the divine mysteries.

Come, holy name of Christ that is *above every name* [Phil. 2.9].
Come, power of the Most High, and perfect compassion;
Come, thou highest gift;
Come, compassionate mother;[28]
Come, fellowship of the male;[29]
Come, thou [fem.] that dost reveal the hidden mysteries;
Come, mother of the seven houses, that thy rest may be in the eighth house;[30]
Come, elder [messenger] of the five members, understanding, thought, prudence, consideration, reasoning,[31]
Communicate with these young men!
Come, Holy Spirit, and purify their reins and their heart,

> And give them the added seal, in the name of the Father and Son and Holy Spirit.
>
> *Acts of Thomas* 2.27, trans. R. McL. Wilson

In some traditions among the Gnostics, pneumatology emphasized the caring and compassionate role of the Spirit. The divine, as the Father–Mother, has not forgotten the offspring (that is the Christian Gnostics), but still tries to communicate with them and guide them out of this current world and experience. It is rather evident that flexible Gnostic traditions represented a different approach to the feminine within the divine from the position of the Church. That 'feminization' of the Spirit and even God provoked severe criticism from representatives of Catholic theology such as Irenaeus of Lyons[32] and later *Epiphanius of Salamis.[33] For Irenaeus, the Holy Spirit has a unique role in the history of salvation as the Spirit revealed Jesus of Nazareth as the Son of God. The Spirit leads people to the Son, the divine Revealer of the Father, therefore through the Spirit people have unique access to the mystery of the Trinity.

> Therefore the baptism of our rebirth comes through these three articles[34] granting us rebirth unto God the Father, through His Son, by the Holy Spirit. For those who are bearers of the Spirit of God are led to the Word, that is to the Son; but the Son takes them and presents them to the Father; and the Father confers incorruptibility. So, without the Spirit there is no seeing the Word of God, and without the Son there is no approaching the Father; for the Son is knowledge of the Father, and knowledge of the Son is through the Holy Spirit.
>
> Irenaeus of Lyons, *Proof* 7, trans. J. P. Smith

Odes of Solomon

In the context of these alternative doctrines of the Spirit, yet another document draws our attention. In the Jewish-Christian poem the *Odes of Solomon*, there is a metaphor for the Holy Spirit which refers to the very maternal function of the divine Parent. The whole narrative expresses the mystery of the Spirit in a context of great intimacy, tenderness and closeness. It does not aim to 'convince', 'explain' or 'prove' the existence of the Spirit, but rather to share with the reader the cherished experience of encountering the might of the Spirit.

> A cup of milk was offered to me, and I drank it in the sweetness of the Lord's kindness.
> The Son is the cup, and the Father is he who was milked; and the Holy Spirit is she who milked him;
> Because his breasts were full, and it was undesirable that his milk should be ineffectually released.
> The Holy Spirit opened her bosom, and mixed the milk of the two breasts of the Father.
> Then she gave the mixture to the generation without their knowing, and those who have received it are in the perfection of the right hand.
>   *Odes of Solomon* 19.1–5, trans. J. H. Charlesworth

The role of the feminine Spirit was to assist in salvation, hidden under the metaphor of 'milk', and to offer it to those who were able to receive it. Based on the Johannine warning that not everyone was prepared to receive salvation (John 1.10), the *Odes* use the image of an intimate relationship between a mother and her child as a reflection of the relationship between the Holy Spirit and a Christian, to exemplify the act of salvation, love and care. This model reassured believers that the divine Parent was directly involved in the process of salvation and sanctification.[35]

Tertullian: God's Spirit as the Third Divine Person

With the second and third centuries, and the growing debate around the nature and functions of the divine persons, mainly the Father and the Son, the character of the Holy Spirit also received more attention. Among theologians representing Western Christianity, *Tertullian contributed to further development of the doctrine of the Holy Spirit. He boldly names the Holy Spirit as the 'third deity'.[36] Protecting the distinction between the divine persons against the error of *Modalism represented by *Praxeas, Tertullian stresses the difference between all three divine persons, alongside their co-existence in the unity of their nature. Praxeas proposed a quite simple and convincing view of God as the one divine being who appeared in the history of salvation in different 'faces' or modes. First, in ancient times, God appeared as 'the Father'; more recently he revealed himself as the 'Son'; while in the latter days as 'the Holy Spirit'. All three names denote the same divine person. This theology, as we can see, protected monotheism, while trying to explain the meaning of the message coming from Christian revelation. Tertullian could not accept this kind of 'compromise' because it led to even more dangerous and bizarre consequences, such as the theory of *'Patripassianism', meaning that it was the Father who suffered on the cross. Tertullian rebuked this theory with all his zeal and intellectual skills. His own theological model of God emphasized the real existence of three persons who exist in a union similar to 'root, branch and fruit' or 'spring, river and stream'.

> For the Spirit is third with God and [his] Son, as the fruit out of the shoot is third from the root, and the irrigation canal out of the river third from the spring, and the illumination point out of the beam third from the sun: yet in no respect is he alienated from that origin from which he derives his proper attributes. In this way the Trinity, proceeding by inter-mingled and connected degrees from the Father, in no respect challenges the monarchy, while it conserves the quality of the economy.
>
> Tertullian, *AP* 8.7, trans. E. Evans

At this stage of theology, for many theologians the Holy Spirit emanated from the Father in a similar way to the Son, that is, eternally. It was Tertullian's important contribution to elaborate the notion of God with the crucial distinction of three persons/individual beings who share the same substance or divine way of being.

Origen: the Spirit and the Divine Hierarchy

Among the representatives of the Eastern branch of Christianity of the third century, Origen's theology of the Holy Spirit is the most sophisticated. Against various opponents, Origen emphasized the real existence of the third divine person[37] and attributed to the Spirit governance over spiritual beings.[38] As a theologian with a clear, although hierarchical notion of the Trinity, Origen placed the Holy Spirit in the 'third position'. The first belonged to the Father of all, the second to the Logos, while the third was for the Holy *pneuma*.[39] However, this 'lowest' rank did not alienate the Spirit from the divine life and nature of God, nor from external acts of salvation. On the contrary, it was the Holy Spirit who was the source of sanctification.[40] This Patristic *leitmotif* finds in Origen yet another enthusiast.

> God the Father bestows on all the gift of existence; and a participation in Christ, in virtue of his being the word or reason, makes them rational. From this follows that they are worthy of praise and blame, because they are capable alike of virtue and of wickedness. Accordingly there is also available the grace of the Holy Sprit, that those beings who are not holy in essence may be made holy by participating in this grace. When therefore they obtain first of all their existence from God the Father, and secondly their rational nature from the Word, and thirdly their holiness from the Holy Spirit, they become capable of receiving Christ afresh in his character of the righteousness of God [1 Cor. 1.30], those, that is, who have been previously sanctified through the Holy Spirit.
>
> Origen, *Princ.* 1.3.8, trans. G. W. Butterworth

The Holy Spirit in the Pro-Nicene Creeds

The Arian controversy over the nature of Jesus Christ gave rise to a number of Creeds, which summarized the belief in the Spirit in just one, short sentence. A brief note on the Spirit contrasted with the much more elaborate doctrine of the Father and the Son pronounced by the same credal statements. Yet the confusion around the exact relationship between the Father and the Son provided the theologians of the Church, as well as their pro-Arian adversaries, with new sets of helpful idioms, philosophical distinctions and intellectual models of the divine.

> [We believe in] one Holy Spirit, the Paraclete, who spoke in the prophets.
>
> The Baptismal Creed of Jerusalem, fourth century CE
>
> In addition to this pious doctrine concerning the Father and the Son, as the divine Scriptures teach us, we confess one Holy Spirit, Who made new both the saints of the old covenant and the inspired teachers of the so-called new covenant.
>
> The Creed of Alexandria, fourth century
>
> And in one Holy Spirit, Who proceeds from the Father, a life-giving Spirit.
>
> The Creed used at baptism by *Theodore of Mopsuestia
>
> And in the holy Spirit, Who is consubstantial [Gr. *homoousion*] with the Father and His Word.
>
> The Egyptian Creed of St Macarius (c.300 – c.390), trans. J. N. D. Kelly

Arius' theology placed the Holy Spirit even further from God than the Logos and closer to other creatures called into being through the mediation of the Logos. Consequently, the being called 'the Holy Spirit' was a creature subordinated to the Logos. Arius' opponents, on the contrary, tried to reaffirm the divine status of the Sprit who, equally with the Father and the Son, offered salvation to all men and women.

Athanasius of Alexandria: the Divine Spirit and Salvation

Athanasius of Alexandria, again, is one of the most important witnesses of the orthodox response to the sort of theology that diminished the nature and the role of the Spirit. The main argument used by Athanasius against the Arian party was focused on the history of salvation. Here, Athanasius, like Irenaeus of Lyons in his polemic against the Gnostics, emphasized the irreplaceable role of the Spirit in the structure or whole plan of salvation. The Spirit spoke through the prophets preparing people for the forthcoming mystery of the incarnation. The same Spirit announced to Mary the coming of the Saviour, then the Spirit works in the Church through sacraments such as baptism to sanctify the believers. In all these and many more ways, the Spirit performs empowering acts, which must be of divine origin if they really have the sanctifying influence claimed by Christians. Otherwise, they are misleading, erroneous and futile. But in Athanasius' view, the Holy Spirit's continuous presence and activity in the history of salvation and his sanctifying power prove and show that he shares divinity with the other two persons of the Trinity. Athanasius emphasizes the stance of mainstream Christian authors that the Holy Spirit is consubstantial (Gr. *homoousios*) with the Father and the Son.[41] Athanasius did not discuss the origin of the Holy Spirit in the Spirit's relationship with the Father and the Son. Nevertheless, in his view the Holy Spirit was divine and had deifying might.[42] Against some Neo-Arians and other theological adversaries, Athanasius criticized the idea that the Spirit was yet another 'creature' of God, a sort of archangel, as previously Arians believed about the Son. Athanasius' contribution at this stage of pneumatology was to bring to light the divine status and nature of the third person of the Trinity by applying to the Spirit the crucial Nicene term 'of the same substance'.

The Cappadocians: the Divine Might and Person

Further terminological and theological advances came with the *Cappadocians. One of the first characteristics of their pneumatology was the belief that all three divine persons shared the same nature, which was incomprehensible to the human mind. While God's substance is beyond the reach of human ability to define, it is possible, through careful examination, to identify the character of these three persons. Second, all three Cappadocian Fathers were involved in the defence of the divine nature of the Spirit. *Gregory of Nyssa composed his *Sermon on the Deity of the Son and the Holy Spirit*, and the title itself reveals the content of this apologetic work; Gregory of Nazianzus referred to the divinity of the Spirit in many of his *Orations*; Basil of Caesarea wrote the first theological treatise dedicated totally to the Holy Spirit, *On the Holy Spirit*. It is quite clear that all three authors were inspired by their common research and the proclamation of their shared belief. It is evident that while some of them only suggested ideas, others further developed the concepts of their friends.

Basil of Caesarea

Basil's pneumatology was based on the Nicene terminology and contained the important difference between one divine essence/substance (Gr. *ousia*) and a person (Gr. *hypostasis*). Now, in the new theological context, Basil underlined the equality of three persons (Gr. *hypostases*),[43] not just the Father and the Son.

> They say [*Macedonians – P. A.-S.] that it is not appropriate to hold as equal the Holy Spirit with the Father and the Son, because he is different in nature and inferior in dignity from them [. . .] When the Lord instituted the baptism of salvation he clearly commanded his disciples to baptize all nations 'in the name of the Father, the Son and the Holy Spirit' [Matt. 28.19]. He did not despise his relationship with the Holy Spirit, but these people say that we should not equate the Spirit with the Father and the Son. Do they not explicitly disrespect God's commandment? If they deny that this agreement of Father, Son and Spirit proves their union and fellowship, let them explain to us why we should accept their opinion. How could Father, Son and the Holy Spirit be united in a more appropriate way? If indeed the Lord did not speak of himself, the Father and the Spirit as united in baptism, then let our adversaries blame us for having invented this doctrine. But no one is so shameless as to deny the obvious meaning of the [scriptural – P. A.-S.] words which clearly declare that the Spirit is one with the Father and the Son. Therefore our adversaries should keep silence; while we shall follow the words of the Scriptures.
>
> Basil of Caesarea, *OHS* 10.24, trans. P. A.-S.

In Basil's presentation, the Spirit was not 'outside' the divine essence/substance, but he participates in it. Yet Basil did not denote the Spirit as equally

divine. This carefulness suggests that for Basil, in the light of pro-Nicene tradition, this term might possibly have been connected exclusively with the Son's
generation. The Holy Spirit was not begotten of the Father, as the Son. Still,
joining together exegesis of the Scriptures, the already established tradition of
the Church and rational investigation, Basil pointed to the unity and harmony
of the divine actions in the history of salvation, when all three persons were
involved, although performing different functions.[44] The crucial <u>inter-dwelling</u>
(Gr. *perichoresis*) of the three divine persons, emphasized by Basil, will find its
further elaboration in the theology of John of Damascus,[45] as it was stressed
that the divine sharing of their nature is not an amalgamation of all three
deities.

> **Inter-dwelling**: 'indwelling of the three divine persons reciprocally in one
> another' (Gr. *perichoresis*, Gr. *peri* – 'around' and *choreo* – 'dance'). Origin-
> ally this term was used by Neoplatonic philosophers to illustrate the union
> of the soul and body. Gregory of Nazianzus applied it to the union of the
> human and divine natures in Christ (*Ep.* 101; *Or.* 38.13). Later Patristic theo-
> logians, such as John of Damascus, referred this notion to the inner divine
> life of the Trinity.

The Holy Spirit was irreplaceable in this process from the beginning, and his
role continued the mission of the Saviour and also well prepared all the circumstances of incarnation. Those actions of the Holy Spirit 'complete' the Trinity.[46]
Basil recalled scriptural metaphors to present the Holy Spirit as the 'breath' and
the 'mouth' of God, but it was the title of 'Spirit of God' which was the most
appropriate to the function of the third person, the source of sanctification, as
expressed in his *Liturgy of Saint Basil*.

> **Liturgy** (Gr. *leiturgia*, from Gr. *leos* – 'people' and Gr. *ergon*, 'work'): denotes
> all forms of the Christian public worship based on a fixed form of prayers
> and actions.

The fundamental connection between dogma and liturgy appears as yet another important axiom of Patristic theology, claiming that 'the way of worship

reveals the nature of belief' (Lat. *lex orandi – lex credendi*). The liturgy was always celebrated in the power of the divine Spirit. But now, with the dogmatic affirmation, the Holy Spirit together with the Father and the Son receives the full attention of Christian worship.

> The Spirit of truth, the Grace of adoption of sons, the earnest of our inheritance which is to come, the first fruit of everlasting blessedness, the quickening Might, the Source of sanctification, through whom every rational creature possessing understanding is able to worship You and to raise to You an everlasting hymn of glory.
>
> *Liturgy of Saint Basil*, trans. P. A.-S.

Gregory of Nazianzus: the Origin of the Spirit

Gregory of Nazianzus, a long-standing friend of Basil and brother of Gregory of Nyssa, emphasized the Johannine idiom[47] denoting that the Holy Spirit 'proceeds' from the Father. In contrast, the Son is begotten.[48] This crucial and definite way of appearing alongside the Father and the Son (not in time but eternally) was attributed only to the Holy Spirit.[49] Gregory emphasized the distinction between the unbegotten (Gr. *agenneton*) divine person, the Father, the begotten (Gr. *genneton*) person, the Son, and the third person who 'proceeds from the Father' rather than being begotten.[50] All three divine beings shared the same substance (Gr. *ousia*), while differing in their individual and real identity (Gr. *hypostasis*).[51] In his view the three ways/modes of divine existence as 'unbegotten', 'generated' and the one who 'proceeds' express the relations within the Trinity and provide each divine person with his unique characteristic. Therefore the distinction of these three persons is valid on the basis of the eternal and mutual relations, which confirm the individuality of each one, while affirming the unity of their substance. In his famous *Oration* 31, Gregory applied the Johannine symbol of light and then assimilated this metaphor to the triune God as threefold light, while he linked the light (i.e. the symbol of all three divine persons sharing the same divinity) with the process of revelation/illumination by which we can perceive the Father, the Son and the Holy Spirit.

'He was the true light which illuminates everyone who comes to this world', that is the Son. 'He was the true light which illuminates everyone who comes to this world', that is the Spirit. These are three persons and three verbs: 'he was'; 'he was' and 'he was'. But the single reality was. There are also three objects: 'the light', 'the light' and 'the light'. But as the light is one, God is one. David's prophetic vision expressed this meaning: 'In your light we see light' [Ps. 36.9]. Therefore we receive the light of the Son from the Father's light, in the light of the Holy Spirit.

Gregory of Nazianzus, *Or.* 1.3, trans. P. A.-S.

As in the case of Basil, so for Gregory of Nazianzus: the Holy Spirit can neither be separated from the Father and the Son, nor be seen as subordinate to them.[52]

Gregory of Nyssa: Affirmation of the Divine Nature

Gregory of Nyssa continued the theological trajectory of his brother Basil. Gregory's main treatise, *On the Holy Spirit: Against the Macedonians, the Spirit Fighters*, offers a highly elaborated theory of the third, divine person. Against his opponents, Gregory openly states that the Spirit is of the same rank as the two other divine persons, with whom he shares all qualities. With great philosophical skill, Gregory reinforced the crucial distinction between divine substance (Gr. *ousia*) and divine personhood (Gr. *hypostasis*). He also further specified the exact nature of the shared substance as opposed to the individual existence of all three persons.[53] He was well aware of the possible separation of the reality of each individual divine being (tritheism), therefore he pronounced a crucial formula of the Trinity as 'one substance and three persons' (Gr. *mia ousia – tres hypostases*).[54] In Gregory's theology there are three, eternal relations, which denote three persons: the one unbegotten who is the Father, the one begotten who is the Son and the one who came through the Son from the Father: the Holy Spirit. This statement approaches a new understanding of the origin of the Spirit as twofold procession. Gregory pronounced: 'in accordance with the Scriptures' that the Holy Spirit is from God the Father and of Christ.

> We acknowledge the Spirit as having equal status with the Father and the Son, so that there is no difference between them in any attribute which piety can ascribe to the divine nature, in thought or name. We acknowledge the Holy Spirit to be indeed *from* God, and *of* Christ, according to the Scriptures; save that in respect of his personal subsistence [Gr. *hypostasis*] he is observed to have his particular attributes. Since he is not ingenerate, he is not to be confused with the Father; nor with the Son, since he is not the Only-begotten. Thus he is distinguished by certain proprieties, but in all other respects he is inseparable from them.
>
> Gregory of Nyssa, *AMac.* 2, trans. H. Bettenson

This crucial distinction denoted as a twofold process of coming 'from/by' was a further clarification of the mystery of the Trinity, which found its place in the Christian doctrine of the Holy Spirit. As an eternal procession it highlighted the life of the Trinity as the divine communion of three persons united in life and mutual giving and receiving. However, co-existing in the relation of 'giving' and 'receiving' does not limit the Spirit to being an object of the divine exchange. On the contrary, it produces his identity[55] as the source of love of the Father and the Son and the bond of their relationship. Then the Holy Spirit 'outside' the Trinity receives as his mission to lead human beings into the eternal, intimate life of God. This idea found its proclamation in the Creed promulgated by the Council of Constantinople (381).

> And in the Spirit, the Holy, the Lord and life-giving One, who is proceeding from the Father, who with the Father and the Son is together worshipped and together glorified, the One, who spoke through the prophets.
>
> The Creed of Constantinople (381), trans. P. A.-S.

Cyril of Jerusalem: Introduction into the Mystery

The emergence, proclamation and further clarification of the faith in the deity of the Holy Spirit did not develop only as a theological speculation. From the beginning mainstream Christians practised baptism in the name of the three divine persons, while in their liturgy they referred unceasingly to the actions of the Father, Son and the Holy Spirit. The liturgy of the Church was 'Trinitarian' even before more advanced theology distinguished the specific nature of each divine person and pronounced it as a dogma. However, the dogmatic statement about the Trinity needed a 'translation', which then stirred up the emotions and minds of believers. One of the best Patristic examples of 'translation' of complex theology into commonly comprehensible language came from *Cyril, the Bishop of Jerusalem. Cyril's catechetical lectures not only give very important evidence of the pastoral and rhetorical skills of the author, but also provide a valuable insight into the development of liturgy in fourth-century Christianity. Among Cyril's 24 addresses, one is specially dedicated to the mystery of the Holy Spirit.

> Magnificent is the Holy Spirit and all-powerful and wonderful in his gifts. Look around, as many of you as are sitting here, each one of you has a soul. At the same time the Holy Spirit prepares each soul to achieve the ultimate goodness. While being present among us, the Holy Spirit is able to see the inclination of each soul. In the same way, he penetrates the thoughts and conscience of each one of us. He knows what we say and what we think as well as what we believe. [. . .] Contemplate the great Protector and Giver of manifold grace, who in the world, offers to one person chastity while to another constant virginity, yet another becomes a generous benefactor as the other is free from care for the material profits, still to another person the Holy Spirit grants the power to cast out evil spirits. Therefore as the one ray of the sun brings light to the whole world, so the Holy Spirit illuminates the sight of all who can see. And if there is somebody who cannot perceive this light because of spiritual blindness, this lack of perception is the result of lack of faith and not caused by the Spirit.
>
> Cyril of Jerusalem, *CL* 16.22, trans. P. A.-S.

Cyril's preparation of the candidate for baptism offers them a hope and vision of a new life illuminated by the light of the Holy Spirit. The Spirit of God is the author of manifold vocations and gifts of grace; the same divine Spirit purifies the believers and guides them through their lives. The Holy Spirit enters into the human soul and makes his dwelling in it. Therefore moved by the Holy Spirit, a Christian disciple is on a journey under the guidance of the divine Sanctifier. That journey begins with baptism. In this way liturgy, theology and spirituality are naturally interwoven within the frame of the Patristic tapestry.

Augustine of Hippo: the Holy Spirit as the Divine Union

*Augustine of Hippo achieved much more than any other Latin theologian while intellectually meditating on the mystery of the Trinity on various occasions,[56] including his spectacular work *On the Trinity*. This *magnum opus* was written over a period of 20 years (399–419) and finally took the form of a highly advanced theory with yet another explanation of the role and person of the Holy Spirit. For Augustine, as for Gregory of Nyssa, the Holy Spirit was the 'common gift' (Lat. *donum*) of the divine Father and the Son.[57] The Holy Spirit is then the divine, perfect *donum* that is love (Lat. *caritas*), which unites the Father and the Son and cannot be inferior to God.[58] The Spirit not only expresses the eternal communion between the Father and the Son, but as *amor* he is a part of that divine union between the lover (Lat. *amans*) and the loved (Lat. *amatur*).[59] The Holy Spirit is more than just a subjective connection (Lat. *conexio*) between the Father and the Son.[60] An individual person, the Spirit, takes his origin from that eternal (as everything in God is eternal), substantial (not accidental) relation (Lat. *relatio*) between the Father and the Son. The Spirit is an inexpressible communion – sharing – fellowship of the Father and the Son, their mutual communion of love.[61]

> It is not without reason that in this Trinity only the Son is called the Word of God, and only the Holy Spirit the Gift of God, and only God the Father is named as the one from whom the Word is born, and

from whom the Holy Spirit originally proceeds. I have added the word originally, because the Holy Spirit proceeds from the Son also. But the Father gave the Son this [i.e. the procession] too, although not given to him when he already existed and did not yet have it; but whatever the Father gave to the only-begotten Word, he gave by begetting him. Therefore he so begot the Son as that the common Gift would proceed from the Son also, and the Holy Spirit should be the Spirit of both. This distinction, then, of the inseparable Trinity is not to be merely accepted in passing, but to be carefully considered; for hence it was that the Word of God was specially called also the Wisdom of God, although both Father and Holy Spirit are wisdom. If, then, any one of the three is to be specially called Love, what more fitting than that it should be the Holy Spirit? – namely, that in that simple and highest nature, substance should not be one thing and love another, but that substance itself should be love, and love itself should be substance, whether in the Father, or in the Son, or in the Holy Spirit; and yet that the Holy Spirit should be specially called Love.
Augustine, *Trin.*, 15.17.29, from *Ante-Nicene Fathers*, modified P. A.-S.

In the seventh book of *On the Trinity* Augustine reaches for an example rather than an argument from anthropology, showing that the co-existence in the human being of 'memory', 'intelligence' and 'will' reflects an image of the divine, Trinitarian community of the Father, the Son and the Holy Spirit.[62] But he was aware of the limits of that analogy, still useful as an illustration of God's mystery. In the human being these three aspects/functions of personhood are not identical with a person, while on the contrary in the case of God, all three are divine. Yet, we cannot simply say that, for instance, the Holy Spirit is the 'divine will', while the Logos is 'intelligence', since each divine person has his own memory, intelligence and will, as part of being a person. Like memory, intelligence and will, they are inseparable, and while human aspects subsist in human nature, the three divine persons subsist in the divine. Augustine added a new and important final note that the Holy Spirit, although proceeding from the Father, also proceeds from the Son (Lat. *filioque*).[63] This new theological inclusion, in Augustine's view, safeguarded the real, not merely nominal, distinction between the Spirit and the Son. The relationship between the Spirit and the Son was not as 'two children' ('twins') of the same Father (generated/proceeding), but rather as the one (the Son) who gives origin to the second (the Spirit).

Later Controversies

Both traditions, Western/Latin and Greek/Eastern, reached their climax with the theology of the Spirit around the Council of Constantinople (381). However, the next, so-called *Priscillianist tendency, which appeared in Spain between the fourth and the seventh century, pressed the Western theologians to a problematic alteration of the Constantinopolitan Creed. In order to highlight the procession of the Holy Spirit, it was added that he proceeds not only from the Father but also from the Son. This insertion, which we already found in Augustine, abbreviated as *filioque*, originating in a local church and its controversy, gradually gained authority in Latin Christendom, while the Greek, Eastern churches expressed their reservation until its open rejection in the ninth century in the Byzantine Empire.

Conclusion

The Patristic theology of the Holy Spirit offers enormous richness of thought upon and approach to the mystery of the third person, and it concludes the doctrine of the Trinity. As has been pointed out, this progress in understanding the triune God was not exclusively an outcome of alternative challenges, as in the case of Christology, but also as a part of the fascination with the divine person who continues Christ's mission to bring humanity back to its origin. Pneumatology, without the very Patristic emphasis on sanctification (deification) as the purpose of human life, remains a dry speculation. But together with Patristic spirituality, it unveils its profound power to inspire personal faith, intellectual growth and the spiritual advance of the believer.

Questions for discussion

- How do you assess the Gnostic effort to present the Holy Spirit as a female divinity?

- Which approach to the mystery of the Holy Spirit do you find the most convincing?
- How do you assess the problem of defining God as one *ousia* and three *hypostases*?
- If the Trinity is a mystery, why does it not need to be comprehended?
- Can a modern formula such as 'Creator, Redeemer and Sustainer' replace the classical, Patristic distinction of three persons in the Holy Trinity?

Further Reading

For beginners
B. Bobrinskoy, 1999, *The Mystery of the Trinity: Trinitarian Experience and Vision in the Biblical and Patristic Tradition*, Crestwood, NY: St Vladimir's Seminary Press.
F. Dünzl, 2007, *A Brief History of the Doctrine of the Trinity in the Early Church*, trans. J. Bowden, London: T&T Clark.

For more advanced students
J. J. Buckley, 2000 '"The Holy Spirit is a Double Name": Holy Spirit, Mary and Sophia in the *Gospel of Philip*', in K. L. King (ed.), *Images of the Feminine in Gnosticism*, 'Studies in Antiquity & Christianity', Harrisburg, PA: Trinity Press International, pp. 211–27 and response by K. Rudolph, pp. 228–38.
S. T. Davis, D. Kendall and G. O'Collins (eds), 2004, *The Trinity*, Oxford: Oxford University Press.
S. M. Hildebrand, 2007, *The Trinitarian Theology of the Basil the Great: a synthesis of Greek Thought and Biblical Truth*, Washington DC: Catholic University of America Press.
A. Marjanen, 2005, 'Montanism: Egalitarian Ecstatic "New Prophecy"', in A. Marjanen, P. Luomanen (eds), *A Companion to Second-Century Christian 'Heretics'*, Supplements to *Vigiliae Christianae*, vol. 76, Leiden: Brill, pp. 185–212.

Internet Resources

Pneumatology (some bibliography):
    http://www.theologicalstudies.org.uk/god_pneuma.php
Augustine of Hippo
    http://plato.stanford.edu/entries/augustine/

Notes

1 Cf. *Didache* 11.7; *EpB* 12.2; *Odes of Solomon* 11.6.

2 For example, Irenaeus, *Proof* 2, 5, 6, 42, 49.

3 For more information, see G. Johnston, 2008, *The Spirit–Paraclete in the Gospel of John*, Cambridge: Cambridge University Press.

4 For example, Athenagoras, *Supplication* 7.2; 9.1.

5 *1 Apol.* 6; 31; 35; 61; *Dial.* 49; 87.

6 For example, Ignatius, *Eph.* 18.2. See more in chapter 3.

7 For example, *Proof* 5; *AH* 3.9.3.

8 Cf. Tatian, *Orat.* 13.3.

9 For example, *Phil.* intro.; *2 Clement* 14.1–5.

10 Ignatius, *Eph.* 17.1–2.

11 Hermas, *Par.* 5.59.5.

12 *Proof* 5.

13 *Princ.* 1.3.8.

14 *EpSerapion* 1.23–4.

15 *DialTrin.* 7.

16 *AEun.* 3.5.

17 *Or.* 31.4; 34.12.

18 *Orth.* 1.8.

19 For example, Hermas, *Par.* 5.6; *2 Clement* 20.5; Justin, *1 Apol.* 33; *Dial.* 61.1.

20 *AI* 9.33–40.

21 *Supplication* 10.3–4; 24.1–2.

22 Cf. *GTh.* 101. More in chapter 3.

23 The Jewish authors who translated the Hebrew text as the *Septuagint* were constrained by the Greek language.

24 Cf. *GPh.* 59.35—60.1.

25 Cf. 64.22–31.

26 Cf. 59.20.

27 Cf. 60.30.

28 'Mother', that is the Holy Spirit, is identified here with 'the Mother of life', 'Sophia', one of the divine Aeons.

29 Possibly, the companion of the divine Father.

30 That is, the Gnostic cosmological idea of the *Ogdoade* ('the eighth heaven'), which was a synonym for eternal rest.

31 Possible a later *Manichaean addition, this title may originally refer to the messenger who embodied the elements of the divine world, which brings salvation.

32 Cf. *AH* 1.30.3.

33 Cf. *Chest* 19.4.1; 30.17.6.

34 The first article is based on faith in One God, the second – in Jesus, the Son of God, the third – in the Holy Spirit who 'prophesied through the prophets'. Cf. *Proof* 6.

35 More in Susan Ashbrook Harvery, 1993, 'Feminine Imagery for the Divine: the Holy Spirit, the Odes of Solomon and Early Syriac Tradition', *St Vladimir's Theological Quarterly* 37, pp. 111–39.

36 *AP* 30.5.

37 *Princ.* 1.1.3.

38 *Princ.* 1.5.7.

39 *ComGJ* 3.25.151.

40 *Princ.* 2.7.2; 11.5; intro. 3; 4.3.14; 4.5.7; 4.3.14.

41 *EpSerapion* 1.27.

42 *OrAA* 3.24; *EpSerapion* 1.23.

43 *Ep.* 214.4.

44 *Ep.* 189.7.

45 Cf. A. Louth, 2004, *St John Damascene: Tradition and Originality in Byzantine Theology*, Oxford: Oxford University Press, pp. 112–13; 174–5.

46 *Hex.* 22.53.

47 Cf. John 15.26.

48 *Or.* 42.17.

49 *Or.* 1.8.

50 *Or.* 30.19.

51 More in T. A. Noble, 1989, 'The Deity of the Holy Spirit: Gregory of Nazianzus', PhD thesis, University of Edinburgh.

52 For more, see C. A. Beeley, 2008, *Gregory of Nazianzus on the Trinity and Knowledge of God*, Oxford: Oxford University Press, pp. 153–86.

53 More advanced readers, see L. Turcescu, 2005, *Gregory of Nyssa and the Concept of Divine Persons*, Oxford: Oxford University Press, pp. 109–14.

54 For example, *AE* 2.12.

55 The Cappadocians argued that gender-type terminology was neither applicable to God nor to the Holy Spirit. See chapter 1 and Gregory of Nazianzus, *Or.* 3.17.

56 For instance, in his *Confessions* 13.9.10, *Letters* 11.4 or his earlier treatise, *OFC* 9.19.

57 *Trin.* 5.12.13; 15.16; 16,17; see also *TR* 13.24.

58 *Trin.* 15.19.36; *OFC* 9.19.

59 *Trin.* 6.5.7; 8.10.14. As love, the Holy Spirit is called by Augustine 'that which the Father and Son share', *Trin.* 15.19.37.

60 Augustine opposes the attribution of feminine gender to the Holy Spirit. He

refuses the notions that the Holy Spirit was 'wife' of the divine Father, or even the divine mother of the Son. *Trin.* 12.5.5.

61 *Trin.* 15.5.12.
62 *Trin.* 15.6.10.
63 *Trin.* 15.26.47.

8

The Holy Church

See also chapters 2, 3, 6, 9, 10, 11.

Consider this Task

Set out, in your own words, the various meanings of the word 'holy'. Find out more about the scriptural images of the Christian community in the New Testament.

Introduction

The early Christians showed a great deal of respect for, if not an explicit emotional attachment to the Church: their Mother and their 'womb'. For those Christians the visible organization was an expression of the ideal fellowship, which included the apostles, the saints, the martyrs and the angels who praise God in heaven. The earthly Church reflected that task, and it was also understood as the source of spiritual life leading to salvation. This great affection is observable in Patristic discussions of the origin, nature and destiny of the Church. The theology of the Church (ecclesiology) developed gradually alongside Christology and the theory of salvation.

> **Ecclesiology** (Gr. *ekklesia* – 'gathering', 'congregation', 'assembly' and ultimately 'church'): a branch of theology which examines the nature and functions of the Church.

In this natural context the mediatory function of the Church was promoted and strongly defended (that is 'there is no salvation outside the Church'). Understanding of the Church with its four marks (one, holy, catholic and apostolic) unveiled the growing significance of its inner structures with various forms of ministry (bishops, priests and deacons) and external mission. This understanding was often seriously questioned by other models of the Church and its role. This chapter addresses only the main factors that make up the Patristic notion of the Church, as a divine–human fellowship with the Holy Spirit, who in and through the Church sanctifies all believers. The specific nature of holiness, while integrated into the unity, apostolicity and catholicity of the Church, was like a theological prism which helped believers to perceive the profound nature of the Christian fellowship.

Opening Question

How do you see the view on the Church depending upon on the understanding of the co-existence of two natures in Christ?

Development of the Argument

Like many of the doctrines we have already examined, any summary of the development of the Church faces the challenge of enormous richness within early Christian literature. With Patristic documents this richness presents a number of dilemmas. While discussing pre-Nicene ecclesiology, the present summary chooses only the most significant theologians, such as *Ignatius of Antioch, *Hermas, *Irenaeus of Lyons, *Tertullian, *Origen and *Cyprian of Carthage.[1] However, it is impossible to discuss their views without a brief account of their opponents' views, which stimulated their apologetic responses. Then while examining the period between the Council of Nicaea (325) and the Council of Chalcedon (451), this chapter will show that the holiness of the Church was not only grounded in the already established doctrine, but expounded into a more elaborate theory of sacraments, salvation and the sanctification of Christians. In this context, the mark of holiness became a visible characteristic shared with the Councils ('holy Councils') and synods ('holy synods'). On the contrary, lack of holiness characterized, in Patristic rhetoric, heresy, schism and disobedience to the Church. As a fall into error, it led to damnation and death.

Ignatius: the Church under the Ecclesiastical Shepherd

Ignatius of Antioch's faith in the holiness of the Church was deeply rooted in his ideal of unity among Christians. The visible, earthly Church reflected the invisible order, including even the relationship between God the Father and the Son. God the Father, whose sole ambassador on earth is the bishop (Gr. *episkopos*) holds the highest position,[2] while his divine Son was entrusted with a mission which he then passed on to the apostles, now the presbyters.[3] Deacons, the third rank, are entrusted with the service of Jesus Christ to the whole community (Gr. *koinonia*).[4] The ecclesiastical 'pyramid' reveals its vertical architecture: the sole bishop represents God the Father. Then, directly under him, there is the council of presbyters; and even lower are the servants of all, the deacons.

As I see it, when you are obedient to the bishop as to Jesus Christ you live your life not according to manner of this world, but according to Jesus Christ's [teaching – P. A.-S.], who died for us in order that by our faith in his death we may escape from death. For this reason it is important that you carry on this kind of life and do nothing without the bishop. Be also obedient to the priests as to the apostles of Jesus Christ, our hope, in him we will be found, if only we live in him. In addition, those who are deacons of the mysteries of Jesus Christ [1 Cor. 4.1] should please everyone in every way.

Ignatius, *Tral.* 2.1–3, trans. P. A.-S.

In this hierarchically organized structure the ordinary Christians are 'the base'. The bishop, priests and deacons administer God's grace (sacraments) and truth (teaching) as all perfection descends from the apex to the base of that ecclesiastical pyramid in an organized way.[5] Christian community exists in historical conditions in this visible world and is bound by an inner unity located in the ministry of the bishop. That unity is the strength of the Church. As God, the Father, the Son and the Holy Spirit exists in unity, the ministers are united under the leadership of their bishop.[6] It is through the *episcopos*, his ministry, and in obedience to his authority, that the whole community participates in the divine holiness. It is evident from Ignatius' letters that he promoted this model of the Church as a parallel structure to what he understood to be a divine co-existence as well as a created hierarchy of spiritual beings. As in the invisible universe all is subjected to God the Father, so in this visible world, and especially in the Christian community, everyone should be subjected to the bishop, who is God's representative and vicar.[7] Ignatius is certain that only within this ecclesiastical framework, which is strongly based on monarchical episcopacy, can believers become 'blameless' and sanctified.[8] It is quite remarkable that Ignatius' over-emphasis on the unity of the Church did not prompt him to elaborate more on its holiness. However, one of the crucial characteristics of Ignatius' ecclesiology is the ministry of the Church, which provides believers with access to God.[9] Only within that community is it possible to communicate with God, and apart from it there is no means of sanctification. The holiness of the Church, local as well as universal/catholic, is then focused on the crucial position of the bishop as the intermediary between the Church and God. Two features of this very early ecclesiology need to be pointed out. First, Ignatius, who defended so strongly Christ's real incarnation, death and resurrection, believed that visible, concrete reality can reflect invisible reality. This reality is a channel of sanctification for the whole community. Second, as the divine world has a clear, unanimous and hierarchical structure, the visible Church needs a similar order. Within this framework God's grace and sanctification come 'down' through the bishop, presbyters and deacons to the rest of the Christian *koinonia*. The 'descending model' culminates in worship, where the bishop is at the centre celebrating the Eucharist and baptism.

Hermas: the Church as an Elderly Woman

At the same time, in Rome, we encounter another imaginative conception of the holiness of the Church: Hermas' the *Shepherd*, which unlike Ignatius' outlook represents a Jewish-Christian ecclesiology. First, the holiness of the Church is openly declared.[10] Second, the Church receives feminine characteristics, where she is sometimes portrayed as an elderly woman, symbolizing her ancient roots, possibly even her pre-existence.

> When I slept, my brothers, a revelation was given to me by a very handsome young man, who said: 'Who do you think the elderly woman is, the one who gave you the little book?' 'The Sibyl' – I replied. 'You are wrong', he answered: 'She is not'. 'Who is she?' – I asked. 'The Church', he answered again. Then I said to him 'Why is she so elderly?' 'It is so' he replied 'because she was created as the first of all created beings. This is the reason why she is so ancient and it was for her sake that the world was established.'
>
> Hermas, *Vis.* 2.4.1, trans. P. A.-S.

> Listen now [the Woman/Church is speaking to Hermas – P. A.-S.] about the stones which are used to build the tower. The stones which are square and white and fit neatly in place, these are the apostles, bishops/ elders, teachers and deacons who walked according to the majesty of God and who served the elect of God in holiness and reverence, in

> the task of leadership, teaching and ministering. Some among them have fallen asleep but others are still alive. They always agreed among themselves and lived in peace as well as listening to one another. This is the reason why they fit into the correct place in the building of the tower.
>
> Hermas, *Vis.* 3.5.1, trans. P. A.-S.

On another occasion, the same Church appears as a very young woman, and this time she represents the renewed spirit of the Christian community.[11] The multilevels of interpretation presented by this document join together the Church/Woman as God's creation with the notion that she is still 'under construction' as a tower, which is being built up and made of various 'bricks', which are the saints, martyrs, confessors and other virtuous people.[12] The most practical and pastoral issue discussed by this apocalyptic document is that of whether or not there is still room in the holy Church for its sinful members. The question is, can the holy Church include sinful members, and if yes, on what conditions? This is the fundamental question of all pre-Nicene ecclesiologies. In the case of Hermas, he provides a positive answer in which he affirms the efficacy of penitence as a remedy that rejoins sinners with their holy Church.[13]

For both Ignatius and Hermas, the Church was at the centre of the relationship with God as revealed by Christ. Both theologians seem to deny any hope of salvation outside this mediator. Its, or rather her ('elderly/young woman'), holiness originated in her providential foundation by God. However, while Ignatius boldly identified the bishop as the visible sign and proof of the Church's connection with the divine life, Hermas did not pay much attention to its hierarchical structure. Instead he emphasized its composition from a diversity of more or less perfect members founded on a single stone: the Saviour.[14]

Irenaeus: the Church as the Dwelling Place of the Holy Spirit

Irenaeus of Lyons' view of the holiness of the Church called attention to the mysterious but real presence of the Holy Spirit in its midst.

The preaching of the Church continues without any change and remains the same everywhere. It has its foundation in the testimony of
the Prophets and the Apostles and all their disciples, as I have proved,
in the same way as through [the witness – P. A.-S.] of those at the beginning, in the middle and at the end. Next, what we believe is a firm
system including all people in salvation. And since it has been received
by the Church, we protect it. This plan has its freshness renewed by the
Spirit of God, as if it were some precious deposit in an excellent vessel; and it causes the vessel containing it also to be rejuvenated [. . .]
In the Church, God has placed 'the apostles, prophets and teachers'
[1 Cor. 12.28], and all the other means through which the Spirit works;
in all of which none have any part who do not conform to the Church.
On the contrary, they [the heretics – P. A.-S.] defraud themselves of life
by their erroneous opinion and most shameful behaviour. For where
the Church is, there is the Spirit of God; and where the Spirit of God is,
there is the Church of every grace. The Spirit, thus, is Truth.

Irenaeus of Lyons, *AH* 3.24.1, trans. P. A.-S.

With Irenaeus, Catholic ecclesiology entered a new, more mature phase, and
his theology shows a greater degree of awareness of the mark of holiness and its
value. First, in a parallel way to Ignatius, possibly because of the similar challenge coming from alternative theories of salvation, Irenaeus defends the structure and authority of the Church with its hierarchical organization. Through
this structured 'channel', holiness and sanctification descend to all believers. For
Irenaeus it was important to highlight the direct link of the visible, local Church
and its leaders with Jesus Christ and God, through the notion of 'tradition'.

Tradition (Gr. *paradosis*): 'teaching or truth handed over from one generation to another'. In the Patristic context it was one of the most crucial and
defended notions of delivering and protecting God's authentic revelation.
It pointed to the prophets of the 'Old Testament' as forerunners of the
Christian revelation, then it highlighted Jesus' teaching passed on to his
apostles and stressed the authority of the Church as the guardian and exclusive interpreter of that legacy.

Only the 'apostolic tradition' safeguarded the faithfulness and genuine character of the Church as well as its sacramental efficacy.[15] Through the tradition,
and only through it, the local church has direct association with the apostles and
Jesus Christ. Only by this proven, historical connection can believers be certain
of their salvation. The holiness of the Church, guaranteed by the presence of
the Spirit, can be recognized in those communities with properly established
authorities. In this logic and rhetoric, those who reject Catholic bishops reject
God's Spirit and consequently cannot participate in sanctification. Irenaeus, like
Hermas, emphasizes that the Church is first and foremost a diverse community
of believers who share the same faith and are obedient to God and, as Ignatius
would add, also obedient to their local leaders. Holiness, or participation in
both the sanctifying might and the activity of the Spirit is achievable within
the framework of that apostolic Church.[16] Holiness as a characteristic became
for Irenaeus, if not the synonym for, at least the expression of the nature and
ministry of the Church. Like the Bishop of Antioch, the Bishop of Lyons saw his
own church as part of the larger Christian network. The catholicity of the local
koinonia was yet another feature to direct people towards to the 'true' Church.
In addition, Irenaeus highlights the Church's unique motherhood. While his
strong emphasis on hierarchy, male leadership and the apostolic tradition show
one line of understanding of the Church, his discussion of baptism, spiritual
regeneration and nourishment reveal the female nature of the same Church.[17]
For Irenaeus, the Church is the Virgin Mother modelled on Christ's Mother.[18]
But his analogy goes further and includes the third woman: Eve. Reference to
Eve, Mary and the Church allows Irenaeus to exemplify his theory of the Church
in an attractive and imaginative way. Eve, in his interpretation, was the mother
of all men and women; she had sexual intercourse and then she gave birth to
her children. Mary receives the title of the Mother of Salvation,[19] because she
did not have sexual intercourse, but nevertheless gave birth to the Saviour (see
chapter 3). The Church becomes the spiritual Mother of all faithful Christians
because, like Mary, she does not have sexual intercourse, but continues Mary's
life-giving act, which is now extended to all humanity. Mary and the Church, the
Blessed Virgin and the Holy Virgin, the former who gave birth to Christ and the
latter who gives spiritual life through baptism, are the embodiment of holiness.
Irenaeus' creative imagery of the motherhood of the Church inspired Patristic
theology for centuries to come.

Tertullian: the Church has no Room for Mediocre Christians

Tertullian's ecclesiology – like the author himself – went through at least two main stages of change: first, with his conversion from paganism to Christianity, and second, with his subsequent conversion to *Montanism (see chapter 4). Despite these two phases, Tertullian's whole theology was accompanied by awareness of the holiness of the Church. In his Catholic period, the Church was seen by him as 'an extension' of the Trinity.[20] Therefore when the fatherhood of God is reaffirmed by faith in the Son and is expressed, for example, by the prayer 'Our Father', the motherhood of the Church is a part of the same Christian belief.[21] Holiness was the mark of the Mother who gave spiritual life to her children and then nourished them with spiritual food.[22] The Church, like a human mother, provides her children with safety and teaches them about the Father as well as introducing them to even greater intimacy with the Son. Tertullian's ecclesiology, including the notion of holiness, became extreme in his second period, with his famous criticism of the Catholic Church as an organization based on the number of bishops, but not on spiritual people.[23] Because the apocalyptic movement Montanism paid special attention to moral discipline and rigour in those 'last days', in contrast to Catholic moral laxity, this radical new ethos appealed to Tertullian, who had already put a strong emphasis on the value of Christian morality, penance and conduct. From that later period comes the important treatise, *On Modesty*, where the author argues against the common Catholic practice of remitting the sins committed by her 'officers' who were not truly spiritual/holy men. He even states that they have fallen into sins such as idolatry, which the Church has no authority to forgive.[24] The holiness of the Church, as first and foremost a community of men and women enriched by spiritual gifts, becomes the sign of its genuine identity. Like Ignatius and Irenaeus, he valued the apostolic origin of the Church.[25] But unlike Ignatius and Irenaeus, Tertullian overemphasized the authority of certain 'spiritual' (or charismatic) lay people, giving them greater authority than the ecclesiastical officers such as bishops, priests and deacons. Like Hermas, Tertullian stressed the value of penitence in the Christian life, but unlike Hermas, he rejected any form of return to 'the spiritual home/tower' by those who committed the gravest sins.[26] Again, in the case of Tertullian, the fundamental question returns: how to reconcile, if possible, sinfulness and holiness in the Christian Church? Tertullian deeply believed that this reconciliation has its limits.

Cyprian: the Church has its Limits

Cyprian, bishop of Carthage, was a theological heir of some of Tertullian's ideas, although he remained faithful to the Church until his martyrdom. In the pre-Nicene period of the development of ecclesiology, including the mark of holiness, Cyprian holds a very special place. His views on the Church were shaped by the cruel circumstances of his life: he faced persecution, fled but then confessed his error and was engaged in an ardent debate about ways of reconciling lapsed Christians with the Church. Cyprian was very close to Ignatius' opinion about the central place of the bishop within the Christian community, and the bishop was responsible for the unity of the Church.[27] Like Irenaeus, Cyprian valued the apostolic tradition very much. Nevertheless, in his view, each local bishop is directly and spiritually linked to the legacy of Peter, and the Church of Rome does not have the same authority as taught by Irenaeus.[28] Like Tertullian, for Cyprian, the Church was the spiritual Mother.[29] Cyprian's awareness of the holiness of the Church emerged with a radical new approach, although less radical than that of Tertullian. After the tragic events during Decius' persecution (250 CE), when many of Cyprian's fellow-believers in North Africa committed apostasy and became *lapsi*, forgiveness of their grave sin was declared by 'confessors', that is Christians, including lay people, who had faced torture, who had survived and gained the highest authority in the Christian communities. At the same time as the Church went through a period of administrative and pastoral turmoil, various Christian heretics baptized converts. After his return to Carthage, Cyprian faced two challenges to his understanding of the holiness of the Church: who has the authority to pardon the sins of the lapsed and open the door of holy Church to the apostates? And, second: can baptism by heretics contain grace and therefore originate growth in holiness? These two questions and two pastoral issues were interconnected in denoting the limits, if not the understanding of the holiness of the Church. Cyprian, against the opinion of Stephen, bishop of Rome, concluded that the nature of the Church requires purity from both clergy and believers. Then, the holy sacraments, such as baptism, can be administered with efficacy as the means of salvation. The Church and only its clerical representatives can proclaim the forgiveness of sins; therefore, the acts of reconciliation practised by the 'confessors' are invalid. Only bishops can open the door of holy Church to sinners.[30] This statement was particularly significant, because in Cyprian's view, like that of Ignatius, Hermas and Irenaeus, and in a certain way of Tertullian, 'there is no salvation outside the Church'.[31] However, unlike Tertullian, and closer to Hermas' intuition, Cyprian believed that the Church is not an elite club and that it contains people who perform penance, and because of God's grace all sins, including apostasy, can be remitted, provided that forgiveness is declared by a minister who is at least reconciled with the Church, if not holy.[32] Like Tertullian, he was certain that it is impossible to 'have God as a Father, if you no longer to have the Church as your mother'.[33] And that spiritual Mother was undefiled.

> The spouse of Christ cannot be defiled, she is inviolate and chaste; she knows one home alone, in all modesty she keeps faithfully to one chamber. It is she who preserves us for God, she who seals for the kingdom the sons whom she has borne. Whoever breaks with the Church and enters on an adulterous union, cuts himself off from the promises made to the Church; and he who turns back on the Church of Christ will not come to the rewards of Christ; he is alien, a worldling, an enemy. You cannot have God for your Father if you no longer have the Church for your mother. If there was escape for one who was outside of the ark of Noah, there will be as much for one who is found to be outside of the Church.
>
> Cyprian of Carthage, *OUCh.* 6, trans. M. Bévenot

So far, these selected, but very important representatives of early pre-Nicene ecclesiology elaborated on the holiness of the Church as a mark that unveils the Church's irreplaceable function in the salvation of all believers. For the majority of these authors, the Church's authority was based on the visible clerical hierarchy. However, some contested this model (Tertullian) by promoting the ideal of the Church as a minority, with greater purity, self-discipline and awareness of the might of the Spirit. In all these documents the visible/invisible aspects of the Church were two sides of the same coin, while the tension between holiness and sinfulness caused more problems with understanding and interpretation of this strain.

Origen: the Church More than an Institution

With Origen's ecclesiology yet another aspect of holiness becomes noticeable.[34] His understanding of holiness, often expressed in his writings by Pauline phrases such as 'with no stain or wrinkle' (Eph. 5.27),[35] combined a very personal devotion ('Mother', 'the Bride of Christ', 'old woman'), like the previous theologians, with a highly metaphysical (Platonic) outlook on the nature of the Church. He believed that the holiness of the Church referred first and foremost to the community that is spiritual and heavenly, which pre-exists the creation of the visible world.[36] If we use the metaphor of the coin as an ecclesiological model of the two dimensions of the Church, Origen concentrates on and promotes the spiritual, invisible aspect of the Church. The administration, practical affairs, discipline and many more aspects of the institutional Church are not at the centre of his ecclesiology. The hierarchy, so precious to Ignatius, Irenaeus and Cyprian, is to Origen only a symbol and reflection of its hidden nature.[37] However, unlike Tertullian, Origen, being a priest himself, was not a radical opponent of the clerical order. He emphasized rather that the ascetic life and virtues are the most important credentials of deacons, priests and bishops. In a similar way to Tertullian the Montanist, Origen had serious doubts about the sacramental efficacy of a minister who is in sin.[38] In brief, an unholy person cannot transmit sanctifying grace to his fellow-believers. Therefore the limits of the Church, visible and invisible, are based on the distinction between sinful acts of a grave nature, which pollute the souls and minds of the transgressors, and the state of grace, which illuminates the souls and minds of God's saints. Those who commit the most serious sins are no longer members incorporated in holy Church.[39] Holiness is thus a mark of the earthly Church, a community that searches for sanctification, repentance and avoiding sinful acts. Even more, the greatest holiness belongs to the pre-existent Church, as the fellowship of originally pure spirits contemplating God. Consequently, holiness will shine in the Church-to-come, as the eschatological union of the saints and angels glorifying the Trinity.[40] Then the unity and holiness of the Church will be complete.[41]

The Church and the Empire Reconciled

The post-Nicene understanding and proclamation of the holiness of the Church, which now became an institution of the Empire,[42] was grounded in important Trinitarian and Christological clarifications. Even more universally than before, the Church was proclaimed as the only repository of orthodox doctrine,[43] the unique distributor and mediator of God's grace, which guarantees salvation for its members, the relationship between believers, and mystical union with God.[44] Ecclesiology based on the Nicene Christological model of the two united natures of Christ leads theologians to affirm that as long as Christians participate in the sacramental life of the Catholic Church, they are sanctified and united by the Spirit with the Saviour. Ecclesiology becomes a part of the theory of salvation and the theory of mystical deification and even of eschatology. On another level, ecclesiastical discipline in the post-Nicene period developed stricter and more elaborate rules (that is canons) about introduction to the Church community, the moral behaviour of its members, possible penance and administrative order, which were justified by the holiness of the Church and its institutional bodies, such as Councils and synods, as well as the leaders. All these increasingly detailed amendments aimed to introduce the catechumen into the sphere of holiness, but also to protect the same sphere of holiness, including the sacraments, against profanation by personal sin, doctrinal disobedience and ecclesiastical disorder. All these new rules and sanctions were the expressions of the authority of holy Church.[45] By the time of the Council of Chalcedon (451), Patristic ecclesiology had matured to openly confessing the faith in 'one, holy, catholic and apostolic' Church. From now on, the holiness of the Church becomes one of the four central marks of the true community of Christ's followers. But Christians still have to believe in it, because in this temporal world its reflection is not perfectly seen. The later Church fathers produced a large amount of exegetical, pastoral and more speculative literature which connected their views on the Church with already established doctrine on Jesus' nature and mission. What was commonly accepted can be summed up in the following analogy: through Jesus' divine nature Christians may participate in the divine life, grace and salvation; so in a similar way, Christ's body, the Church, roots its members in communion with the Saviour.

> We proclaim the death, in the flesh, of the only-begotten Son of God,
> Jesus Christ, and acknowledge his return to life from the dead and
> his ascension to heaven, and as we do this we perform the bloodless
> sacrifice in the Churches: and thus we approach the consecrated gift
> of the sacrament, and we are sanctified by partaking the holy flesh and
> the precious blood of Christ, the Saviour of all.
>
>   Cyril of Alexandria, *Ep.* 17, trans. H. Bettenson
>
> It is necessary for him to be present in us in a divine manner through
> the Holy Spirit: to be mixed, as we were, with our bodies by means of
> his holy flesh and precious blood, for us to have him in reality as a
> sacramental gift which gives life, in the form of the bread and wine.
> And so that we should not be struck down with horror, at seeing flesh
> and blood displayed on the holy tables of our Churches.
>
>   Cyril of Alexandria, *ExpGLk* 22.19, trans. H. Bettenson

Sacramental participation in the life of the Church gives its members access to its holiness.[46] Holy Church and its authorities taught believers about the correct matrix of worship; for example, the concept of priesthood and moral judgement over ethical issues, which helps to sanctify their lives and actions. In this context, yet another important contribution must be noted.

Augustine: the Church for Sinners and for Saints

*Augustine of Hippo's defence of the Church's holiness against the Donatists presented the Christian community as a mixed community of sinners and saints.

> Donatism: a radical Christian movement, later schism, in the African church
> which started at the beginning of the fourth century CE during the persecu-
> tion of Diocletian. The main theological and ecclesiological idea of this group,

founded by a certain Donatus, was focused on the rigorist understanding and protection of the purity of the Church and the sacraments. Their main opponent was Augustine of Hippo.

This idea had already appeared with Hermas, Tertullian, Cyprian and to some extent Origen, but with Augustine's rejection of the Donatist ideal of a 'pure' Church, it gained its final form. While their ecclesiological ideal promoted the radical rejection of any compromise of the holy Church with sin, betrayal and apostasy, Augustine's exegesis of the Scriptures[47] convinced him that in the earthly Church there is still room for 'grain and chaff', good and evil, saints and sinners, 'pure and impure', but that its current condition will change in its eschatological stage.

Catholics prove false their [that is the Donatists – P. A.-S.] accusation about the existence of two Churches, proving each time even more clearly what Catholics affirm, that is, the Church contains mixed membership, including the sinful. However this is not a reason to call itself 'a Church foreign' to the kingdom of God, as there will not be this mixture containing evil members. But the same Church, One and Holy, at the present moment exists in a certain condition, while then, it will be in another. At the moment it is mixed and has evil members; then it will not have such partakers. Now it is mortal because it is made up of mortal people; then it will be immortal, because there will be nothing corporeal in it, nothing that can die.

Augustine, *BCD* 3.10.20, trans. P. A.-S.

Augustine's understanding of the holiness of the Church does not suggest that this mark was undermined by sin and evil, but rather that within the Church, which has a divine origin and is full of grace, containing a majority of holy men and women, there are some who are less than perfect individuals. Those 'impure' people take part in the sacraments, but they are excluded from the communion of saints.[48] It is clear that in Augustine's view, the Church is on a journey towards ultimate holiness, and during its earthly life it contains some elements of imperfection, which later, at the final, eschatological stage, will be purified by God's judgement.[49] This development, in comparison with Tertullian's and especially Cyprian's stance, was welcomed by the Catholic Church.

The Manifold Functions of the Church in the Syriac Tradition

The final example of the understanding of the holiness of the Church in the Patristic era comes from the richness of the early Syriac tradition, which emerged from its Jewish-Christian roots.[50] The Syriac documents show a significant parallel to early Jewish-Christian imagery, and then to the Graeco-Latin fathers, in portraying the Church in very devotional terms as 'the Mother',[51] 'the bride of Christ',[52] but they also explore other metaphors, such as the holy 'Noah's Ark',[53] 'Mystic Vineyard', 'Medicine of Life',[54] 'New Paradise'[55] and 'Bridal chamber'.[56] However, unlike other Christian interpretations, the perfect Church, with its crucial mark of holiness, belongs to the age to come. The visible reality of the Church is waiting for its fulfilment in eschatology, and therefore the Church's perfection, including holiness, is not fully realized.[57] Christians needed to be aware of this interim stage, which does not allow any room either for triumphal celebration, or a compromise with heresy, or any other distraction.[58] It looks as if Syriac theology found one of the best ways of expressing the paradox of 'already partaking'–'not yet achieving' the holiness of the Church in the eucharistic liturgy. The holy Eucharist is the holy Church proclaiming Christ's death, resurrection and life with the saints, but it is also a celebration of the eschatological event: the wedding feast of the divine Bride with her Bridegroom. In addition, the prayers of intercession express the desire to be united with the holy Church which glorifies God in heaven, but at the same time the prayer commemorates the holy bishops who preached the orthodox word of truth in this, that is the earthly, holy Church. The Syriac understanding of the Church has at its heart not a speculation, or systematic elaboration of its nature, functions and missions, but rather a very ascetic self-preparation of its members to participate in its eschatological realization: life in a paradise to come. The noticeably ascetical background of the Syriac documents suggests at least two degrees of holiness in which Christian may participate. First, the highest degree belongs to the saints, confessors, hermits, celibates and virgins. The second, much more common level belongs to those who sanctify their lives living in families and begetting children. While 'the heavenly Church' is the embodiment of pure holiness, the Church on this earth contains some degree of that holiness, but is also marked by sin and penance and is not fully united with its prototype. This distinction reflects the tension between the kingdom of God, which has already come to this world, and the kingdom which is not yet here and will only be realized at the end of time. Syriac theologians did not produce a systematic elaboration of the theology of the Church comparable with Irenaeus' (such as catholicity) or Ignatius' and Cyprian's models (the episcopacy). In the heart of their understanding of the nature of the Church was the distinction between the holy Church, the kingdom of God already established in the souls of believers, and the Church in heaven. The main ethical and spiritual effort was then focused on building up the Church, 'the temple of the Spirit', in human hearts, creating a prophetic community among them, while waiting for the heavenly Church to come. The earthly life of faith and virtue was promoted as the best way of 'doing' ecclesiology.

Conclusion

Faith in the holiness of the Church unveils a number of theological assumptions which were very important to the Patristic authors. They include the understanding of salvation, Christology and the relation between the Church and the world outside, as well as the tension between sinfulness/impurity, and blamelessness/purity. Among those assumptions, under the pressure of conflicts, debates and new catechetical needs, already known aspects of faith were proclaimed with a new strength. Some Church fathers loudly affirmed the exclusive role of the Church in salvation, apart from which there was no hope. But it must be stressed: the reflection on the nature of the Church, which shows such a passionate attachment among the Church fathers, was not an intellectual speculation but rather a multifaceted expression of their ethical, spiritual, sacramental and liturgical life.

Questions for Discussion

- Why did Patristic authors have to put so much emphasis on the 'holiness' of their Church?
- Does the holiness of the Church, in a Patristic context, 'deify' a historical, socio-political institution?
- Where is there room for the human element in the 'holiness' of the Church?
- Comment on the notion of the 'pre-existence' of the Church. Was humanity created for the Church, or the Church for humanity?
- 'There is no salvation outside of the Church.' Re-examine the value of this Patristic axiom.
- How was the holiness of the Church connected with the Christian liturgy? Was it an essential or a marginal part of it?

Further Reading

For beginners
M. Bockmuehl and M. B. Thomson, 1998, *A Vision of the Church*, Edinburgh: T&T Clark.
R. Haight, 2004, *Christian Community in History: Historical Ecclesiology*, vol.1, London and New York, Continuum.

For more advanced students
R. M. Jensen, 2008, 'Mater Ecclesia and Fons Aeterna: The Church and Her Womb in Ancient Christian Tradition', in A. J. Levine and M. M. Robins (eds), *Feminist Companion to Patristic Literature*, London and New York: T&T Clark, pp. 137–55.

On Ignatius
C. A. Hall, 2002, *Learning Theology with the Church Fathers*, Downers Grove, IL: InterVarsity Press, pp. 226–33.

On Origen
F. Ledegang, 2001, *Mysterium Ecclesiae: Images of the Church and Its Members in Origen*, Leuven: Peeters.

Internet Resources

Early Christian symbols of the Church:
   http://www.jesuswalk.com/christian-symbols/

Notes

   1 Among those authors, *Ignatius, *Irenaeus and *Cyprian were bishops; therefore their view on the Church and its ministry had a particular bias as the shepherds of the people of God. While *Tertullian was a lay person and *Origen was ordained to the priesthood.

   2 *Mag.* 3.1.

   3 *Mag.* 6.1.

   4 *Mag.* 6.1; *Tral.* 2.4.

   5 It is interesting to note the opposition between Ignatius' theology of the Church and the chronologically parallel theology of 'John's Gospel', or rather the Johannine tradition. While the Bishop of Antioch promotes the ideal of a structure centred around the most important figure, that is the elder or the bishop of the community, the Johannine ecclesiology emphasized the model of equal partnership of all disciples gathered around 'the beloved disciple'. Further, while Ignatius highlighted the central role of the Eucharist, the Johannine model stressed the non-sacrament model of ministry expressed by the symbolic action of 'washing the feet' (John 13.12–15).

   6 For example, *Phil.* 4; *Smyr.* 6.2; 8.1; 8.2.

   7 *Mag.* 6.1.

   8 *Eph.* 5.2; *Phil.* 3.2.

   9 *Eph.* 4.2.

   10 *Vis.* 1.3.4.

   11 *Vis.* 3.9.1; 3.21.1.

   12 *Vis.* 3.11.3; 3.12.3—15.4.

   13 *Man.* 4.31.1–7.

   14 *Vis.* 3.2.6.

   15 *AH* 4.26.2.

   16 *AH* 3.38.1.

   17 *AH* 3.24.1; 5.20.2.

   18 *AH* 4.33.4.

   19 *AH* 3.22.4.

   20 *Bap.* 6.

   21 *Prayer* 2.

   22 *AM* 4.40.1; and on baptism, *Bap.* 10.5–6.

23 *Mod.* 21.17.

24 *Mod.* 1.6; 5.14; 18.18.

25 For example, *PH* 20.7; 32.6; *AM* 1.21.5.

26 *Mod.* 20.2.

27 *OUCh.* 5.

28 *OM* 21.

29 *Ep.* 15.2; 43.6.

30 *Ep.* 17.1.

31 *Ep.* 73.21.

32 The controversy between Cyprian and the Bishop of Rome led to the question of the personal holiness of the minister who administers the sacrament. Later Catholic authorities attributed the correct teaching to the Bishop of Rome, against Cyprian.

33 Tertullian, *Prayer* 2 and Cyprian, *OUCh.* 6.

34 On Origen's general ecclesiological outlook, see H. Crouzel, 1989, *Origen*, trans. A. S. Worrall, San Francisco: Harper & Row.

35 See, for example, *ComEph.* 19.33–40; 30.6–13.

36 *ComSS* 2.8.3–7; *ComGMat.* 14.7.

37 *ComGMat.* 14.22.

38 *ComGMat.* 12.14.

39 *ComGMat.* 2.

40 For example, *HomNum.* 23.11.

41 *ComGMat.* 27.15.

42 Cf. Eusebius of Caesarea, *OEC* 2.5.

43 Gregory the Great, *MDJ* 18.11.18.

44 John Chrysostom, *Hom1Cor.* 32.1.

45 Cf. the acts and canons of the Council of Nicaea, such as canons 14; 15; 17 with the emphasis on the Holy Council. Then the *Letter of the Council of Nicaea to the Egyptians* 1; 11, which highlighted the holiness of the Church in Alexandria. From now on, the self-understanding of the Councils of the Great/Catholic Church was directly connected with its status of holiness.

46 Cyril of Jerusalem, *CL* 22.1–6; 23.15; 20–2; Basil of Caesarea, *Ep.* 8.4; Gregory of Nyssa, *CO* 40; Theodoret of Cyrrhus, *ComPs.* 109.

47 *Ep.* 93.2; *CG* 18.49; *Serm.* 264.5.

48 *Ep.* 98.28; *Serm.* 233.2.

49 *CG* 20.1.

50 Cf. D. G. K. Taylor, 2004, 'The Syriac Tradition', in G. R. Evans, *The First Christian Theologians*, Oxford: Blackwell Publishing, pp. 201–24. My brief account of the holiness of the Church in Syriac ecclesiology is indebted to R. Murray, 1975, *Symbols*

of Church and Kingdom: A Study in Early Syriac Tradition, Cambridge: Cambridge University Press.

51 *HN* 25.5.

52 *HV* 19.2.

53 *HN* 1.45.

54 *HP* 6.

55 *BookCT* 20.7—22.5.

56 This motif appeared first in the *Odes of Solomon*, for example 42.8–9, and in *Gnostic literature, for instance *GPh.* 65.10.15.

57 *Odes of Solomon* 11.

58 *SF* 6.315–330.

9

Forgiveness of Sins

See also chapters 2, 5, 6, 7, 8, 10, 11.

Consider this Task

Find out the Christian, modern Order of the Service of Baptism and study
its theological content (for example in *Common Worship*, 'Holy Baptism').
Set out in your own words the baptismal promises, such as 'rejecting the

devil and rebellion against God', 'renouncing the deceit', 'corruption of evil' and 'turning to Christ'.

Introduction

To many, not only modern observers, the theory of 'sin' and a fascination with repentance and forgiveness are important factors in making Christianity appear unattractive. This strong criticism highlights one important observation: it is through the Church fathers that the notion of <u>original sin</u> and sinful human nature spread widely in the late Hellenistic world.

'**Original sin**': this theory, based on a Pauline idea (Rom. 5.12–21; 1 Cor. 15.22), denoted the present condition of human nature as marked by the first sin of Adam and Eve. The original act of disobedience to God's commandment by the first couple brought on to all humanity an inclination towards evil, suffering and death. Various early Christian theologians discussed the degree of destruction of human nature or deformation of the image of God imposed on human beings in the act of creation.

The devastation of all men and women by original sin, as the Fathers claimed, called for the redemption and healing which came only in Jesus Christ. This fundamental link between sin and the Saviour, or in a larger picture, the link between the original evil act and its restitution in the climax of the history of salvation, are omnipresent in Patristic thought. But this article of faith points to yet another aspect of sin which is committed after baptism. How can sins be forgiven after baptismal purification? Should they be? Which ones? All of them, or just the less grave? Who has the authority to minister forgiveness? The current declaration seems to be a very realistic theological response to the experience of human imperfection after the initial stage of enthusiasm. As with all the previous articles, this one also steadily grew alongside the Church's more mature self-understanding and its mission to declare God's salvation open to all. Finally, it is not a coincidence that this credal article appears after the previous statements on the nature of the Church and the might of the Holy Spirit. As we shall see, these statements offer specific hope of forgiveness of sins.

Opening Question

Which of God's mighty acts in the history of salvation prefigured forgiveness of sins, and which actually forgave?

Development of the Argument

To all early Christians the act of baptism meant a new life and a new relationship with God through the Saviour Jesus Christ. In addition, in the pre-Nicene period, this total commitment may have led to persecution, suffering and even death. Therefore the conscious step to accept 'the new faith' signified a profound existential decision. The earliest documents, for example *Hermas' Shepherd*, put repentance and forgiveness at the core of the Christian life. In his view, even in the case of such a grave sin as apostasy after baptism, it is possible to do penance and return to communion with the Church, but only once.

> I said 'Sir, I would like to ask yet another question.' 'Speak on', he said. And I said, 'I have heard that some teachers believe that there is no other repentance than that which takes place, when we descended into the water and received remission of our former sins.' He answered, 'That is correct, for that is really the case. The one who has received forgiveness of sins ought not to sin any more, but to live in purity. However, as you inquire diligently into all things, I will point out this also to you, not as giving occasion for sin to those who are to believe, or have lately believed, in the Lord. For those who have just believed, and those who are to believe, have not repentance for their sins; but they have remission of their previous sins. For to those who have been called before these days, the Lord has established repentance. As the Lord knows the heart, and knows all things before they happen, he knew the weakness of people and the manifold craftiness of the devil, that he would inflict some evil on the servants of God, and treat them in a wicked way. The Lord, therefore, full of mercy, has had mercy on the work of his hand, and has set opportunity for repentance; and he has entrusted to me the authority over this repentance. Even so I have to warn you, that if anyone is tempted by the devil and sins after that great and holy

> call in which the Lord has called his people to everlasting life, he has only one opportunity to repent. But if the person should sin again, and then repent, to such a sinner his repentance will be of no use; for with difficulty will he live.' And I said, 'Sir, I believe that life has returned to me while listening carefully to your instruction; for I know that if I avoid sin in future, I shall be saved.' And he said, 'You will be saved, you and all who act in this way.'
>
> Hermas, *Man.* 4.3.1–7, trans. P. A.-S.

This 'one' chance to be readmitted to the Church may have prompted some candidates to postpone their baptism to a later phase of their lives. At the same time, a growing number of converts and catechumens from a pagan background asked the important question: what is the meaning of baptism and its 'purification'? Therefore, the issue of the pollution caused by individual sinful acts, as well as the notion of 'original sin', surfaced very early in the Patristic doctrine. In this introduction one more thought should be added. While the Patristic doctrine of sin, including original sin, as a part of Paul's theological legacy, did not change dramatically 'before' and 'after' Nicaea, the understanding of forgiveness as 'offered to all in Jesus Christ' showed a number of specific developments. Similarly, teaching related to baptism revealed various theological nuances, which Latin and Greek, Alexandrian and Antiochene, Coptic and Syriac theologians explored with great interest.

Irenaeus of Lyons: Original Sin as a Real Event

Some of the earliest evidence of the developed theory of original sin can be found in *Irenaeus of Lyons. Against his *Gnostic adversaries, who understood original sin as an allegory of a cosmological catastrophe, Irenaeus stressed the human participation in this real event, which originated human exile from God's closeness, as well as God's mercy in bringing all humanity back to the original participation in divine grace. We are by now well acquainted with his crucial theory of 'recapitulation' (see chapter 2). In Irenaeus' understanding, original sin, as an evil human act, produced the greatest act of goodness. While the sinful act committed by the first Adam created the gulf between humanity and God, the second act of 'the second Adam' (Jesus Christ) brought reconciliation. More careful insight into Irenaeus' theory reveals his specific awareness of the gravity of original sin as well as his understanding of God's forgiveness. The first sin was the archetype of all transgression because it contained at its core disobedience to God.[1] It was an evil act because it rejected the authority of God, the good Creator, and as an act it turned Adam to the devil and placed him under the dominion of Satan.[2] That disobedience brought its direct consequence: death.

> The fact that God spoke the truth, while the serpent was a liar, came out in the outcome: those who had eaten the fruit encountered death. Together with the fruit they had fallen into dominion of death as their action was the result of disobedience, so consequently that disobedience brought both of them to death.
>
> Irenaeus, *AH* 5.23.1, trans. P. A.-S.

In Irenaeus' theory, sin and death are interconnected. Therefore the whole of humanity lives in the shadow of death, certainly in suffering. However, Irenaeus' theology is quite ambiguous about the way in which original sin is inherited. Original sin, like a thorn, wounds all people. However, the gloom of the first transgression did not undermine the love and care of the good Creator. God offered forgiveness and promised salvation.[3] The first Adam responded with penitence, shame and fear. The realization of God's promise came with the second Adam, who was totally obedient to God, and who, through his own passion, death and resurrection, liberated humanity from the dominion of Satan. Irenaeus believed that Mary's purity was the source of regeneration of humanity (see chapter 3).[4] So the second Adam, born of a pure mother, was not marked by sin. However, this does not mean that his humanity was 'unreal', but only that in his nature there was no inclination to disobey his Father's will, as he was united with his divine Parent. Jesus saved all from the illness, weakness and inability to live in communion with God.[5] This new fellowship of holiness and salvation is re-established by the Saviour, but each individual must choose to accept it in the sacrament of baptism as regeneration.[6] Then each believer should take care of the new life under the guidance of the holy Church,[7] by participating in the sacraments such as the Eucharist.[8] Irenaeus' understanding of the forgiveness of sins is well integrated into the larger framework of his famous theory of salvation. It combines an original exegesis of the scriptural evidence about the dramatic events in Eden with a very positive, if not optimistic, model of correction and further perfection of all by the Saviour. Therefore forgiveness of sins is a liberating experience of baptism as well as the strong, eschatological hope which will allow participation in eternal life.

Tertullian: Original Sin – Serious Damage to the Human Condition

*Tertullian, whom we have already met on many occasions, has to answer for the very problematic legacy of his theology on this subject. His conversion from paganism to Christianity, as expressed in his treatise *On Penance*, was a step from 'darkness' to 'light', or from 'slavery to sin' to 'deliverance and forgiveness' in baptism.[9] It is quite remarkable that this document from his earlier Catholic phase already focuses on one of the most important aspects, in Tertullian's view, of Christian life. Awareness of sin in its various forms and an equally strong conviction of God's forgiveness given to people in baptism were among the most characteristic features of Tertullian's moral theology. Both sin and forgiveness drew a lot of his time and theological attention. This scrupulous interest in the nature of both appears throughout the whole of Tertullian's life and was one of the elements that led him into conflict with the Catholic doctrine and ultimately allegiance to *Montanism (see chapter 8), as a rigorist movement of early Christian puritans. His general view was that each human being is deeply marked by original sin passed from parents to their offspring. However, people are still able to make moral choices, are therefore responsible for their actions, and ultimately will be judged, punished and rewarded by God.

Turning to Tertullian's concept of original sin: in his view, it has totally changed human nature by, for example, if not destroying, seriously undermining man's rational faculty.[10] Original sin can be compared to a malicious virus which weakens the natural resistance of the soul against evil, or even, while growing, deforms the nature of human being. It originates in Adam's and Eve's sin and is transmitted in the soul, which is already contaminated with the deadly virus. As Tertullian had quite a material understanding of the human soul, the transmission and infection of original sin was direct and embraced all humanity. The essence of sin was, in Tertullian's analysis, impatience. Then it produced various evil transmutations, such as malice, murder, hate, anger and adultery. However, in another treatise, this time from his Montanist period, Tertullian named seven grave sins as the outcomes of original sin: idolatry, blasphemy, murder, adultery, rape, false witness, fraud.[11] Yet in another treatise from the same period, Tertullian suggested only three: idolatry, fornication and murder.[12] The precise number of grave sins is not the most important point. Both catalogues open with idolatry as the principal sin, which suggests that apostasy from the Christian faith in one God to the pagan worship of idols was the most serious betrayal of the baptismal oath.

However, Tertullian and many other theologians of this period faced two fundamental issues: what was the role of baptism as the first proclamation of forgiveness? And, second, in the case of post-baptismal sins, which ones can be forgiven by the Church, and which ones cannot be forgiven? For Tertullian, in the later stage of his life, the Church did not have authority to forgive the most serious transgressions after the first penitence and baptism.

> I know of a certain edict issued recently which claims even the highest ecclesiastical authority. The Pontiff that is the bishop of bishops has declared: 'I remit the sins both of adultery and of fornication, for this individual has done penance.' Oh, dear edict of which it is impossible to say 'a good deed'!
>
> Tertullian, *Mod.* 1.6, trans. P. A.-S.

According to the teaching in the treatise written in his Montanist period against *Marcion, Tertullian reaffirms the Catholic view that one of the four gifts of grace given to the baptized person is the forgiveness of sins. The other three gifts are deliverance from death, spiritual regeneration and the bestowal of the Holy Spirit.[13] Baptism is thus a perfect remedy for the illness caused by original sin and its transmutations; it washes sins away.[14] But some people then re-offend and commit the same or new sins. Tertullian, the Montanist, remained unconvinced by any arguments about the Church's authority to proclaim forgiveness in the case of such grave sins as adultery and fornication.[15] Furthermore, he not only attacked his Catholic bishop and fellow-theologians on this matter, but also part of the tradition of the Church, which treated with respect the idea of further forgiveness taken from Hermas' *Shepherd*.[16] For Tertullian, forgiveness of the gravest sins was beyond the Church's power and mission. Pastorally, it was confusing and erroneous because it gave a false hope. At this radical stage, post-baptismal forgiveness of sins, from being a purely theological notion became, for Tertullian, very ecclesiological and political. The Church, the one declared by Tertullian, by now a Montanist, was the spotless Bride of Christ. It therefore could not contain any pollution caused by the most evil acts of those who believed in 'the second chance'. Logic, coherence and moral perfection fused at this point with Tertullian's theory of salvation and the Church. That fusion, as a legacy, left its mark on many Christian theologians in centuries to come.

Cyprian of Carthage: Conditions of Forgiveness

We have already encountered the serious dilemmas faced by *Cyprian of Carthage about the proclamation of reconciliation with the Church after Decius' persecution (250 CE). The public apostasy of some Christians and the act of offering a pagan sacrifice (idolatry) – which included not only burning incense to a god or gods, but also roasting of meat, saying prayers and taking part in a banquet after the service – were the most outrageous disloyalty to the Christian faith, in the eyes of the Church fathers. Cyprian's homily, *On the Lapsed*, provides us with evidence of similar practices, while it debates the crucial question about the nature of the forgiveness of sins. The Bishop of Carthage, although a disciple of Tertullian, argued for proper ways of reuniting lapsed Christians with the Church, and therefore for a second chance to be given to sinners. Forgiveness can be offered when the appropriate penance has been applied, and transgressors can enter again on board the ship that is the holy Church. While forgiveness is given to adult offenders, Cyprian also called for the baptism of infants, in order to wash away original sin.

> However, if in the case of the worst sinners and of those who sinned much against God, when afterwards they believe, the remission of their sins is granted and no one is prevented from baptism and grace, how much more, then, should an infant not be prohibited, who having been born recently, has not committed sin, except that, born of the flesh according to Adam, he has contracted the corruption of that old death from his first birth [that is sharing the nature of Adam – P. A.-S.]? For this very reason he approaches more easily to receive the remission of sins because the sins forgiven him are not his own but those of another.
>
> Cyprian, *Ep.* 64.5, trans. P. A.-S.

It is evident from Cyprian's argument that he believed that original sin is transferred from parents to children and has to be remitted by baptism.

Origen: Multiple Ways of Cleansing

*Origen, although in a different theological context from Irenaeus, Tertullian and Cyprian, confirmed the 'apostolic' tradition of teaching that original sin is washed away by baptism and the Spirit.[17] But he also developed an original theory of seven ways of forgiveness of sins.

> As you have heard how many sacrifices for sin there were in the Law; now hear how many remissions of sins are in the Gospel. First remission comes with baptism as we are baptized 'for the forgiveness of sins' [Mark 1.4]. A second remission comes with the suffering of martyrdom. Third is that which is given because of almsgiving [Luke 11.41]. [. . .] Fourth remission is obtained when we forgive our brothers their sins [Matt. 6.14]. [. . .] Fifth remission is given when 'someone converts a sinner from the error of his way' [1 Peter 4.8]. [. . .] There is also a sixth remission of sins, through an abundance of charity [Luke 7.47]. [. . .] In addition, there is also a seventh remission achieved by penance, although it is hard and laborious, when the

> sinner washes 'his pillow in tears' [Ps. 6.7], when his tears become his bread 'day and night' [Ps. 41.4], when he is not ashamed to declare his sin to a priest of the Lord [Ps. 31.5].
>
> Origen, *HomLev.* 2.4.5, trans. P. A.-S.

In the context of the various forms of sacrifice prescribed by the book of Leviticus, Origen proposes a number of penitential acts which bring effective remittance. Some of them are public, others more private. But as highlighted by the case of the declaration of sins to a presbyter, forgiveness of sins is related to the Church community and takes place within the ecclesiological context; that is, it is not 'a private matter' between the sinner and God. This 'social' reference was important not only to Origen. One brief note is appropriate here. Among Origen's recommendation of seven means, there is one which recalls the scriptural notion of forgiving our brothers their sins against us. This attitude, mentioned for the first time in the present chapter, will be explored further by later monastic literature; life in a community of monks provides plenty of opportunity to practise this specific way of forgiveness.

Athanasius of Alexandria: The Darkness of Sin Illuminated by the Light of the Divine Redeemer

Post-Nicene theology brought a number of important elucidations in the Catholic understanding of the forgiveness of sins. These further explorations grew up alongside the greater awareness of Christology, the theory of salvation, and the nature of the Church, its ministry and the sacraments. *Athanasius of Alexandria, the great champion of orthodoxy, provides us with a good example of strong and positive theological belief in forgiveness of sins. At the centre of this belief is his Christology. The original history of humanity shows the dramatic and deteriorating fall into sin, corruption and death.[18] But despite that tragedy, the incarnation of the Logos has changed everything. Taking on 'flesh', which experienced sin, death and corruptibility, the Son of God not only ameliorated the weakness of the bodily element, but directed it towards the divine. The Saviour's act of ascension reaffirmed the value of the human body. Corrupt human nature was 're-created' by the Logos' resurrection and then clothed with incorruptibility. On the basis of Christology, forgiveness of sin is thus not only real and efficient in baptism, but also a strong eschatological anticipation because all will be subordinated to the Saviour, covered with his glory and ultimately transformed into the state of perfection. Liberation from death and sin, which has already begun with Christ's resurrection/ascension, will be fulfilled in deification of the body and the soul. That transformation will allow 'pure' but 'in body' human beings to participate in God's holiness.

Cyril of Alexandria: Liberation from Corruption

Many of these motifs were further clarified by *Cyril of Alexandria, for whom Christ's incarnation liberated human flesh from corruption. The crucial event in the history of salvation, related to Christ's incarnation, offered to all believers a new status of adopted children,[19] which is a result of purification by the Holy Spirit. This new position and dignity includes a brave hope that human sins have been forgiven and is fully expressed by participation in the Eucharist. Already baptism restored in Christians the divine image, deformed and overshadowed by sin, but in the current daily life it is through the Eucharist that human beings are restored to incorruption.[20]

Theodore of Mopsuestia: The Human Condition Purified by the Sacraments

For the Antiochene school, belief in forgiveness of sins was related to more 'existential', direct experience of sins committed after baptism. *Theodore of Mopsuestia assumed the presence of sins in daily life, but he suggested that the remedy lay in prayer, repentance and, again, in the spiritual purifying power of the Eucharist.

[If we have committed a sin], the Body and Blood of our Lord [. . .] will give us strength. If we have committed some wrong acts involuntarily, and they appeared against our will having its origin in the frailty of our human condition or when we have fallen against our wish and because of those transgression we feel remorse and then we prayed to God with the spirit of repentance for our sins [. . .] certainly we will receive the grace of forgiveness for our sins by receiving the Holy Sacrament.

Theodore of Mopsuestia, *CH* 16, trans. P. A.-S.

He believed in and recommended the 'medicine of penitence', which renovates the strength of the human spirit and commitment to God. In Theodore's approach there is a real effort and concern to reconcile the sinner with God before his or her death, because the Church was commonly understood to be the exclusive way to salvation. Theodore, like many other fathers, emphasized free will, which either allows the commission of sins, or brings even more personal, freely accepted attachment to God and salvation. This element of realistic self-assessment as well as devotional loyalty to God, including confession of sins and trust in their forgiveness, also appeared in *John Chrysostom's instructions.

Not only is it wonderful that He forgives us our sins, but also that He neither uncovers them nor does he make them stand forth clearly revealed. Nor does he force us to come forward and publicly proclaim our misdeeds, but He bids us to make our defence to Him alone and to confess our sins to Him. [. . .] God forgives our sins and does not force us to make a parade of them in the presence of others. He seeks one thing only: that he who benefits by the forgiveness may learn the greatness of the gift.

John Chrysostom, *BI* 12.36, trans. P. W. Harkins

Augustine of Hippo versus Pelagius: the Central Theological Battle

*Augustine of Hippo's contribution to the Christian notion of original sin and the efficacy of forgiveness in baptism established yet another theological milestone. In relation to our theme, Augustine's polemic against *Pelagius, an ascetic monk, articulated the essential understanding of original sin as well as God's merciful forgiveness. Augustine's dramatic personal life and experience of God deeply shaped his theology. He stressed total dependence on and surrender to God, and he encouraged Christians to put their trust in a forgiving Father and divine grace. This view contrasted with Pelagius' opinion, which promoted human confidence, moral effort and self-reliance and which opposed the laxity common among Christians. To Pelagius, who arrived in Rome with a wave of refugees around 410 CE, contact with the Christian community of the city was a rather shocking experience. In the heart of the Christian Empire, at least around the Holy See of Peter and Paul, Pelagius found Christians, neither 'hot or cold', showing signs of decadence and pessimism as their world was about to be changed by the approaching wave of barbarian armies. For them the current world looked temporary, unstable and almost apocalyptic. Among Roman Christians, many excused their sinful behaviour because they believed in 'a defect in human nature itself'; some Christian form of determinism and false idea of God's commandment. At the centre of that was the idea of original sin, which in Pelagius' view excused Christians from responsibility for their moral acts and placed the blame on Adam. Therefore, in order to restore the original Christian zeal, Pelagius presented his own interpretation of Adam's sin. Pelagius and his supporters, such as Celestius, presented their 'reformed' version of Christian morals, which can be summed up as a correct understanding of human nature and achievement of salvation. Unlike the common views on original sin, which 'marked' all humanity, Pelagius and his followers stated that Adam's sin was only 'a bad example' of disobedience. There is no excuse for magnifying its role, and baptism does not 'clean' us from any 'stain'. Attaching forgiveness to the baptismal act is an abuse of the idea of God, as the newborn baby has not committed any atrocious act which calls for mercy. As 'an example', original sin was not transferable to later generations of human beings, as some believed; furthermore, basic human nature is strong enough to perform virtuous actions. To Pelagius' ears, the baptismal terminology such as 'remission of sins' together with slogans such as 'trust in God's grace' sounded rather like apologetic excuses used by lazy preachers. A human being is born, in Pelagius' view, as a clean slate, and all that happens is an outcome of his and her free will and moral action.

> [Pelagius claims – P. A.-S.], that 'all good and evil acts on the basis of which we are either praised or blamed, are done by us and are not born with us. We are not born in our full potential, but with ability to commit good and evil action. We are born without virtue in the same way as without fault.'
>
> Augustine, *Grace* Ch. 14, trans. P. A.-S.

The response from the Church came immediately, as those innovative views not only undermined the commonly accepted teaching on original sin, baptism and forgiveness, but also challenged the role of sacraments and the understanding of salvation. Augustine's reply to the Pelagian challenge took him a number of years (412–30 CE) and a great deal of literary effort. One of his earliest works against Pelagius, *On Forgiveness of Sins and on the Merits of Infant Baptism*, aimed to clarify what, in his view, Pelagius had misunderstood. Augustine reaffirmed what he believed to be the Catholic and apostolic teaching[21] on original sin, its effects including death and the vital role of child baptism.[22] In another work, Augustine magnified Christ's salvation as the divine response to Adam's sin and justification of all in Christ. He encouraged his readers to put their trust in God's grace, Christ's redemption and liberation from sin.[23] Christ is the Mediator of the salvation given to all believers. Consequently, apart from Christ, there is no hope either in another 'mediator' or even in a human's own assumed potential to be reconciled with God on the basis of the goodness of their nature and the strength of their natural skills.[24] The clash between Augustine and Pelagius was not a simple confrontation between pessimistic and optimistic assessments of the human condition; rather at its centre was the value of self-confidence in the quest for salvation. Sin and forgiveness were a crucial part of that conflict of exegesis and anthropologies. Augustine's effort was accepted by the Church and conquered the imagination of many Christians in his generation and in generations to come. As for Pelagius and his followers, the

Synod of Carthage (418) condemned six so-called 'Pelagian' statements, rather than Pelagius' own view.

Anyone who denies that newborn infants are to be baptized or who says that they are baptized for the remission of sins but do not bear anything of the original sin of Adam which is expiated by the washing of regeneration, so that as a consequence the form of baptism 'for the remission of sins' is understood to be not true but false in their case – let him be anathema.

Synod of Carthage (418), Canon 2, trans. J. Pelikan

This was only one among many public condemnations of the Pelagian heresy and declaration of the doctrine of original sin.[25]

Struggle against Sin and the Devil: Early Christian Monasticism

In this context it is important to note briefly the eruption of the monastic movement with countless male and female hermits, monks, nuns and various charismatic leaders who searched for Christian perfection. Those passionate men and women put awareness of sinful nature, penitence and hope for forgiveness at the centre of their ascetic life. As the Church of the Empire became increasingly a conventional institution, a number of Christians wished to return to the 'original zeal' of the apostles, martyrs and confessors.[26] The post-baptismal struggle against the Devil and sin soon became expanded in a new kind of literature which encouraged the ascetic life. Athanasius of Alexandria's hagiographical work on the life of Saint Anthony provided a matrix of a heroic effort to struggle with temptations based on trust in God's grace or even becoming a second Christ, by a rigorous life of penitence, renunciation and self-discipline.[27] This paradigm found its various versions in emerging monastic communities and literature as the new category of Christian authorities, the so-called 'Desert Fathers', provided countless examples of penitence for sins as well as enhanced faith in the crucial value of forgiveness of sins of the brothers as an expression of God's act of mercy to the monk/nun/sinner.

Once there was a meeting of monks in Scetis, and they discussed the case of a guilty brother but Pior said nothing. Afterwards he got up and went out, took a sack, filled it with sand, and carried it on his shoulders. He put a little sand in a basket and carried it in front of him. The monks asked him, 'What are you doing?' He answered, 'The sack with a lot of sand is my sins; they are many, so I put them on my back and then I shall not weep for them. The basket with a little sand is the sins of our brother and they are in front of me, and I see them and judge them. This is not right. I ought to have my own sins in front of me, and think of them, and ask God to forgive me.' When the monks heard this, they said, 'This is the true way of salvation.'

The Desert Fathers, trans. B. Ward

The Coptic Tradition

Among the Coptic documents from the Patristic period, one author, *Shenoute of Atripe (fifth century CE), delivers a great deal of material on the understanding of sins and the value of repentance and forgiveness. This theme appears in the context already discussed, namely, the purifying power of sacraments, including the Eucharist.[28] But also, in the monastic milieu, unceasing prayer asking for the forgiveness of sins (later known as the 'Jesus prayer') helped to create an even greater awareness of the grace contained in the sacraments such as the Eucharist. The Coptic sources constructed the ideal of monastic life, which imitated the angels in heaven and their innocent, sinless existence. As in other monastic traditions, in the Coptic narratives the monks are portrayed as the 'angels' on earth whose lives are focused on glorification of the Lord. This image echoes Jewish and Christian apocalyptic[29] and the later Christian ideal of life,[30] namely, that the righteous, whose sins have been forgiven, are assimilated to the angels who participate in God's glory and, although still on earth, worship the Almighty Creator and his Messenger. But this highly ambitious purpose did not mean an idyllic serenity of life. On the contrary, it was a rigorous daily struggle to keep bodies and souls 'clean' from any form of pollution as well as an ability to forgive the sins of the fellow-monks on many occasions. In this context, forgiveness of sins emerges not as a straightforward, easygoing practice, but rather as the ultimate reward after severe, long and unceasing penitence.

Syriac Tradition

The Syriac authors and documents, such as Ephrem the Syrian, *Aphrahat and *The Book of Steps*, highlighted again the reality of original sin[31] as well as the value of the sacrament of baptism since it allows the Holy Spirit to indwell the newborn Christian.[32] Aphrahat accepted that later transgressions can be forgiven within the frame of penance and on an even larger canvas, in relation to the Catholic/Universal Church, who received this authority from Christ. Ephrem's polemic against his theological adversaries, such as the *Manichaeans, stressed the correct authority of proclamation of the forgiveness of the sins.[33] The characteristic call coming from those sources addressed both sides: the sinners, or 'the wounded', and the people in authority, or 'the physicians' who have the power to heal.[34] To receive the 'wounds' means, in the ascetic framework of these narratives, the outcome of spiritual warfare, falling into sin as a result of demonic temptation, to show weakness. But human vulnerability calls for the remedy: God's healing and the remission of sins. Aphrahat's theology, as far as we can reconstruct its main characteristics, encourages people to take the opportunity of repentance and reconciliation with God by the means given to the Church. However, he seems to be quite certain that if people die without reconciliation, their fate is tragic and reminds us of the suffering of the rich man from the Gospel story (Luke 16.26).[35] *The Book of Steps* locates the forgiveness of sins as one of the tasks for the 'Perfect', who aim to follow Jesus' commandment and search for ultimate closeness to God.[36] In these Syriac sources, the proclamation of the forgiveness of sins has two aspects: it is strongly recommended in daily life when Christians encounter the sins of others, and it is related to the ministry of the Church, as well as the power of the Spirit. First, it is the divine Spirit who cleans the soul, and remission of sins is given at the baptism. Second, as a member of the ecclesiastical community, the sinner can receive absolution, after appropriate penance, from the 'superiors', who have the promised authority to forgive the sin and reunite the offender with fellow-Christians as well as with God.

Conclusion

Forgiveness of sin was, for Patristic theology, one of the greatest gifts of the Saviour to his Church. This appraisal was based on a strongly pro-orthodox Christological and ecclesiological premise, when through Christ's incarnation and the authority given to the Church, as an extension of Christ's mystical body, forgiveness was ministered to the whole community of believers. But this positive catechesis also had its controversial aspect: ubiquitous, profound awareness of original sin and its consequences. Therefore the sacrament of baptism became the principal means of restoring the purity of the divine image in the baptized. Later sins, except the most serious offences such as adultery and heresy, were understood by the majority of the authors to be within the range of forgiveness. This credal article reminded ancient Christians about both opportunities: about the transforming power of baptism, as well as about the strength of their hope – as long as they repent, God's mercy will be declared to them.

Questions for Discussion

- Which among the ancient documents quoted do you find closest to your understanding of forgiveness of sin? Explain your choice.
- Reflect upon the place of this article in the structure of the Creeds and explain its position as well as its relation to the previous and following articles.
- If baptism in Patristic interpretation did play the pivotal role in purifying the soul from original sin, why was the same soul still vulnerable to transgressions?
- Which among the ancient authors explain the theory of original sin in the most comprehensive way?
- Among the Church fathers, Augustine of Hippo had the greatest impact on the Catholic doctrine of original sin. Why did this theologian put such a strong emphasis on the value of God's grace in Christian life?

Further Reading

For beginners
P. C. Finney, D. Scholer and E. Ferguson (eds), 1993, *Studies in Early Christianity: Doctrine of Human Nature, Sin and Salvation in the Early Church*, vol. 10, New York and London: Routledge.

On Augustine
P. Rigby, 1999, 'Original sin', in A. D. Fitzgerald (ed.), *Augustine through the Ages*, Grand Rapids, MI: Eerdmans.

For more advanced students
E. Ferguson (2007), *Baptism in the Early Church: History, Theology and Liturgy in the First Five Centuries*, Grand Rapids, MI: Eerdmans.

On Monasticism
D. Brakke, 2006, *Demons and the Making of the Monk: Spiritual Combat in early Christianity*, Cambridge, MA and London: Harvard University Press.
R. Krawiec, 2002, *Shenoute and the Women in the White Monastery: Egyptian Monasticism in Late Antiquity*, New York: Oxford University Press.
C. T. Shroeder, 2007, *Monastic Bodies: Discipline and Salvation in Shenoute of Atripe*, Philadelphia: University of Pennsylvania Press.

Internet Resources

Baptism in Early Church: the patristic documents and recent studies
http://www.earlychurch.org.uk/baptism.php
Sin in the early Church: some patristic documents and recent studies
http://www.earlychurch.org.uk/sin.php
Adam and Eve in early Christian art (the sarcophagus from the fourth century CE)
http://www.kean.edu/~jtuerk/images/4_Byzantine/01_EChSalvationalImagery/21.jpg

Notes

1 *AH* 4.39.1.
2 *AH* 5.21.1.
3 *AH* 5.21.3.
4 *AH* 4.33.11.

5 *AH* 3.18.7.

6 *AH* 3.17.1.

7 *AH* 1.10.2; 3.24.1; 4.13.2.

8 *AH* 3.17.3.

9 *Pen.* 1.1.

10 *AM* 5.5.4–6.

11 *AM* 4.9.6.

12 *Mod.* 5.

13 *AM* 1.28.2.

14 *Bap.* 8.1.

15 *Mod.* 4.

16 *Mod.* 10.

17 For example, *ComGLk* 14.5.

18 *AHeathen* 8.

19 *ExGJ* 1.9.

20 *ExGJ* 6.3.

21 For example, *AJ* 2.10.33.

22 *For.* 2.27.43.

23 On Paul's influence of Augustine's thought on the role of grace, see for example *Conf.* 7.5.10–11.

24 *GraceCh.* 2.24.28.

25 Pelagian theology was condemned by the Synod of Diospolis, in Palestine (415); the Synods at Carthage and Milevis (416); again by the Synod at Carthage (418); the Ecumenical Council of Ephesus (431), and the Second Synod of Orange (529).

26 Because the literature on the origin of Western and Eastern monasticism is vast, I would recommend for a less advanced reader, G. Clark, 2004, 'Body and Soul', in *Christianity and the Roman Society*, Cambridge: Cambridge University Press, pp. 60–77 with bibliographical references.

27 More in T. G. Weinandy, 2007, 'Anthony the Perfect Image of Christ', in his *Athanasius: A Theological Introduction*, Aldershot: Ashgate, pp. 129–32.

28 *IAA* 354–55.

29 For example, *2 Enoch* 22.10; *AI* 9.10.

30 For example, Clement of Alexandria, *Strom.* 6.105.1; 7.78.6; 84.2.

31 Ephrem, *Hymns* 4.1, Aphrahat, *Tr.* 6.14; 23.3.

32 Aphrahat, *Tr.* 6.14; 12.6.

33 *HaH* 2.3.

34 For example, *Tr.* 7.3.

35 *Tr.* 20.12.

36 *BS* 2.2.

10

Resurrection of the Body

See also chapters 2, 5, 6, 7, 8, 11.

Consider this Task

Read carefully the story of Lazarus' resurrection (John 11.1–44). What are the similarities between Lazarus' and Jesus' resurrections? What are their greatest differences?

Introduction

Faith in resurrection of the body implied a belief in resurrection of the dead. At the same time it clarified the condition of the deceased. They were not 'ghosts' but rather human beings in transformed 'form'. To many ancient philosophers, intellectuals and critics this belief was yet another example of Christian naivety, as if flesh had a value in the immaterial, perfect and eternal world which awaits all people. Still, the bold and public proclamation of this article of faith was rooted in the previous, fundamental assumption that Jesus rose in his body (see chapter 6), not just in his soul. Although centuries passed in the Patristic period, the same credal belief remained unchanged and became, for the later Church fathers also, a crucial part of Christian doctrine. However, later interpretations of this belief explored different aspects of its content, as the theological and pedagogical interest of the Church responded to the new imagery, inquisitiveness and expectation of fellow-believers.

Opening Question

What is new and different in the Christian idea of the resurrection of the dead in comparison with Greek mythological representations of life after death?

Development of the Argument

Belief in life after death was commonly accepted by early Christians of all tendencies, as the Saviour not only promised life after death, but he himself returned to the eternal kingdom. It is thus not surprising that the most ancient Creeds contained this belief and that the whole confession of faith concluded with it. Christian eschatology declared the universal resurrection of the dead, not only the resurrection of Christians.

Eschatology (Gr. *ta eschata* – 'the last things'): the part of theology that reflects upon the final stage of history: the second coming of Christ, the final judgement and either eternal life or condemnation.

Moreover, that final event will include, according to the emerging Catholic doctrine, human bodies, not just souls. Christ's resurrection was here a paradigm. This belief, either in relation to Christ's new life or to the destiny of all humanity, sounded, as we know from the reaction of a pagan philosopher, Celsus, unbelievable.[1] It does not look as if this article was formulated to attract Jews and pagans to Christianity; rather its role was to reaffirm the specific hope of those who were already convinced that Jesus was the Saviour, that he rose from the dead and would return to take the righteous to his kingdom. One of the earliest interpretations of the resurrection of the body can be found in the so-called *Letter of Romans to the Corinthians*, where Christian faith in the ultimate restoration of the unity between the soul and the body is painted with characters borrowed from pagan mythology.

Let's see that wonderful sign which is noted in Eastern regions, around Arabia. There is a certain bird named 'Phoenix'. This unique bird lives five hundred years. When the time of its termination and death comes, it builds itself a nest of frankincense, and myrrh, and other spices, into which, when the time is completed, it enters and dies. But as the flesh decays a certain kind of worm is born, which is fed by the juices of the dead bird, and grows wings. Then, as it gains some strength, it takes up that nest with the bones of its parent, and carrying them away, travels from Arabia to Egypt, to the city called Heliopolis. In this place, in open day in the presence of all, it flies to the altar of sin, where it leaves the bones. Having done this, it returns to its original place. The priests then examine the registers of dates, and conclude that the bird returned exactly in the five hundredth year. Can we, then, not believe that it is a truly great and wonderful thing that the Creator of all things will bring about the resurrection of those who have served him in holiness, in the assurance of good faith, when he shows – through the story of a bird – the wonder of his promise? For he says in a certain place: 'You shall raise me up, and I will praise you' [Ps. 27.7] and again, 'I lay down, and slept; I rose up, for you are with me' [Ps. 3.5]; and again, Job says, 'You shall raise up my flesh, which has suffered all these things' [Job 19.26].'

1 Clement 25.1—26.3, trans. P. A.-S.

As we can see from that imaginative picture, ancient myth and wisdom has been assimilated into the frame of the Christian hope. As such, it inspired the vision of the eschatological event among those who were already baptized, but it also served as an illustration in order to explain the belief to outsiders.

Athenagoras of Athens: The Impossible which is Possible

One of the earliest documents which dealt with explanation of the faith in physical resurrection of the dead is *Athenagoras' treatise[2] On the Resurrection. This was dedicated to those who had heard of the bizarre Christian idea and rejected it. It is plausible that Athenagoras the philosopher aimed to argue the rationality of this belief against some Christians with a dualistic tendency. The main argument of the narrative begins with a reaffirmation of the unquestionable might of God, on which subject Athenagoras' opponents seemed to agree with him; from the premise of unlimited divine might he concludes that raising the dead is not beyond the divine power.[3] God's will is thus able, in his view, to call all the dead back to life.[4] Next he turns towards the aim of resurrection, and again he provides logical argumentation, which may be sketched as follows: resurrection, which includes bodies, confirms the human destiny to live in union with the flesh, as that union of soul/mind and body has to face the final judgement which is a part of God's governance, his providence over his creatures.[5] Within that rhetorically well-structured framework, Athenagoras provides a number of proofs to support the idea of resurrection. They are based on:

1 the purpose of creating human beings for eternal life;
2 the nature of human beings, who are made up of body and soul, therefore both elements must survive physical death;
3 God's justice, since everyone will face judgement and the consequences of good and evil actions;
4 the aim of human life, which is directed towards the contemplation of God.

Athenagoras is convinced that by the very fact of being created by God, men and women cannot 'simply' die and be annihilated. People will continue their existence when God's might brings them back to life. This conviction includes the human body, which is not alien to the human soul, but rather a companion in their temporary life here and, as such, will be present at the resurrection and after it. This controversial point leads Athenagoras to consider the potential 'chain of consumption': human remains are eaten by animals, which in turn are consumed by other beasts of prey, but this natural process still does not and will not limit God's power to raise human beings with their bodies.[6] Athenagoras' treatise holds a very important place among the early apologists of this doctrine, as his mature reflection affirms the essential intuition that fulfilment of human life in the world to come cannot happen without the flesh. The body, however, will be transformed into a new reality, since communion with God does not need any material element.

Irenaeus of Lyons: Resurrection and its Place in the History of Salvation

As we might expect, the same line of polemic against some dualistic, possibly Gnostic theologies is also found in *Irenaeus of Lyons' account of heresies. But Irenaeus incorporated the whole idea of the resurrection of the body into his great theory, adding some details, which from the perspective of later, post-Nicene doctrine, sounded problematic.[7] First, within the acceptable part of Irenaeus' interpretation, bodily resurrection was certain and welcome.[8] It accomplished God's plan of salvation open to all humanity, not just the elite, and included the flesh, not exclusively the immaterial soul. In the spectacular panorama of the last events painted by Irenaeus, Christ, 'the second Adam', will accomplish in flesh what the first man destroyed. The salvation of humankind, which was inaugurated in Christ's incarnation, in the resurrection of the flesh will reach its climax.

> Consequently, those people [Irenaeus' adversaries – P. A.-S.] undermine the power of God, and do not consider what the Logos declares, when they overemphasize the weakness of the flesh, but do not take into consideration the power of God who raises it up from the dead.

For if God is not able to raise to life what was mortal, and if he does not have power to change what was corruptible into incorruption, then he is not Almighty. But the fact that God is powerful in all these aspects we can conclude from our own creation, when God took dust from the earth and created the first people. It was much more difficult and incredible to create from non-existent bones, and nerves, and veins, and the rest of the human organism, which later became part of the human being, and to shape first man and woman, as animated and rational creatures, than it was to reintegrate again what had been previously created and then afterwards decomposed into earth [for the reasons already mentioned]. [. . .] For the One who in the beginning caused the first human being to have existence out of non-existence as it pleased the Creator, will much more call to life again those people who had a former existence, when the Creator's will decides as they [may receive] the life now again offered to them. So the flesh also will be found fit for and capable of receiving the power of God, which at the beginning received the skilful touches of God.

Irenaeus of Lyons, *AH* 5.3.2, trans. P. A.-S.

The ultimate restoration cannot take place without flesh as human existence from its beginning in the Paradise was connected with the body. Briefly, what came from God as his good creation has to return to its Creator at the last day. Adam and Eve were created with their bodies, therefore they and their 'offspring' will go back to God as complete human beings with the corporeal element. Irenaeus highlights what, in his view, his Gnostic opponents misunderstood or even deformed in their perverse teaching. In order to make his claim even more convincing, if not natural, Irenaeus saw a prefiguration of that eschatological event in the agricultural process of growth, where a grain of wheat first dies, then appears to our eyes in a new form, but still with the same, original essence.[9] Death, what we would call 'biological death', is not the ultimate event in human existence, and again, Christ's paradigm as well as his real victory over death's dominion will restore life to all human beings.[10] As if the natural order of visible things were not sufficiently convincing, Irenaeus also refers to the well-known scriptural stories of Elijah, Enoch, Jonah and the three Jewish young men (Dan. 3.1–30), who all survived death and reappeared in the body.[11] To Irenaeus, against his Gnostic adversaries, human flesh will certainly rise and glorify its good Creator.

Tertullian: Reassurance of Resurrection

In his *Montanist phase, Tertullian composed another important treatise, the title of which unveils its content: *On the Resurrection*. But a more careful look into Tertullian's work reveals that its author was still close to his earlier Catholic phase. First, in the larger context of Tertullian's eschatology, the return of the Saviour, as a paradigm of Christian faith,[12] will bring an end to this world and its institutions.[13] The ending of the visible world announces the beginning of another world: the true kingdom of God, which starts with the resurrection of the body. In his treatise *On the Resurrection*, Tertullian revealed his exegetical skills, as he elaborated the crucial theme in many, rather imaginative ways. All of them highlighted his anti-dualistic convictions and presented the human body with dignity, respect and due appropriate admiration.[14] Referring to the Apostle Paul's teaching (2 Cor. 5.1), Tertullian found an analogy between the material tabernacle[15] and the human body: both contained the spiritual element. As people live in their bodies, and Christians are baptized/sanctified in their flesh, the body is the 'tabernacle' in which the soul resides.

> And now that the flesh is protected by warrants strong enough to es-
> tablish its claim to be worthy of salvation, must we not also reckon
> up the power, the authority, the liberty of action of God himself, asking
> whether he is not great enough to be competent to rebuild and restore
> the tabernacle of the flesh after it has fallen down or been swallowed
> up or in whatsoever manner been dismantled?
>
> Tertullian, *OR* 11, trans. E. Evans

Therefore this 'tabernacle' will be restored to its true and original glory at the end of time. Christ's second coming brings a new breath which will penetrate all that is dead and, as in the prophetic image from the prophet Ezekiel (37.1–14), the dry bones will be revitalized.[16] The eschatological 'spring', this time with reference to Isaiah (66.4), heralds a new, eternal season where bodies will flourish 'like grass'.[17] Moving towards Paul's direct message on the resurrection of the dead (1 Cor. 15.35), Tertullian shared with his readers the belief that the mythological figure of the Phoenix signified this Christian hope.[18] The use of this poetic symbol to communicate the mystery of resurrection directed the imagination of the readers to that ultimate event, confident of its realization. Yet Tertullian uses this opportunity to put the emphasis on his belief that this end will not be only a spectacular closure of the world. He also proclaims that the last judgement will be a crucial part of the eschatological state of affairs. After the resurrection of the body, everyone will be judged and face either punishment or glory for all his or her works. God's justice and goodness will be revealed at this event,[19] and it is this judgement which is the true reason for necessary universal resurrection.[20] Like Irenaeus of Lyons, Tertullian too believes in Christ's thousand-year reign on earth with the saints.[21] Montanism, with its strong emphasis on spiritual gifts and surrender to the power of the Holy Spirit, gave hope of a new period of time on earth with the Lord. Finally, after the blessed period of the millennium, this world will be burnt down, as the Stoics predicted; however, not annihilated, but again transformed into a spiritual substance as part of the kingdom of God. Then, eternal life shall begin (see chapter 11). It is quite clear that Tertullian's strong anti-Gnostic stance inspired him to acclaim the value of the flesh right up to the last phase of history. While his Catholic past located the whole event within the frame of scriptural hope, Montanist enthusiasm magnified the penetration of the visible, redeemed reality by the presence of Spirit, who shall make everything 'new'. That will include the body and the heaven.

The three theologians quoted so far have unanimously rejected the dualistic interpretation of the resurrection of the body. Therefore, before we go further towards the post-Nicene catechesis on this article of faith, we shall look briefly at *Gnosticism.

Gnostic Alternative Views on Resurrection

Paradoxically, with the Gnostic Christians, the case was much more complicated than that presented by the representatives of the Great Church. Since 'Gnosticism' was a multifaceted phenomenon, there were groups who believed only in the resurrection of the spiritual element, either the soul or the divine 'spark' in it, but equally, there were others with views quite similar to the Catholics.[22] As Irenaeus and Tertullian seem to point to the *Valentinian school, we can mention just one document, which represents this tradition: the *Gospel of Philip*. This narrative, which elaborates the theme of resurrection in reference to Paul's teaching that 'flesh shall not inherit the kingdom of God' (1 Cor. 15.50), demonstrates that earthly, material flesh cannot enter into the spiritual. However, if 'the body' is nourished by the Saviour by, for instance, his teaching, then it will access the divine realm.

> Some are afraid lest they rise naked. Because of this they wish to rise in the flesh, and they do not know that it is those who wear the flesh who are naked. It is those who [. . .] to unclothe themselves who are not naked. 'Flesh and blood shall not inherit the kingdom of God' [1 Cor. 15.50]. What is this which will not inherit? This which is on us. But what is this, too, which will inherit? It is that which belongs to Jesus and his blood. Because of this he said, 'He who shall not eat my flesh and drink my blood has not life in him' [John 6.53]. What is it? His flesh is the word, and his blood is the Holy Spirit. He who has received these has food and he has drink and clothing. I find fault with the others who say that it will not rise. Then both of them are at fault. You say that the flesh will not rise. But tell me what will rise, that we may honor you. You say the Spirit in the flesh, and it is also this light in the flesh. [But] this too is a matter which is in the flesh, for whatever you shall say, you say nothing outside the flesh. It is necessary to rise in this flesh, since everything exists in it. In this world, those who put on garments are better than the garments. In the Kingdom of Heaven, the garments are better than those that put them on.
>
> GPh. 56.30—57.20, trans. W. W. Isenberg

It is the Christian Gnostic soul 'clothed in' the spiritual/sacramental body that will be raised and then ascend to heaven. This rather sophisticated concept of the resurrection of the body was not easily understood by the theologians of the Great Church, some of whom resorted to mockery as the only way of dealing with its intellectual complexity.[23] Still, this brief reference to the complexity of Gnostic thought shows that those Christians also believed strongly in life after death. Unlike the Catholics, however, they did not pay, at least according to the existing Gnostic documents, the same attention to the final judgement. They certainly did not expect to live on earth for a millennium after the last judgement. Gnostic symbolism, if it is possible to use this example, argued in its various forms of eschatological hope, that the Redeemer would draw spiritual elements and all those like him to himself as a magnet draws up tiny, scattered particles of metal. Then, united with him and with one another they would return to the spiritual, original homeland. That would be the central event of restoration: everything reverting to its original condition.

Origen and the Controversy

Origen has acquired a problematic reputation, not only with modern scholars, but also with ancient authors, due to his controversial, often misunderstood, theory of universal salvation (see chapter 11). In the present context, our main interest is in his contribution to the development of doctrine on the resurrection of the body. Therefore I shall only sketch his eschatological framework of the event. The final moment of history will reflect the original order: everything must return to its original 'position', as this is the way divine wisdom and providence will complete the whole plan of salvation. After death, as Origen believed, all human souls except perfect Christians such as martyrs, go through a process of purification, thanks to which they ascend higher and closer to God.[24] It is arguable that Origen here hints at ideas that would later develop into the classical Roman Catholic doctrine of purgatory. Rather, he considered the eschatological encounter with God as a meeting of 'like with like'; therefore everything that was unlike God's holiness and purity must be cleansed and transformed into 'a spiritual being', if this state has not been achieved in the earlier life. The final event, resurrection of the body, would follow the Pauline idea of the 'spiritual body',[25] which was again drawn from the famous passage already quoted by the Gnostic Christians (1 Cor 15.44). The risen body will be 'spiritualized', unlike the present one: incorrupt, in honour and in power.[26]

> If it is certain that we are to possess bodies, and if those bodies which have fallen are declared to rise again – and the expression 'rise again' could not properly be used except of that which had previously fallen

– then no one can doubt that these bodies rise again in order that at the resurrection we may once more be clothed with them. The one thing, therefore, is bound up with the other. For if bodies rise again, undoubtedly they rise again as a clothing for us, and if it is necessary, as it is certainly is, for us to live in bodies, we ought to live in no other bodies but our own. And if it is true that they rise again and do so as 'spiritual', there is no doubt that this means that they rise again from the dead with corruption banished and mortality laid aside; otherwise it would seem vain and useless for a man to rise from the dead in order to die over again. Finally, this can be the more clearly understood by carefully observing what is the quality of the 'natural body' which, when sown in the earth, can reproduce the quality of 'a spiritual body'. For it is from the natural body that the very power and grace of the resurrection evokes the spiritual body, when it transforms it from dishonour to glory.

Origen, *Princ.* 2.10.1, trans. G. W. Butterworth

It is quite clear from Origen's systematic theology that this 'spiritual body' will facilitate direct contact, vision and communion with God. Therefore it must have appropriate qualities.[27] This ultimate fellowship with God requires transformation of the body in order to fulfil God's plan of becoming 'all in all' (1 Cor. 15.28).[28] The aim of the whole assimilation includes and transforms the human body. Later, a controversy arose among theologians representing various approaches to Origen's legacy: will this eschatological transformation have only allegorical meaning or was Origen suggesting the ontological amalgamation of 'all in one' and 'one in all'?

The Early Christian Dilemma

So far, in the pre-Nicene period two approaches have emerged, which characterized the earliest understanding of the resurrection of the dead/body. Both approaches are strongly based on exegesis of the Scriptures and pressure from alternative Christian theologies. The first approach, represented by Irenaeus of Lyons and Tertullian, emphasized the direct connection between the resurrection and final judgement, then added the problematic notion of the thousand years of God's kingdom on earth (Rev. 20). This interpretation, evidently created to counter some dualistic tendency which depreciated the material world, aimed to re-value its status. At the same time it highlighted God's providence and the justice which would be served out to those who promoted blasphemous views. The second approach, represented here by the Gnostic narrative and a brief encounter with Origen's complex eschatology, stressed the value of the resurrection as the final episode in the ascension of purified human beings towards the divine realm. This interpretation was constructed to counter Christians who held to literal exegesis of the Scriptures. Yet both approaches, together with that Athenagoras of Athens, saw the final event of the resurrection as the fulfilment of true human nature: to share eternity with God and contemplate his glory.

Further Developments

Post-Nicene theology commonly accepted the notion of the second coming of Christ, resurrection of the body and judgement as an already established essential part of Christian orthodoxy. With acceptance of Christ's real flesh, death and resurrection, the corruptible human body achieved its incorruption for good. Therefore its resurrection reflected the central mystery of Christ's incarnation and extended the consequences of Christ's passion and death to all humanity. So the Paschal mystery provided believers with hope of life without end in the body on the model of Christ. This common teaching received a very significant further development in the contribution of *Augustine of Hippo and the *Cappadocian Fathers.

Augustine of Hippo: Bodily Resurrection as the Axiom of Christian Hope

Augustine of Hippo, as a former Manichaean hearer[29] and certainly as a scholar influenced by Neoplatonism,[30] was intrigued by the nature of Christian hope already expressed in the Creeds as the 'resurrection of the body'.

> **Manichaeism**: a religious and philosophical system based on teaching of Mani or Manes (c.216–76 CE). It presented a radically dualistic view of reality, the material/evil or darkness and the spiritual/good or light. Salvation was understood as the liberation, or self-liberation, of the spiritual spark (light) from the prison of the material body (darkness). The movement spread rapidly in the fourth century in Rome and North Africa and presented a variation of the Gnostic traditions of eastern Persia.

> **Neoplatonism**: a complex philosophical system, which originated in the third century CE in Plotinus' (c.205–70 CE) commentaries on Plato's philosophy. This school of thought claimed that the whole of reality emanated from its original, transcendent Source known as 'the One' (Good). In the ongoing, eternal emanation, there first appeared the hypostasis of Mind/Intellect (the realm of perfect ideas), then the hypostasis of the Soul (the realm of all souls). While the outward movement or emanation introduced multiplicity of beings, the inward movement or ascent through contemplation leads to achievement of higher unity and integrity of contemplative life. The end of that inward movement leads to the encounter with its beginning: the One. In Neoplatonic ethics the bodily element should be controlled by human mind/intellect.

Both traditions, even if rejected (Manichaeism) or critically re-examined by Augustine, accompanied his theology, including his understanding of resurrection of the body. For Augustine, this article of faith was one of the pillars of Christian identity, underpinning ethics, theology and spirituality, history and future. A correct understanding of the content of this article helped to shape the present life in a form and direction that would facilitate the final encounter with God after the resurrection. As a result, 'resurrection of the body' was not a sophisticated speculation about the end of the world. On the contrary, it was a belief that influenced the present existence of Christians and was a preparation for this eschatological event. It involved Christian doctrinal struggle and a daily life of virtue and grace; all these aspects are engaged in realization of the ultimate communion with God. Augustine's views on the resurrection contained and addressed these and other assumptions. In a sincere effort to participate in eternal life with God, and against Manichaeans and Neoplatonic philosophers, Augustine proclaimed the distinctive character of Christian belief in the 'resurrection of the body'.[31] Augustine strongly reaffirmed the immortality of the soul, which has much in common with the realm of perfection and eternal beauty.[32] So far the Neoplatonic philosophers and the Manichaean theologians would have agreed with the Catholic bishop of Hippo. But then Augustine developed his argumentation further and, using scriptural passages, he reminds us of the Christian view that the soul as the true image of God's own beauty was given to human beings in the act of creation and united with the body. Augustine rejected the Neoplatonic argument that ultimate happiness comes from the liberation of the soul from the body,[33] and unlike Manichaeans, he did not see in this union any evil. Nonetheless, the body marked by original sin gravitates towards moral evil and sinful acts.[34] The union between the soul and body is the most natural for both and it is a part of God's providence. In this way, even after the body is dead, the soul looks forward to entering into that union again and wishes resurrection to happen as soon as possible.[35] As a result, on the last day, at the second coming of Christ, that union will be recreated, because the soul cannot exist without the body. The saints will continue their existence in human bodies, by now purified and uncorrupted.[36] In this elaboration Christ's risen body presents the perfect example for Christian faith.[37] Against Platonism, including Origen's Platonic stance, Augustine did not amplify the 'spirituality' of the risen body with reference to the Pauline idea, but rather commented on it in a way which suits his whole teaching. The risen body will be free from any stain of sin, purified and free from clumsiness.[38] Like current flesh, it will have a material element, but this 'physical' dimension will be in its perfect form.[39] Augustine's theory advertises first and foremost the positive value of the human body as created by a loving God – 'the Artisan', although this value is overshadowed by the drama of sin and its consequences.

> But, for example, if an object made of soluble metal should be either melted down by fire, or pounded into dust, or squeezed into a shapeless mass, and then an artist wished to make it over from the same metal, it would make no difference to the wholeness of the renovated object, whichever particles of metal were restored to whichever part of the object, so long as the restored object took up the whole of that

> material of which it was originally made. Similarly, God, the Artist who acts in wonderful and inexpressible ways, will restore our bodies with a wonderful and inexpressible speed. He will restore our flesh from the entirety of the material of which it was made, and it will make no difference to its reconstruction whether hair becomes hair or nails become nails, or whatever of these had perished be changed to flesh and be assigned to other parts of the body. What is crucial is that the providence of the Artist will take care that nothing inappropriate happens.
>
> Augustine, *Enchir.* 23.89, trans. P. A.-S.

Still, it is possible to see that the present corruption will be redeemed and the same, not another, body together with the soul will attain eschatological communion with its Creator, Saviour and Sanctifier. Augustine's interpretation presents a carefully crafted doctrine of the resurrection of the body. The author, although he was acquainted with other philosophical and religious interpretations of the crucial union between the soul and the body, aimed to navigate between, as he saw it, two dangerous doctrines: the pagan Platonism of his time and Manichaeism. This final cautious but attractive vision is yet another reason for Augustine to be looked on as the foremost Church father and the authority on Christian eschatology.

The Cappadocian Fathers: Christian Hope in a Philosophical Frame

*Basil of Caesarea, *Gregory of Nazianzus and *Gregory of Nyssa, while continuing to reflect upon this article of faith alongside the main theological line of the Catholic Church, explored new aspects of this belief. Like a majority of previous theologians, the Cappadocians placed the current statement in the context of creation achieving final perfection, which fulfils God's plan of salvation. Basil, for instance, in his treatise *On the Holy Spirit*, openly declared the direction of human history to be a progress towards the ultimate perfection[40] and universal purpose established by the Creator.[41] This gradual movement, which includes growing understanding (Gr. *gnosis*) and wisdom (Gr. *sophia*), advancement in virtue (Gr. *arete*), transformation from 'darkness' into 'the share of the saints in light' (Col 1.12–13),[42] also includes the human body. The expectation of the last day to come, waiting for the climax of history, encompasses every dimension of the created order, as nothing can be lost, annihilated or forgotten in God's project of salvation. The Cappadocian Fathers, although inspired by the above Neoplatonic paradigm of ascent/return to the original Source of reality, protected the necessary Christian character of this eschatological vision with great success. First, like the Neoplatonists, the Cappadocians put a strong emphasis on the role of human freedom because through the life of virtue people participate in advancement towards the ultimate Source of reality. Any Stoic element of belief in fate or even a Christian version of predestination had to be rejected.[43] Second, this whole cosmological transformation was not an 'automatic' process. It was rather an outcome of God's carefully elaborated plan of salvation, which includes 'many dwelling places' for different people.[44] Hence human individuality will not be destroyed at this final stage of union with the divine. Third, the Cappadocians highlighted the role of virtues, such as *apatheia*, which already unites with Christ in this life and to an even greater degree after the resurrection.[45] Fourth, as in the case of Basil, sanctification, which starts with baptism and is performed by the Holy Spirit, not only sanctifies the human soul or mind, but also transforms the body.[46] Consequently, after the final resurrection the human body will participate in the contemplation of God (Gr. *theoria*) and in deification.[47] Gregory of Nyssa composed a treatise, *On the Soul and the Resurrection*, which elucidates his understanding of the resurrection of the body arising directly from Paul's well-known proclamation (1 Cor. 15.35–49). To Gregory the resurrection of human flesh signifies a rediscovery of the original lost stage of human nature, in which each human body and soul were united in continuing, uninterrupted harmony.

> For we learn from the Scriptures, in the first cosmogony, that the earth first brought forth the green plant, then seed was produced from this plant, and from this, when it had been shed on the ground, the same form of the original growth sprang up. Now the inspired Apostle says that this is what happens also at the resurrection [1 Cor. 15.35–49]. Thus we learn from him not only that human nature is changed into a far nobler state, but also that what we are to hope for is just this; the

> return of human nature to its primal condition. The original process was not that of an ear from the seed, but of the seed from the ear, the ear thereafter growing from the seed. The order of events in this simile clearly shows that all the happiness which will burgeon for us through the resurrection will be a return to our original state of grace. Originally we also were, in a sense, a full ear, but we were withered by the torrid heat of sin; and then on our dissolution by death the earth received us. But in the spring of the resurrection the earth will again display the naked grain of our body as an ear, tall, luxuriant, and upright, reaching up as high as heaven and, for stalk and beard, decked with incorruption and all the other godlike characteristics.
>
> Gregory of Nyssa, *OSR*, trans. H. Bettenson

The return to life of the body will be linked with the last judgement and its two ultimate consequences: the eternal bliss of the vision of God[48] or punishment.[49] The body as well as the soul has to face the consequences of all moral action during this transitory life as it cannot be omitted in either glorious reward or shameful retribution. To the Cappadocian Fathers the eschatological event of the resurrection of the body gave an enormous, positive inspiration not only to their anticipation of this occasion but also in their preparation for it, which included theological reflection, liturgical and sacramental celebration and spiritual maturing.

Conclusion

This credal article elaborates on the nature of human beings in the context of eschatology. It affirms that all men and women, as individuals, not just en masse, will face God's judgement and then either reward or punishment. This final assessment is expressed by a specific connection between soul and body. Soul alone, although more appropriate to encounter the reality of the kingdom of God, cannot be cut off from its earthly and material 'cloth' since it was created in this 'cloth' in the first place. The body alone, although created as good by the Creator, cannot exist without the individual soul to which it is attributed from its beginning. That union, 'for better and for worse', will survive the temporary separation caused by the physical death, but then, recreated by the might of God, will enter into 'the endless day'.

Questions for Discussion

- How do you assess the Patristic effort to explain the mystery of the resurrection of the body by reference to Greek mythological figures, such as the Phoenix?
- If the resurrection of the body was so central to early Christian eschatology, what kind of body, shape and form can those who die in infancy or before birth expect?

Further Reading

For beginners
J. J. Collins, 2002, 'Death and Afterlife', in J. Barton (ed.), *The Biblical World*, vol. 2, London and New York: Routledge, pp. 363–6.
B. E. Daley, 1991, *The Hope of the Early Church: A Handbook of Patristic Eschatology*, Cambridge: Cambridge University Press.

For more advanced students
H. G. Reventlow (ed.) 1997, *Eschatology in the Bible and in the Jewish and Christian Traditions*, London and New York: T&T Clark.
C. Setzer, 2004, *Resurrection of the Body in Early Judaism and Early Christianity: Doctrine, Community, and Self-Definition*, Leiden: Brill.

Internet Resources

Eschatology in the early Church: selection of the original documents and recent studies:
   http://www.earlychurch.org.uk/eschatology.php

Useful Patristic chronology and iconography, including many motifs on death and resurrection
   http://academic.brooklyn.cuny.edu/history/dfg/jesu/topic%205.htm

Notes

1 *AC* 2.55.

2 I refer to Athenagoras of Athens as the author of this work. There are, however, other views as well; for more detail, see the introduction to the English edition of the work: W. R. Schoedel, 1972, *Athenagoras,* Legatio *and* De Resurrectione, Oxford: Clarendon Press, pp. XXVI–XXXII.

3 *Res.* 3.

4 *Res.* 10.

5 *Res.* 18.

6 *Res.* 4.

7 The early Christian notion of millenarianism will be discussed in chapter 11.

8 *AH* 5.13.3.

9 *AH* 5.7.2.

10 *AH* 3.18.7.

11 *AH* 5.5.1–2.

12 *OR* 1.1.

13 *Scapula* 2.6.

14 *AM* 5.9.3.

15 *OR* 41.

16 *OR* 30.

17 *OR* 31.4.

18 *OR* 13.3.

19 *AM* 2.11.3.

20 *OR* 17.9.

21 *AM* 3.24.3–6.

22 For example, see *TRes.* 48.3—49.35.

23 Epiphanius, *Chest* 31.7.6; 7.10.

24 For example *HomJer.* 12.3.

25 *Princ.* 2.11.2; *AC* 6.29.

26 *AC* 5.18–19.

27 *Princ.* 2.3.2.

28 *Princ.* 3.6.2.

29 See P. Brown, 1967, *Augustine of Hippo: A Biography*, Berkeley: University of California Press, pp. 46–60.

30 More in M. J. Edwards, 1999, 'Neoplatonism', in A. D. Fitzgerald (ed.), *Augustine through the Ages*, Grand Rapids, MI: Eerdmans.

31 *OFC* 10.23.

32 *IS* 1.1—6.11.

33 *Ep.* 166.9.27.

34 *CG* 13.16.1.

35 *CG* 13.20.

36 *CG* 13.19.

37 *CG* 22.12; 22.18.

38 *CG* 20.21.

39 *CG* 22.19.

40 *OHS* 8.18.

41 Gregory of Nyssa, *ComSS* 15; Gregory Nazianzus, *Or.* 33.9.

42 *OHS* 8.18.

43 Gregory of Nyssa, *ComSS* 4; 9; *OMM* 16; Basil of Caesarea, *Hex.* 1.2; Gregory of Nazianzus, *Or.* 4.44. As to the Christian version of predestination, here mainly Augustine's theory of 'God's prescience', see *CG* 5.9.

44 Gregory of Nyssa, *ComSS* 15.

45 Gregory of Nyssa, *OLP* 3.

46 Basil of Caesarea, *OHS* 9.

47 Gregory of Nazianzus, *Or.* 7.23.

48 Gregory of Nyssa, *ComSS* 1; 6; 12.

49 Gregory of Nazianzus, *Poems* 34; Basil of Caesarea, *HomPs.* 33.4; Gregory of Nyssa, *LM* 2.

11

Life Everlasting

See also chapters 1, 2, 3, 5, 6, 8, 9, 10.

Consider this Task

Find some examples of Christian iconographical illustrations of heavenly bliss. What do you find most attractive, surprising and disconcerting in those illustrations of heaven?

Introduction

The last chapter of this book elaborates on the destiny of humankind when the saints attain everlasting fellowship with God. According to Christian logic, if there were no original sin which alienated men and women from the Paradise, the description of heaven would denote the life in the first stage, before innocence had been lost. However, the Patristic authors shared the intuition that the 'life everlasting' would not be a simple 'repetition' or 'a copy' of the original bliss. This life to come was presented as a glorious encounter between God and men and women sanctified by God's grace. The patristic authors were aware of the various stages of the history of salvation as summarized in the previous chapters. As we shall see in this chapter, the content of this belief developed within the framework of Christian theology, from its early form, including the controversial theory of *millenarianism, towards the problematic contribution of Origen, the rather systematic vision presented by Augustine, and led towards the orthodox understanding of ultimate fellowship with God among the Cappadocian Fathers.

Millenarianism (Lat. *mille* – 'thousand', or Gr. *chilioi*, – 'chiliasm'): the theory that the reign of the Messiah will last 'a thousand years' on earth before the final end of time was intended to include this transitory material world into God's spiritual kingdom. As a theory it addressed some dualistic and nihilistic tendencies within Christianity.

Opening Question

Can 'life everlasting' be understood as yet another synonym and name of God?

Development of the Argument

The earliest theology, particularly in its Jewish-Christian tradition, was deeply inspired by the apocalyptic literature with its vivid imagery of the last judgement and then the dramatic end of the present world, which precedes the forthcoming of God's kingdom (e.g. 2 Tim. 2.12; 1 Thess. 4.17; 2 Thess. 1.7; 1 Cor. 15. 23–8). In this chronological framework, after the judgement and punishment of the wicked, the next stage was described as 'a thousand years of Christ's reign' on earth before the triumphant return of all saints with their Saviour to the realm of God.

The Theory of a Thousand Years: The Feast on the Earth

The second-century theologians were already convinced that the return of the Saviour would not happen immediately. As the 'day of the Lord' (e.g. 1 Thess. 5.2) was delayed, new questions emerged about the signs of its inauguration, the direct political and theological context and its length in time. Millenarianism, as an outcome of a particular exegesis, offered some convenient answers. Therefore it became a part of early doctrine professed by such theologians as *Papias,[1] *Justin Martyr,[2] *Irenaeus of Lyons,[3] *Tertullian[4] and *Methodius of Olympus.[5] All these theologians, although they seemed to share the same hope, supported their belief by different arguments. Millenarianism attracted the attention of others besides the representatives of Catholic Christianity. In the second century, for example, the same idea was also confessed by *Montanists (see chapter 4), which shows that belief in the beginning of heavenly kingdom on earth appealed to various groups of Christians. The theory, although it has some local variations, in its core predicted the second coming of the Saviour with his angels. The coming of the celestial army introduced the final battle with the Antichrist, the ruler on the earth, and his servants. After the final conflict between good and evil, all the dead are raised and join the company of the righteous who survived the rule of the Antichrist. Then, the Saviour establishes his kingdom on the earth (the 'earthly Jerusalem'), in which he and his saints rule for a thousand years in peace and harmony. After a thousand years the wicked will be raised for judgement and they will receive punishment in hell. Finally, the Saviour and his saints together with the angels will ascend to heaven. It is possible to find some variations on this general picture, but its core remains the same; it is on this visible earth that the Lord, now the mystical Lamb, will reign with the holy men and women for a thousand years as a preparation for eternal rest and happiness. According to Irenaeus of Lyons, the whole idea originated in Johannine circles and was then transmitted as 'the tradition of the Elders' to the next generation of disciples, including Papias, 'the hearer of John and the companion of Polycarp'.[6] This theological pedigree established millenarianism as the belief of the Church, soon popularized by Irenaeus of Lyons in his anti-heretical writings. This apology included the notion of 'the eschatological festive meal' with the Saviour. Millenarianism affirmed the important anti-Gnostic and anti-dualistic thesis on the value of the visible world as God's magnificent handiwork and its participation in the initiation of everlasting life. Therefore it is also necessary to include in our presentation of the doctrine the Gnostic view of 'everlasting life'.

Life Everlasting and Gnostic Interpretation

Gnostic eschatology, of which some elements were mentioned in the previous chapter, understood 'life everlasting' in a rather different way from the representatives of the Church. Gnostic comprehension was much more suspicious of the possibility of participation of the bodily, material element, such as human flesh, in the spiritual realm and bliss. The Gnostic paradigm excluded any reconciliation between 'spiritual' and 'material' as these two elements belong to two opposite realms. This paradigm influenced Gnostic views on 'life everlasting' of the most mature, advanced Christians.

As Catholics, Gnostics were also waiting for the fulfilment of time, though the classical tension between participation in 'the world to come' as *already* present but *not yet* realized, was understood as initiation to salvation.[7] The main characteristics of everlasting life, in Gnostic interpretation, emphasized such metaphors as 'enthronement' of the purified soul,[8] when the soul ends its exile and receives 'the throne of glory'. The eschatological events only briefly mentioned the 'second coming of the Lord'. The Gnostic narratives stressed instead ascent of the soul to the realm of light, which is often related to progress in the spiritual spheres of the universe (various numbers of 'heaven'), until the ultimate realm of rest is reached. This ascent was also perceived as universal reintegration of the spiritual elements, which was the synonym of the Christian perfects. Only those mature Christians who developed an allegorical understanding of the Scriptures and history would be able to enter into the 'bridal chamber'. There, in this sphere of delight they would be united as brides (the souls) with the bride man (the Saviour).[9] On the other hand, those Christians who are less perfect will wait for hope either in uncertainty or, in grave cases of total ignorance, shall perish. Therefore, all divine 'particles' (i.e. the souls of the Gnostics) dispersed in this material world, like the sparks of light imprisoned in darkness, will be reunited and re-established to their original glory at this moment beyond time.[10] It is not surprising that those Gnostic Christians did not express any attraction to the idea of millenarianism, as all of them wished to return to their homeland without any delay or nostalgia for this corruptible world, which jailed their souls for so long.

Origen: Christian Hope

Origen, like the Gnostics, rejected the idea of millenarianism as the opening phase of 'everlasting life' consistently throughout his entire life.[11] Origen's understanding of the Scriptures, including the problematic passage from the Book of Revelation (20.1–10), did not leave any room for this 'literal' view.[12] First and foremost, from Origen's stance, millenarianism was too literalistic, if not too naïve, to be a divinely inspired understanding of the end of the world. This kind of literalistic exegesis according to 'the flesh' and not to the 'spirit'[13] miscomprehended God's plan of salvation. Origen prioritized the spiritual dimension of the scriptural narratives. Therefore the forthcoming everlasting life was not related to a chiliastic 'material' and 'political' configuration, but it meant that the spiritual realm of the world to come was 'great and hard to explain'.[14] Although Origen affirmed faith in the 'resurrection of the body' (see chapter 10), he interpreted the life everlasting and communion with God as a spiritual fellowship, rather than an earthly feast in a corporeal world.

Origen's theology suggested another theory which attracted much attention in the Patristic period. It was based on his particular interpretation of God's promise to restore the whole universe as prefigured by Jesus' resurrection,[15] and it had two stages. First, universal restoration (Gr. *apokatastasis*; Lat. *restitutio*) designated the ultimate perfection of all human beings after the resurrection and submission of all men and women to the Son of God as the entire body of Christ, which has many members.

> 'Restoration' (Gr. *apokatastasis*), later in the Christian context: 'consummation', 'fulfilment': *apokatastasis* appeared in the Stoic philosophy and denoted the appearance of the next, identical world after destruction of the present by an eschatological fire. As such, *apokatastasis* was a part of the natural process of the never-ending cycles of destruction/re-emergence of the universe. In the Christian context, particularly in Origen's vocabulary, this notion emphasized the fulfilment of God's plan of salvation, when all spheres of realities and all intelligible beings will be subjected to Jesus Christ and God's might.

Then in the second phase, even the Son with his risen 'body' (i.e. all humanity) will be subjected to the Father, and this final act closes the history of the world. This optimistic theory became highly contentious in the later fourth-century Origenist controversy because some of Origen's disciples included sinners and even evil spirits in the act of reconciliation with God.

> **Origenist controversy**: a conflict over a number of theological theories ascribed to Origen by his theological opponents. Among them, the chief doctrines were on pre-existence of the souls (human souls exist in a spiritual realm before they descend into bodies) and eschatology (restoration and salvation of all human beings, including sinners). These views were promoted by some of Origen's radical disciples, but were condemned by a Council at Alexandria (400). Later in the sixth century the controversy over Origen's legacy broke out again, this time initiated by Palestinian monks. At the Fifth Ecumenical Council of Constantinople (553) both theories claimed by Origen's disciples were found to be heretical and as such condemned.

This outline of Origen's complex theory hints at the spiritual nature of the eschatological culmination, with no room for any material, historical extension as exemplified by the chiliastic hope. Rejecting the tendency to see the beginning of the everlasting life as an earthly kingdom, Origen placed the final event within his hypothesis of the history of the universe. First, the visible universe had its pre-historical beginning as the community of created beings contemplating God. Then, or rather now, it has its moment/time as a religious and spiritual passage towards perfection. Third, it will have its glorious accomplishment in the final restoration. Its end in time must bring the balance to the beginning in time; however, it will go back even further to recapitulate the original perfection of all. Within this structure, everlasting life appears to Origen as universal restoration of the primordial order of the whole created reality. Origen, an exegete who explored the spiritual, deepest meaning of the Bible, noted that on various occasions the Scriptures hint at God's economy of salvation: restoration of the original and perfect fellowship of all with God.

> If, however, there is something greater than the ages – so that among created beings we think of ages, but among those who exceed and surpass visible created beings, something still greater – which will perhaps exist at the 'restitution of all things' [i.e. Gr. *apokatastasis*, Acts 3.21] when the universe reaches its perfect end, then possibly that period in which the consummation of all things will happen is to be understood as something more than an age. [. . .] Now when it says 'still more' [i.e. 'from this time forth and for evermore' – the translator] undoubtedly it wishes something more than an age to be understood. And see whether that saying of the Saviour, 'I will that, where I am, these also may be there with me' [John 17.24] and 'as I and thou are one, that they also may be one in us' [John 17.21] does not seem to point to something more than an age or ages, perhaps even more than the 'ages of the ages' [Gal. 1.5; 1 Tim. 1.17], to that period, namely, when all things are no longer in an age, but 'God is all and in all' [1 Cor. 15.28].
>
> Origen, *Princ.* 2.3.5, trans. G. W. Butterworth

In an anthropological context, Origen's idea promoted the return of the human soul to its original warmth, the status of contemplation and closeness to God.[16] Everlasting life is thus a restoration of the human soul, as well as others, to their unity with God, a new heat of love which binds the souls with their Creator. In this eschatological and mystical stage, all souls become one with the Lord and the Saviour.[17] Then in the Trinitarian context, through the Holy Spirit and the Son they shall participate in the divine.[18]

Life Everlasting: Contemplation in Love

So far the main attention has been focused on the preliminary stage of everlasting life denoted by the controversial idea of millenarianism. Yet the pre-Nicene theologians also hinted at some images of the eternal happiness. To many early authors, everlasting life was represented by a vision/contemplation (Gr. *theoria*) and love (Gr. *agape*) of God. As the earthly journey was guided by faith (Gr. *pistis*) and obedience (Gr. *hypotage*) to God, the arrival at the destination offered the highest degree of intimacy expressed by 'contemplation in love'. This understanding had already appeared in Irenaeus of Lyons[19] and in *Clement of Alexandria.[20] The symbol of 'vision' denoted not just a new, eternal 'perception', but a degree of closeness, intimacy and direct encounter with the incomprehensible God. This image, as has been pointed out, was precious to Origen, but a similar understanding also appeared among Latin authors such as Tertullian[21] and later *Cyprian of Carthage.[22] Tertullian put a special emphasis on everlasting life being a reward for courageous victory in the present life.[23] Therefore Tertullian belongs to those theologians who perceived the present existence as a competition, battleground, or even a sport, where only winners gain the ultimate and only prize: the crown[24] and victory.[25] As this often dramatic struggle includes bodily suffering, everlasting life will bring glory to human flesh and make it incorruptible. All saints (who will continue exist as individual people, although in community with angels and other saints) will receive their place in God's kingdom according to their merits.[26] Everlasting life was not seen as a quiet, dreary and static dwelling in the Father's house, but rather, as for example Clement of Alexandria suggested, a deification and mutual friendship between the one who knows and the one who is known.[27]

Later Interpretation of Heaven

Among the post-Nicene authors who dealt with the idea of everlasting life, a special place belongs to Augustine of Hippo and the Cappadocian Fathers. However, this motif was commented on by many other authors of catechetical interpretations of this belief. Among those lectures, Cyril of Jerusalem provides us with one of the best examples.

> Only when we are taught by the holy Catholic Church and by leading a righteous life, shall we inherit the kingdom of heaven with everlasting life. This reward is the purpose of all efforts, so that we may enjoy it while receiving it from the Lord. This purpose is not at all insignificant. We are seeking out eternal life. [. . .]
>
> The true and real life is God the Father, the Source of life itself. He bestows his heavenly gifts on all creatures through the Son and the Holy Spirit and the blessing of everlasting life is promised to human beings as he loves us. There should not be any doubt about that, and we ought to believe, as our mind should be focused on God's might not on our weakness.
>
> Cyril of Jerusalem, *CL* 18.28–9, trans. P. A.-S.

Augustine of Hippo: Heaven and its Citizens

Augustine reinterpreted the notion of millenarianism to which he was attracted in the first phase of his life and theological reflection. Second, Augustine, the great orator reaffirmed and emphasized certain images related to life eternal. Augustine as a theologian was well aware of the earliest Christian form of millenarianism, which, as he pointed out in *City of God*, he accepted at some point.[28] As a Platonist, however, he was not keen to believe that after the second coming of the Lord, the promised celestial banquet would take the form of a literal consumption of abundant food as, for instance, Papias and Irenaeus of Lyons expected.[29] Therefore, Augustine, while cherishing the allegorical method, interpreted the vision of the eschatological feast after the thousand years as a symbol of spiritual satisfaction of all human needs. In his view, the idea popular among early Christians of the millennium with the Lord could be explained either as the last period of time before the final judgement, and then the promised 'Sabbath', or as the perfect denotation of the whole history of the world which will take a thousand years.[30] Both interpretations 'corrected' the earlier bold Christian idea and as such provided the Church with new understanding of the eschatological hope. Augustine's view on history in relation to eschatology established yet another important part of Christian self-understanding. In the same treatise, *City of God*, the crucial distinction between God's realm (Lat. *Civitas Dei*), that is the holy Church, and 'the city of this world' (Lat. *Civitas terrena*) appeared on a full theological scale. The former will survive the latter, as it is a synonym of the kingdom of God. However, it is manifested by the Church rather than identified with it. The *Civitas Dei* as already present in this age is totally directed and focused on the age to come. Augustine highlighted on many occasions the essential part of Christian belief that the true fulfilment of human life is beyond this life, therefore the whole earthly existence has in its core an eschatological dimension and realization. While promoting this basic intuition in a new rhetorical form and with attractive new images, Augustine pictured everlasting life with fresh colours. In his *Confession* he stated that God is the final end and the ultimate happiness of human being.[31] The *City of God* confirms that perception and adds that the saints will enjoy the company of the unchanging goodness and have rest in God himself.

> God himself is the source of our happiness, he is the end of all our desire. By our choice of him as our end – or rather by our re-choice (as we have lost him by our disregard); [. . .] we turn to him with love so that in reaching him we may rest in God, and find our happiness as we have reached our fulfilment in him.
>
> Augustine, CG 10.3, trans. P. A.-S.
>
> Anyone can easily understand that the happiness which is desired by the intelligent beings as their proper object is effected by the conjunction of two elements: interrupted enjoyment of the unchangeable Good, which is God, together with the certainty of remaining in God in eternity without any doubt, hesitation, error and disappointment. This is, as we earnestly believe, the happiness of the angels of light.
>
> Augustine, CG 11.13, trans. P. A.-S.

Here, Augustine saw that eschatological day without end combined intellectual knowledge and passionate love of the Father, Son and the Holy Spirit.[32] That experience of undisturbed bliss, peace and mystical ecstasy will include transformed, glorified post-risen human bodies since Augustine the Platonist included scriptural motifs in his theology. Then in communion with the angels and all saints, the new creation will praise its Creator, Redeemer and Sanctifier, in an act of worship on the endless Sabbath day. As may be noted, Augustine saved as much as he could from the original millenarian notion, while he added fresh ideas based on his personal devotion and religious experience. His genius allowed him to hold the integrity of that personal experience and a larger eschatological vision, which attracted attention and received the respect of many theologians in ages to come.

The Cappadocians: the Hope of the Universal Salvation Revised

The Cappadocian Fathers, whose theology expressed the general Alexandrian outlook and in various degrees was dependent on Origen's legacy, placed the theme of universal restoration either in the centre, or on the margin and even outside of their eschatology. All of them expressed a great theological, pedagogical and ascetic interest in teaching about the eternal life with God as fulfilment of human destiny and achievement of the highest assimilation to God (Gr. *theopoiesis*, Gr. *theosis*), which begins in the present life. All of them emphasized the reality of the resurrection of the body, the final judgement and then consequently either punishment or eternal life. All three theologians held in the heart of their eschatological hope the communion with the Saviour and the other divine persons. But these shared views also contained explicit differences in details. While *Gregory of Nyssa welcomed the core intention of universal restoration, which allowed God to triumph in all creation in a similar way as he was recognized by all nations not just the Jews,[33] his brother *Basil of Caesarea rejected it and emphasized the role of the last judgement, which will seal the fate of the saints and the sinners.[34] Between these two poles was Basil's friend *Gregory of Nazianzus, who had some interest in the value of the concept for orthodox eschatology. However, he was neither as enthusiastic as Gregory nor as critical as Basil. For him restoration, when interpreted carefully, may reveal important aspects of the forthcoming new stage of reality as a communion with God. In Gregory of Nazianzus' opinion, universal restoration denoted the ascension of the whole dispersed creation towards divine unity and harmony. In this eschatological stage, 'in heaven' all will become one, or rather all will become God and in this way deification (Gr. *theosis*) will be achieved as a form of restoration.[35] Gregory of Nyssa, the greatest enthusiast for this theme, understood it as an extension of Christology which embraced in its universal dimension all intelligent creatures. For Gregory, the purpose, history and future of the universe can be accomplished when all will be reunited with Christ's Father. This aim was the Saviour's reason for coming to this world, redeeming it and turning its direction towards God's kingdom. Christ's mission will be fulfilled by the eschatological reconciliation of all with God.[36] The hope in restoration is then an expression of that divine purpose, mission and destiny. But it includes a necessary period of preparation for the glorious future, a limited period of penitence and amelioration involving purification by fire.[37] To the Cappadocian Fathers, everlasting life was a synonym of never-ending communion with God as the pure and highest beauty and goodness. That life will reach the transcendent God who will become the most intimate, illuminating and loving presence. The mystical treatise of Gregory of Nyssa, the *Life of Moses*, unveils some helpful analogies of the eschatological stage.[38] Heaven can be understood as the most profound experience of God the Holy Trinity, who dwells in the soul of the Christian. But it is not the Christian saint who will possess God; rather it is God without limits who will inhabit the saint. This heavenly occurrence originates in the earthly consent allowing Christ to grow in the soul of the Christian and achieve its final greatness in the life beyond this world. Everlasting life would then be a full and perfect participation in God's life, but it would not amalgamate human and divine. It would realize the greatest paradox: gaining access to the inaccessible God, achieving understanding of the One who transcends all notions, and it would allow seeing him who cannot be contained by any vision.

> This is the real vision of God: never become saturated in the desire to see him. However, while looking at what can be seen, one has to rekindle desire to see ever more. Therefore no boundaries will limit progress in the ascent to God as neither Good has boundaries nor the growing desire for Good possesses limits as it cannot be satisfied.
>
> Gregory of Nyssa, *LM* 2.239, trans. P. A.-S.

Therefore the apex of life 'with' and 'in' God, which is the greatest desire of the Christian, is not a vision of God (Gr. *theoria*), but rather an experience of immense divine presence or participation in God. This original point made by Gregory of Nyssa can also be applied to his view of everlasting life. A similar, although less apophatic motif, appeared in Basil's catechesis on everlasting life as the fundamental direction to human existence.[39] Gregory's brother elaborated the Pauline motif of the distinction between the present stage of knowledge of God ('dim glass/mirror', see 1 Cor. 13.12) and the heavenly, pure and direct contemplation of God's mystery, the true experience of the paradox 'seeing that consists of not seeing'.[40]

> 'Blessed are the pure in heart, for they shall see God' [Matt. 5.8.]. Brethren, think of the kingdom of heaven as just this, the genuine contemplation of realities. This is what the inspired Scriptures call blessedness: for 'the kingdom of heaven is within you' [Luke 17.21]. Now the inner man consists simply of contemplation: it follows that the kingdom of heaven must be contemplation. Now we behold 'as in a glass' [1 Cor. 13.12] the shadows of things, the archetypes of which we shall behold later, when we are set free from this earthly body and have put on an incorruptible and immortal body [1 Cor. 15.54]. Then we shall see, that is, if we steer our life's course towards the right, and if we take heed of the right faith; for otherwise no one will see the Lord. [Hebr. 12.14]
>
> Basil of Caesarea, *Ep.* 8.12, trans. H. Bettenson

It is clear from Basil's exegesis of the famous passage that the present life and world are only 'shadows' of the true and forthcoming existence in God's kingdom, which provide the saints with the heavenly citizenship and a place in the chorus of the angels.[41] To Basil, the author of the first treatise on the Holy Spirit as the divine person (see chapter 7), eternal life is achieved through sanctification by the Holy Spirit, which as the gift of grace increases growth in virtues and leads to the full participation in God's life or 'becoming like God'.[42] Of course this notion was not understood as literal, but rather as a metaphor of the final metamorphosis and sanctification. Therefore although 'everlasting life' or 'heaven' refers to the eschatological stage of union with God, it originates in the present existence. In Basil's view everlasting life, although a forthcoming and new reality, will be a continuation and amplification of the present fellowship with God. Again, this communion will protect the individual identity of human being, while penetrating the human with the divine grace. The third of the great Cappadocians, Gregory of Nazianzus, saw the eschatological happiness again as the climax of steady moral and spiritual development, including the role in this life of sacraments such as baptism[43] and the Eucharist.[44] These divine means lift up the human mind towards its true object of reflection and help to free human attention from attraction to the material world. The current ascent towards the divine by moral purification[45] receives further support and energy from the sacraments and the fact of Christ's incarnation, as the divine Saviour took on the conditions of human nature.[46] These aspects of spiritual development are various stages and expressions of growth into divinity.[47] It leads towards the heavenly Jerusalem and contemplation of the Holy of Holies.

> Let us direct our mind not to the earthly city, but the heavenly Jerusalem [Heb. 12.22]; not to the one which is now crushed by armies, [Luke 1.20–4] but to that glorified by angels. Let us not make offerings with young calves and lambs with horns and hoofs; the slaughtered animals. On the contrary, let us offer to God the sacrifice of praise upon the heavenly Altar, with the heavenly dances. Let us put aside the first veil; let us come close to the second, and look into the Holy of Holies.
>
> Gregory of Nazianzus, *Or.* 45.23, trans. P. A.-S.

Conclusion

Hope of everlasting life with God, although it took different forms and expressions, was one of the pillars of Patristic theology. While the drama of original sin introduced a substantial obstacle to communion between the Creator and his creatures, the act of redemption by God's incarnate Son brought a new potential to attain the lost fellowship. Eternal life was seen by the Church fathers as realization of the spiritual potential given by Christ to each Christian, or even more, offered to the whole of humanity. Hope of everlasting life was not, as later popularized by Christian iconography, a static uniformity of stiff heroes, but it contained the intention of becoming God's dwelling place with unceasing, overwhelming radiant joy, for good and for ever.

Questions for Discussion

- How do you understand 'death'? What kind of symbols and images are used in the Gospels to exemplify death?
- What kind of evidence do we find in the New Testament which argues that we shall experience life everlasting as individual beings not just as humanity?
- As all 'models' of 'heaven', 'eternal life', 'intimacy with God' and 'bridal union' were elaborated by male theologians, where do you see the limits of those metaphors and how female experience of love, happiness and intimacy may contribute to hermeneutics of eternal communion with God?
- Why must 'everlasting life' happen in the realm outside of this visible, material and redeemed world? Is this not a hidden dualism which disallows the eternal happiness to happen in this visible world?
- Can you propose a theory which would save the doctrine of millenarianism?
- Can the theory of *apokatastasis* convincingly embrace the free choice of some creatures to reject God as the source of goodness and happiness?

Further Reading

For beginners
J. M. Court, 2008, *Approaching the Apocalypse: A Short History of Christian Millenarianism*, London and New York: I. B. Tauris.
A. E. McGrath, 2003, *A Brief History of Heaven*, Malden, Oxford: Blackwell.

For more advanced students
C. Hill, 2001, *Regnum Caelorum: Patterns of Millennial Thought in Early Christianity*, Grand Rapids, MI: Eerdmans.

C. Rowland, 'The Eschatology of the New Testament Church' in J. L. Wallis (ed.), 2008, *The Oxford Handbook of Eschatology*, Oxford: Oxford University Press, pp. 56–72.

B. McGinn, J. J. Collins and S. J. Stein (eds), 2000, *The Encyclopaedia of Apocalypticism*, vol. 1, London and New York: Continuum International Publishing.

J. E. Wright, 2002, *The Early History of Heaven*, Oxford: Oxford University Press.

On Augustine

M. J. Scanlon, 1999, 'Eschatology' in A. J. Fitzgerald (ed.), *Augustine through the Ages*, Grand Rapids, MI: Eerdmans, pp. 316–18.

On Neoplatonism

R. T. Wallis, 1995, *Neoplatonism*, London: Duckworth.

Internet Resources

Iconography of Eschatological Feast with the Lamb:
http://personal.stthomas.edu/plgavrilyuk/PLGAVRILYUK/Art/Lamb/Lamb%20Rome.htm

Society for later Antiquity (a number of very useful web pages, discussion groups and documents related to cultural and philosophical context of the book):
http://www.sc.edu/ltantsoc/

Worlds of Later Antiquity (similar collection of useful references):
http://www9.georgetown.edu/jod/wola.html

Christian Origins (Internet Ancient History Source Book):
http://www.fordham.edu/halsall/ancient/asbook11.html

Byzantine Studies on the Internet:
http://www.fordham.edu/halsall/byzantium/

Diotima (Material for the Studies of Women and Gender in the Ancient World):
http://www.stoa.org/diotima/

Notes

1 According to Eusebius, *EH* 3.39.11–12, and Jerome, *Lives* 18, Papias accepted the theory.

2 *Dial.* 80.5 and in 81 where Justin comments on Isaiah 65.17–25, and possibly on Ps. 90.4 and 2 Pet. 3.8. This exegetical effort shows that, at least for Justin, millenarianism was intrinsically related to Christian revelation and doctrine. In addition, Justin's polemic against his Jewish opponent revealed a certain rhetorical construction: while the first advent brought Christ the cross, the second coming will be his glorification.

3 *AH* 5.33.3–4. Irenaeus' adaptation of millenarianism may be seen as a part of his theory of 'recapitulation' (see chapter 2). The final reign of the Saviour on earth signifies the abundance of this visible world, which was created as a garden full of fruits and good things, but because of human sin, it suffered decay. The forthcoming thousand years of prosperity on earth emphasizes the original goodness of this world, which in the eschatological stage gains its final glory. This interpretation of Irenaeus' intention can be supported by the fact that to Irenaeus this belief was a part of the apostolic tradition, which he inherited from his teachers.

4 *AM* 3.24.3–6. Tertullian expressed interest in millenarianism not only as a fervent enemy of *Marcion who might have denied it as a Jewish legacy, but also as an equally committed follower of Montanism in the later stage of his life when he wrote his treatise. Tertullian the Montanist shared the belief of the group in the imminent end of this world and the descent of the heavenly Jerusalem to earth for a thousand years.

5 *Symp.* 9.1 and 5.

6 *AH* 5.33.4.

7 For instance, in the Valentinian document, *TT* 123.5.

8 *TP* 1.45.13–20.

9 *GPh.* 84.14—85.21.

10 *TT* 123.3–22.

11 For instance, in *Princ.* 2.11.2; *ComGMat.* 12.34; 17.35; *AC* 7.29. The last reference suggests that Origen understood millenarianism as 'a Jewish mythological interpretation', that is literalistic not allegorical (or spiritual) understanding of the prophetic message, see *AC* 7.28–30.

12 *OP* 27.13; although this passage presents a riddle, it shows Origen's critique of chiliasm.

13 Origen distinguished three kinds of exegesis, which referred to his anthropological theory. As human being is composed of the flesh, mind and spirit, so the scriptural narrative contains its literal ('flesh of the Scripture'), edifying or pedagogical (the mind) and, the most important, spiritual (the soul) dimensions. More in *Princ.* 4.2.4.

14 *AC* 5.59 and *Princ.* 2.11.2–3.

15 *AC* 2.77; *ComGMat.* 17.19.

16 To Origen the soul (Gr. *psyche*) takes its name from the Greek verb which denotes gradual growth in cold (Gr. *psychesthai*), as the soul lost its original heat at the stage of contemplation of God, and then becoming heavier it had fallen to the lower part of the universe (this visible world) to continue its existence. In the eschatological stage this process will be reversed, as the same soul will become 'hotter' and will ascend to its proper and natural position in relation to God. See, *Princ.* 2.8.3.

17 *Princ.* 3.6.1.
18 *Princ.* 4.4.9.
19 *AH* 4.20.5.
20 *Strom.* 5.14.2; 19.4; 67.3; 6.86.1.
21 *AP* 23.4.
22 *EpTh.* 58.10.
23 *OR* 40.9.
24 *Crown* 14.
25 *Apology* 50.2.
26 For example, Tertullian, *Scapula* 4.8; *Scorpiace* 6.7.
27 *Strom.* 7.56.4—57.5.
28 *CG* 20.7.
29 *AH* 5.33.3–4.
30 *CG* 20.7.
31 *Conf.* 1.1.1.
32 *CG* 8.4–8.
33 *LM* 1.
34 Basil of Caesarea, *Moralia* 1.1.
35 *Or.* 30.6.
36 *ComSS* 4.
37 *OSR* (*Patrologia Graeca* 46.160).
38 Although the literary gender of the *Life of Moses* qualifies this treatise within ascetic-spiritual literature, I see in Gregory's work some elements which hint at his understanding of eschatology and the everlasting life.
39 *Ep.* 42.1.
40 *LM* 2.163.
41 *OHS* 9.23.
42 *OHS* 1.2.
43 *Or.* 7.22.
44 *Or.* 45.19.
45 *Or.* 30.4.
46 *Or,* 30.3.
47 *Or.* 21.2.

Index of Ancient Theologians cited in the book

Glossary

Ambrose of Milan (*c.*339–97) Bishop of Milan and outstanding orator. As a theologian he supported the pro-Nicene doctrine and was famous for his preaching skill. His political power was so great that he was able to oppose the emperors, excommunicating one of them (Theodosius), while protecting the autonomy of the Church from the secular power. Among his many writings are *The Duties of the Clergy,* the *Mysteries,* various treatises on virginity and many epistles as well as hymns.

Aphrahat (third – early fourth century CE) One of the first Syrian Fathers, known as the 'Persian Sage', possibly a bishop. His treatises contain catechesis and reveal the interests of the author in ascetic life.

Apologists The title of the early Christian theologians (second century CE) who defended the Christian faith against their Jewish and pagan critics. The apologists presented new faith as superior to pagan philosophies and Judaism. Among them are: the anonymous author of the *Epistle to Diognetus,* Aristides of Athens, Athenagoras of Athens, Justin Martyr, Hermas, Melito of Sardis, Tatian, Tertullian and Theophilus of Antioch.

Apollinarius or **Apollinaris** (*c.*310 – *c.*390) Bishop of Laodicea/Turkey. Apollinarius' views on Christ emphasized that the impassible Logos was incarnate in human body and soul, but within tripartite distinction of the mind, soul and body, Jesus' mind was divine, not human as his soul and body. This opinion was classified as heretical and condemned by the Council of Constantinople (381).

Apostolic Fathers A title coined in the seventeenth century to denote the Christian writers who wrote in the period immediately following the New Testament authors. They include Clement of Rome, Ignatius of Antioch, Hermas, Papias of Hierapolis, Polycarp of Smyrna and the anonymous authors of the *Epistle of Barnabas, Second Epistle of Clement* and the *Didache.*

The Apostolic Tradition (third century CE) A treatise which deals with the liturgy of the early Church, possibly written by Hippolytus of Rome. The document presents in detail a number of rites related to the ordination of various ministers as well as to the way of celebrating the Eucharist.

Aristides of Athens (second century CE) An apologist. His *Apology* presents the Christian faith as holding more mature understanding of God than the philosophy of the Greeks and the religion of the Jews.

Arius (*c.*250 – *c.*336) Alexandrian presbyter who did not accept the divinity of Jesus of Nazareth and taught that the Saviour was a created being, not consubstantial with God. Together with his supporters Arius was condemned and excommunicated first by a Synod at Alexandria (*c.*320), then again condemned by the first Council of Nicaea (325).

Athanasius (*c.*296–373) Bishop of Alexandria. The most important opponent of **Arius** and Arianism, the author of many highly significant works in which he promoted the true, orthodox doctrine, among which are: *On the Incarnation of the Logos, Orations against Arians, On the Decrees of the Synod of Nicaea* and *Life of Anthony.*

Athenagoras of Athens (second century CE) An apologist. He wrote the *Supplication for the Christians* and possibly *On the Resurrection of the Dead.* His theology presented Christianity as a religion compatible with rational philosophy and purifying it from idolatry while offering the believer access to higher wisdom.

Augustine (354–430) Bishop of Hippo Regius (North Africa); one of the most important Latin Patristic theologians. Although he was brought up by his Christian mother Monica, in his adolescence Christian faith lost its value in his life. Then in a more religious phase, he turned first to Manichaeism and later was attracted to a Platonic version of Christianity. Augustine was baptized by Ambrose of Milan (387), returned to North Africa, where he was ordained to the priesthood (391) and later consecrated as bishop. His substantial theological legacy includes his contribution to the Catholic doctrine of the Church, sacraments (against **Donatist** teaching), original sin, grace (against **Pelagianism**) and the Trinity.

Basil of Caesarea (*c.*330–79) Also known as Basil the Great, Bishop of Caesarea in Cappadocia. Basil was one of the three **Cappadocian Fathers**. His theology defended pro-Nicene orthodoxy and contributed especially to the Christian understanding of the nature of the Holy Sprit (*On the Holy Spirit*) as a divine person.

The Book of Steps An anonymous Syriac collection of 30 discourses on the spiritual life. A significant part of it is devoted to describing, instructing and enhancing two basic levels of the Christian life, first of 'the Perfect' and second of 'the Righteous'.

The Cappadocian Fathers The common title of three theologians of the fourth century CE: Basil of Caesarea, Gregory of Nazianzus and Gregory of Nyssa. Because they lived in 'Cappadocia', a district of modern Turkey, the title contains this geographical notion. Their doctrine of the Holy Trinity, theory of salvation and moral as well spiritual writings contributed to the development of orthodox doctrine.

Celsus (second century CE) Philosopher and critic of Christianity, probably of Platonic orientation, who wrote *True Word against Christians*, where he criticized, among other beliefs, the doctrines of incarnation and crucifixion.

Clement of Alexandria (*c.*150 – *c.*215) An eclectic theologian who tried to present Christian faith as acceptable to the educated pagans, as it combined the spirit of Hebrew wisdom and Greek philosophy. In the centre of his theology was the divine Logos, the educator of humanity and guide to his Father.

Clement of Rome (end of first and the beginning of the second century CE) Bishop of Rome. Traditionally two letters to Corinthians are ascribed to him, but his authorship is still the subject of discussion. A Christian legend tells the story of his expulsion to the Crimea and martyrdom.

Cyprian (d.258) Bishop of Carthage/North Africa. During the Decian persecution (250) he escaped. After his return he expressed his opposition to easy reconciliation of lapsed Christians. Cyprian became a martyr in 258. His theological legacy includes the treatise *On the Unity of the Church*, *On the Lapsed* and a number of letters.

Cyril of Alexandria (d.444) Bishop and Patriarch of Alexandria; an important defender of orthodoxy against **Nestorius**, the Patriarch of Constantinople. He participated in controversy over Christ's nature, opposing Nestorius' views. His Christology contributed to reaffirmation of the pro-Nicene doctrine, while developing even further new aspects of the co-existence of the two natures of the one divine person.

Cyril of Jerusalem (*c.*315–87) Bishop of Jerusalem and author of a series of lectures for catechumens. These commentaries express not only Cyril's orthodox views but also provide an insight into liturgy practised in his city.

The Didache, (second century CE) A Christian handbook on morals and the organization of the Church, which elaborated the issues of fasting, baptism, prayer and the Eucharist and clarified the ways of dealing with prophets, bishops and deacons.

Ebionitism A Jewish-Christian heresy held by the Ebionites (Hebr. 'the poor men'). According to this view, the Saviour was merely the natural son of Joseph and Mary who possessed some charismatic gifts.

Ephrem the Syrian (*c*.306–73) Patristic theologian and exegete, author of over 500 hymns. He was involved in defence of orthodoxy against, for example, Marcion and Mani.

Epiphanius (*c*.315–403) Bishop of Salamis/Cyprus and supporter of the Nicene Creed. He wrote the *Panarion* ('Medicine Chest'), also known under the title *Refutation of all Heresies*. His work is a specific 'encyclopaedia' of all heresies from the beginning of Christianity.

The Epistle of the Apostles An apocryphal account (*c*.150–70) of the post-resurrection teaching of the Saviour passed on to his apostles. The document attacked **Gnostic** theology and encouraged faith in the reality of Christ's incarnation and resurrection.

The Epistle of Barnabas A Christian document (second century CE) by an anonymous author. The epistle aimed to clarify the value of the Old Testament to Christians. By use of allegory, the document interpreted 'the Old Testament' events as useful metaphors for Christian life, ethics and doctrine.

The Epistle to Diognetus (150–225) An anonymous document which addressed concerns of pagan intellectuals about Christianity. At the same time, the Epistle promoted the Christian ethos of life as 'the soul of the world'. It also claimed the exclusive character of Christianity as the religion which contains the ultimate revelation of God.

Eusebius of Caesarea (*c*.260 – *c*.340) Bishop of Caesarea; the historian of the early Church. Eusebius supported Arius' theology in the earlier phase of the conflict and was condemned by the Council of Antioch (324/325). Later he was inclined to accept the Nicene Creed, while still opposed to **Athanasius'** model of Christology.

Eutyches (*c*.378–454) Christian theologian who, while rejecting **Nestorius'** model of two separated natures in Christ, assimilated its radical opposition and claimed that Christ has only one nature: human–divine. Another consequence of his doctrine was that Christ's humanity was not consubstantial with other human beings; therefore, from the Catholic perspective, his theory denies the redemption of humankind. Eutyches was ultimately condemned by the Council of Chalcedon (451), and his heresy became known as one of the versions of monophysitism.

Gnosticism (Gr. *gnosis*, 'knowledge') An amalgam of philosophy and religion in later Antiquity, which also appeared in a Christian form. The central doctrine was related to the acquisition of 'knowledge' about the nature of the visible and invisible reality in the context of religious salvation/liberation. Christian Gnosticism brought together various elements taken from Greek, mainly Platonic, philosophy and Hebrew scriptural imagery, and provided an original interpretation of Christian revelation, including Christology, ecclesiology and eschatology. As an inner-Christian movement, Gnosticism was ostracized by authors representing the Great Church. Our main source of direct knowledge about Gnosticism comes from the Coptic collection of documents known as the **Nag Hammadi Library.**

Gregory of Nazianzus (329/330–389/390) One of the three **Cappadocian Fathers**; Bishop of Nazianzus. Gregory was a close friend of **Basil of Caesarea**, with whom he studied in Caesarea, Alexandria and Athens. Gregory's *Five Theological Orations* contributed to the Christian doctrine of the Holy Trinity, especially to the doctrine of the Holy Spirit. He also composed theological poems.

Gregory of Nyssa (*c.*330 – *c.*395) One of the **Cappadocian Fathers**; the brother of **Basil of Caesarea**; Bishop of Nyssa. Gregory's theology elaborated on many fundamental doctrinal issues, including incarnation, salvation, sacraments, moral and spiritual life and dogmatic theology. As the leading defender of the Nicene Creed he challenged many alternative views on the nature of Christ and the Holy Spirit.

Gregory the Great (*c.*540–604) Bishop of Rome, a skilful politician, an excellent administrator. Earlier in his life, Gregory had an outstanding secular career in Rome, but after his conversion, he accepted a radical Christian life. He sold his possessions and the money he distributed to the poor as well as founding seven monasteries, in one of which he led the monastic life. Soon he was ordained as a deacon, then served as the Pope's ambassador and finally he was elected to be the Bishop of Rome (590). Among his works we have a great number of letters, homilies and commentaries on selected Old Testament books. His theology was dominated by the ideal of monastic, contemplative life.

Hermas (second century CE) One of **the Apostolic Fathers**. He wrote the enigmatic, visionary treatise the *Shepherd*. Among the theological themes of this treatise are Christian morality with the idea of forgiveness of sins committed after baptism, salvation and ecclesiology.

Hippolytus of Rome (*c*.170 – *c*.236) One of the most important defenders of orthodoxy, as presented by his treatise the *Refutation of all Heresies*. To him is also attributed the *Apostolic Tradition*. His zeal for theological correctness inspired his opposition to various opponents, including the modalists and Zephyrinus, the bishop of Rome (198–217).

Ignatius (*c*.35 – *c*.110) Bishop of Antioch and Apostolic Father. Ignatius wrote seven letters to the local Christian communities and to Polycarp of Smyrna on his way to Rome where he was executed, during the reign of Trajan (98–117). Ignatius' emphasis on a monarchical type of episcopacy is one of the characteristics of his ecclesiology.

Irenaeus (*c*.130 – *c*.200) Bishop of Lyons/France (*c*.177/8). He is well known as a defender of Great Church against Gnostics, whose theology is the subject of his scrutiny in his *Against the Heresies*. He also commented on the Christian faith and doctrine in his *Proof of the Apostolic Preaching*.

Jerome (*c*.342–420) An outstanding exegete and one of the greatest biblical scholars among the Patristic theologians. He is the author of the Latin translation of the great part of the Bible known as the *Vulgate*. Among his enormous literary legacy there is an important biographical work on ecclesiastical theologians, *Lives of Illustrious Men*. Jerome was an ardent opponent of Arianism, Pelagianism and **Origenism.**

John Chrysostom (*c*.347–407) Famous preacher ('golden-mouthed'), theologian and the Patriarch of Constantinople (398). His theology was formed by the Antiochene approach to the Scriptures, and his exegesis combined moral teaching with theological outlook. The political intrigues of his ecclesiastical enemies led to his deposition and sent him into exile. Among his works the leading place belongs to his homilies on the Scriptures.

John of Damascus (*c*.655–750) One of the most significant theologians of the late Patristic period. John wrote, among other works, the *Fountain Head of Knowledge* composed of three sections: a treatise on logic, a list of heresies and an exposition of Christian doctrine (*On the Orthodox Faith*). The last part elaborates many issues related to theological issues, such as the creation of the world, human nature and Christology.

Justin Martyr (*c*.100–162/168) An **apologist**. He was the author of the *First*

and *Second Apology* where he defended Christian faith in front of pagan intellectuals. He also wrote the *Dialogue with Trypho*, a treatise in which he promoted
Christian doctrine as based on the Hebrew Scriptures, against Trypho, who
represents Jewish critics of Christianity.

Lactantius (*c.*250 – *c.*325) A teacher of rhetoric in Nicomedia (Turkey) and important advocate of the Christian ethos. Lactantius' main work was the *Divine
Institutes*, which aimed to present Christianity as an attractive, convincing and
coherent model of life for the educated classes. His other work, *On the Death
of the Persecutors*, presents the circumstances of the death of the persecutors of
Christianity, which as a rhetorical treatise serves the apologetic purpose of the
author.

Macedonians (also known as pneumatomachians, 'fighters against the [Holy]
Spirit') Fourth-century theologians who denied divinity to the Holy Spirit;
some of them also held pro-Arian views. The name of the group comes from
Macedonius, Bishop of Constantinople (d. *c.*362), although this connection is
doubtful. Macedonius is seen as a theologian inclined to semi-Arianism (Gr.
homoiousios not the Nicene *homoousios*). Therefore it is possible that he did
not share the orthodox view on consubstantiality of the Holy Spirit with the
other two divine persons. Macedonians were condemned first by Damasus, the
bishop of Rome in 374, and later excommunicated by the Council of Constantinople (381).

Marcion of Sinope/Turkey (d. *c.*160) Theologian and founder of an ecclesiastical organization who claimed that Christianity had to be separated from the
legacy of Judaism. This radical separation included rejection of the Hebrew
Scriptures as well as rigid selection of the Christian documents which later
composed the New Testament. Marcion believed that the God revealed by Jesus
Christ had nothing in common with the characteristics of the Creator of the
world revealed in the Hebrew Bible. Consequently, the main Christian principles, including love, were irreconcilable with the prescripts of the Mosaic Law.

Martyrologies Catalogues of martyrs, composed and edited from the fourth
century CE in order to commemorate the heroism of persecuted Christians in
the earlier period.

Melito (d. *c.*190) Bishop of Sardis/Turkey; the author of the *Paschal Homily*.
Melito's Christology expressed the orthodox view on Christ's two natures,
while his polemic addressed the Jewish and Gnostic tendencies in Christian
communities.

Methodius of Olympus (d. *c*.311) Bishop of Lycia/Turkey. His treatise the *Symposium* or the *Banquet of the Ten Virgins* promoted virginity as a model of Christian perfection as well as allegorically describing the union of Christ with the Church as a marriage.

Minucius Felix the Apologist (end of the second and beginning of the third century CE) His main treatise, the *Octavius*, presents a debate between a Christian called Octavius and a pagan interlocutor who accepts Octavius' arguments and converts to Christianity. This conversation allows the author to present a number of Christian views, including belief in the unity of God, providence, resurrection of the dead, while attacking pagan religious practices.

Millenarianism (Lat. *mille* – thousand) or *chiliasm* (Gr. *chilias* – 'thousand') A doctrine based on exegesis of the twentieth chapter of the Book of Revelation, which declared 'a thousand-year' reign of Christ with his saints on the earth.

Modalism (Lat. *Modus* – 'mode', 'form') An early Christian doctrine which reduced the three divine persons to one God, interpreting the appearance of the others, as 'ways' of manifestation of the divine being. *Modalism* was proclaimed by **Noetus** (Rome), **Praxeas** (North Africa) and **Sabellius** (Libya). Modalism was a version of **Monarchianism.**

Monarchianism (Gr. *monos*, 'sole' and Gr. *arche*, 'rule') An early Christian doctrine which overemphasized the unity of God, rejecting the real existence of the second divine person: the Son. Monarchianism was taught by **Noetus, Praxeas** and **Sabellius**, who claimed that God does not share his governance with any other (divine) being, while Dynamic Monarchiansim claimed that Jesus was endowed with divine powers (Gr. *dynamis*) and so only *proxy* divine; therefore, it was a version of adoptionism. Monarchianism assumed suffering of the Father: **Patripassianism.**

Montanus (second century CE) Founder of Montanism; a charismatic Christian prophet and theologian from Phrygia (Asia Minor). His preaching emphasized the forthcoming abundance of grace given by the Holy Spirit to his Church.

The Nag Hammadi Library A collection of 13 codices (ancient 'books' made of papyrus sheets) found near Nag Hammadi in Upper Egypt in 1945/6. The tractates from this collection written in the Coptic language give a unique access to the complexity of Christian Gnostic theologies, metaphysics, ethics and anthropology.

Nestorius (*c*.351 – *c*.451) Patriarch of Constantinople (428); theologian and exponent of the Antiochene school of exegesis. His exegesis and Christology led him to proclaim that Mary was the Mother only of Christ's humanity (Gr. *Christotokos*), not his divinity (Mary was not 'God-birth-giver', Gr. *Theotokos*). Therefore he seemed to believe that the incarnate Saviour contained two persons: human and divine. This view received the name 'Nestorianism' and was labelled heretical.

Noetus of Smyrna/Turkey (b. *c*.200) Christian theologian, possibly the inventor of the doctrine that claimed that the divine Father was incarnate, suffered and died on the cross (*patripassianism*). Noetus was a **Modalist**.

Novatian (third century CE) Theologian, whose main work was *On the Holy Trinity*. He established a rigorist ecclesiastical party, which rejected any concessions for lapsed Christians during the Decian persecution. Although Novatian and his followers held orthodox views, they were excommunicated from the Catholic Church.

Origen (*c*.185 – *c*.254) Born in Alexandria, one of the most educated and original theologians of the Patristic era. His enormous theological legacy includes commentaries, homilies and treatises on various aspects of Christian doctrine such as Christology, ecclesiology, soteriology and eschatology, together with his important contribution to Christian spirituality. His theology combined excellence in biblical scholarship (exegesis) with a Platonic outlook (metaphysics).

Papias (*c*.60–130) A bishop in Hierapolis/Turkey. His theology is known only from fragments preserved by other authors, such as Irenaeus of Lyons and Eusebius of Caesarea. According to those excerpts, Papias promoted the theory of **Millenarianism**.

Patripassianism (Lat. *pater* – 'father', *passio* – 'suffering') A version of **Monarchianism**, which claimed that God the Father suffered on the cross as there is only one God and Saviour.

Pelagius (fourth – fifth century CE) A British theologian who emphasized in his theology the goodness of human nature, freedom of choice and the ability to grow in sanctity without the special support of God's grace. At the same time, he denounced the idea of transmission of the consequences of the original sin from one generation to another. His theology was radicalized by his followers.

Philo of Alexandria (*c*.20 BCE – *c*.50 CE) An eclectic Jewish philosopher (Platonism, Aristotelism, Stoicism, Neopythagoreanism), theologian and exegete. Philo's theology assimilated a number of Platonic ideas in their contemporary, that is Middle Platonist, form (such as the purpose of life as the assimilation to God, free will, providence). His most significant contribution to the later

Christian, especially Alexandrian, theology was his theory of exegesis (the allegorical interpretation) and the theory of the Logos (various parallels with the Platonic *demiurge*), as God's instrument in creation and governance over the existing world as well as the mediator of God's revelation. Philo's theology inspired many theologians, particularly **Clement of Alexandria.**

Praxeas (b. *c*.200) Christian theologian, mainly known from Tertullian's treatise *Against Praxeas*. Tertullian accused Praxeas of holding the view that the Father was crucified (*patripassianism*), therefore, Praxeas is regarded as a Modalist.

Priscillianism (fourth – fifth century CE) The doctrine of spiritual renewal originating in Priscillian's teaching and ascetic example of life. As a doctrine it seems to be a variation of dualistic theology combined with a strong **modalist** tendency. Theology and movement were condemned at the Synod of Toledo (400).

Rufinus of Aquileia/North Italy (*c*. 345–411) Translator and historian of the Church. The most important of his translations is the Latin version of Origen's treatise *Peri Archon*. Rufinus' theological stance was influenced by his spiritual master, Origen. Rufinus wrote a commentary on the Apostles' Creed, which is partly based on Cyril of Jerusalem's *Catechetical Lectures*.

Sabellius (third century CE) A theologian, possibly inventor of **Modalism.**

Sibylline Oracles (second century BCE – second century CE) Collection of prophecies, which were modelled on pagan oracles of divinely inspired Greek clairvoyants. Many Church fathers accepted the authority of these testimonies as useful pagan prophecies foretelling various elements of Christian faith.

Shenoute (fifth century CE) One of the Coptic fathers, a leader (abbot) of the monastic community in Athribis/Atripe in Egypt from 388. He supported Cyril of Alexandria against Nestorius and took part in the Council of Ephesus. His writings promoted the monastic ethos of discipline and quest for virtue.

Tatian (b. *c*.160) A Christian apologist; the author of *Discourse to the Greeks* and *Diatesseron*. Tatian is famous for his extreme opposition to assimilation of Greek culture, particularly philosophy, into the Christian ethos.

Tertullian of Carthage/North Africa (*c*.160 – *c*.225) The father of Latin theology. Tertullian converted from paganism to Christianity and then used his excellent intellectual skills to enhance and protect the Christian faith against various opponents. In the second part of his life Tertullian joined the **Montanist** movement.

Theodore of Mopsuestia (*c*.350–428) One of the leading Antiochene exegetes and theologians. Theodore was also the Bishop of Mopsuestia/southern Turkey. His approach to the Scriptures was dominated by historical, philological methods. Some of his Christological views were recognized as unorthodox by the Ecumenical Councils of Ephesus (431) and Constantinople (553).

Theodoret of Cyrrhus (*c*.393 – *c*.460) Bishop of Cyrrhus/Syria. As a theologian he supported **Nestorius** against **Cyril of Alexandria**; a leading representative of the Antiochene school of exegesis.

Theophilus of Antioch (second century CE) Bishop of Antioch; an apologist. His treatise *To Autolycus* elaborates various elements of Catholic theology as well as containing one of the first expressions of belief in creation of the world 'out of nothing'.

Valentinus (second century CE) Theologian and exegete who taught in Rome. His followers became known as the Valentinians and formed two schools within the same tradition. Although there is no treatise written by Valentinus, the **Nag Hammadi Library** contains a number of works which express the Valentinian doctrine on incarnation, salvation and other doctrinal issues, including Christology.

Chronology and Synopsis of the Ecumenical Councils

The title 'Ecumenical' or 'Oecumenical' signifies here the assembly of the Church leaders from the Patristic period (second – sixth century CE), which established the doctrine binding upon the whole of Christendom. Therefore these five Councils, whose doctrine is related to this book, differ from the local, that is provincial, synods, whose teaching and disciplinary statements were not recognized universally in Christendom.

1 First Ecumenical Council of Nicaea (325)

The Council of Nicaea/Turkey was summoned by the Emperor Constantine and attended by between 220 and 250 bishops. The main, but not the only, theological challenge addressed by the Council of Nicaea was the Arian controversy. While the pro-Arian confession of faith was rejected, the Council promulgated another version of the credal statement, which contained the word 'consubstantial' (Gr. *homoousios*), affirming the divinity of the Son of God. This Creed became known as the Nicene Creed. In addition, the Council issued four anti-Arian anathemas. See chapters 2 and 10.

Sources
Eusebius of Caesarea, *Life of Constantine* (II 61—III 23).

Athanasius of Alexandria, *On the Decrees of the Synod of Nicaea* (19–20).
Rufinus of Aquilea, *Ecclesiastical History* (X 2–6).
Socrates Scholasticus, *Ecclesiastical History* (I 5–13).
Sozomen, *Ecclesiastical History* (VII 7–9).

2 Second Ecumenical Council of Constantinople (381)

The Second Ecumenical Council of Constantinople was summoned by the Emperor Theodosius I and attended by 150 bishops, all representing the Eastern churches. Its main task was to bring unity to the Eastern part of Christendom in the aftermath of the Arian crisis. The doctrine of Christ's divine origin established by the Council of Nicaea was reaffirmed, while against the view of **Apollinarius** the complete humanity of Jesus was safeguarded by doctrinal statements. The Council also confirmed the divinity of the Holy Spirit. See chapters 2, 3, 7 and 10.

Sources
Theodoret of Cyrrhus, *Ecclesiastical History* (5, 9, 13).
Socrates Scholasticus, *Ecclesiastical History* (V.8).
Sozomen, *Ecclesiastical History* (VII 7–9).

3 Third Ecumenical Council of Ephesus (431)

The Council of Ephesus was called by the Emperor Theodosius II with the task of responding to **Nestorius**' teaching on the relation between the two natures of Christ as well as on the role of the Virgin Mary. Under **Cyril of Alexandria's** leadership, the Council deposed **Nestorius** and proclaimed his teaching heretical. It also affirmed Mary's title as the *Theotokos*, confessing that she was the mother of Christ's divinity not only humanity. See chapters 2 and 3.

Sources
Socrates Scholasticus, *Ecclesiastical History* (VII 34).
Evagrius Scholasticus, *Ecclesiastical History* (I 3–7).

4 Fourth Ecumenical Council of Chalcedon (451)

The Council of Chalcedon was summoned by the Emperor Marcian and addressed the Christological theory of **Eutyches** on one nature of Christ. The Council proclaimed the belief in two natures of the one person of Jesus Christ, while denoting in details five characteristics of their co-existence ('united, unconfused, unchangeable, indivisible and inseparable'). See chapter 2.

Sources
Evagrius Scholasticus, *Ecclesiastical History* (II 2–4; IV).

5 Fifth Ecumenical Council of Constantinople (or the Second Council) of Constantinople (553)

The Second Council of Constantinople, also known as the Fifth Ecumenical Council, was summoned by the Emperor Justinian and attended mainly by Eastern bishops. Its aim was to restore unity in Christendom ('one Christian Empire – one Christian religion') in the aftermath of the previous crisis and excommunication of those Christians who believed in only one nature of Christ (i.e. 'Monophysites'). It condemned some views ascribed to **Origen** and in an effort to gain acceptance from some theological opponents, the Council also condemned some works of **Theodoret of Cyrrhus, Theodore of Mopsuestia** and Ibas of Edessa (the so-called 'Three Chapters'), which were thought to be pre-Nestorian. It also confirmed the authority of the first four Councils, especially that of Chalcedon, contested by some theologians.

Further Reading
Evagrius Scholasticus, *Ecclesiastical History,* (IV 38).

Bibliography

L. Ayres, 2006, *Nicaea and its Legacy: An Approach to Fourth-Century Trinitarian Theology*, Oxford: Oxford University Press.

M. J. Edwards, 2007, 'Synods and Councils' in *The Cambridge History of Christianity: Constantine to c.600*, Cambridge: Cambridge University Press, pp. 367–85.

P. l'Huillier, 1996, *The Church of the Ancient Councils: The Disciplinary Work of the First Four Ecumenical Councils*, Crestwood, NY: St Vladimir's Seminary Press.

J. Meyendorff, 1989, *Imperial Unity and Christian Divisions: The Church 450–680 A.D.*, Crestwood, NY: St Vladimir's Seminary Press.